Yours, Plum

BOOKS BY P. G. WODEHOUSE

Aunts Aren't Gentlemen
The Adventures of Sally
Bachelors Anonymous
Barmy in Wonderland
Big Money
Bill the Conqueror
Blandings Castle and Elsewhere
Carry On, Jeeves
The Clicking of Cuthbert
Cocktail Time
The Code of the Woosters
The Coming of Bill
Company for Henry
A Damsel in Distress
Do Butlers Burgle Banks?
Doctor Sally
Eggs, Beans and Crumpets
A Few Quick Ones
French Leave
Frozen Assets
Full Moon
Galahad at Blandings
A Gentleman of Leisure
The Girl in Blue
The Girl on the Boat
The Gold Bat
The Head of Kay's
The Heart of a Goof
Heavy Weather
Hot Water
Ice in the Bedroom
If I Were You
Indiscretions of Archie
The Inimitable Jeeves
Jeeves and the Feudal Spirit
Jeeves in the Offing
Jill the Reckless
Joy in the Morning
Laughing Gas
Leave It to Psmith
The Little Nugget
Lord Emsworth and Others
Louder and Funnier
Love Among the Chickens
The Luck of the Bodkins
The Man Upstairs
The Man with Two Left Feet
The Mating Season
Meet Mr Mulliner
Mike and Psmith
Mike at Wrkyn
Money for Nothing
Money in the Bank
Mr Mulliner Speaking
Much Obliged, Jeeves
Mulliner Nights
Not George Washington
Nothing Serious
The Old Reliable

Pearls, Girls and Monty Bodkin
A Pelican at Blandings
Piccadilly Jim
Pigs Have Wings
Plum Pie
The Pothunters
A Prefect's Uncle
The Prince and Betty
Psmith, Journalist
Psmith in the City
Quick Service
Right Ho, Jeeves
Ring for Jeeves
Sam the Sudden
Service with a Smile
The Small Bachelor
Something Fishy
Something Fresh
Spring Fever
Stiff Upper Lip, Jeeves
Summer Lightning
Summer Moonshine
Sunset at Blandings
The Swoop
Tales of St Austin's
Thank You, Jeeves
Ukridge
Uncle Dynamite
Uncle Fred in the Springtime
Uneasy Money
Very Good, Jeeves
The White Feather
William Tell Told Again
Young Men in Spats

OMNIBUSES
The Golf Omnibus
The World of Blandings
The World of Jeeves
The World of Mr Mulliner
The World of Psmith
The World of Ukridge
The World of Uncle Fred
Tales From The Drones Club
Wodehouse Nuggets
   (edited by Richard Usborne)
The World of Wodehouse Clergy
The Hollywood Omnibus
Weekend Wodehouse
The Jeeves Omnibus
   Volume 1
The Jeeves Omnibus
   Volume 2
The Aunts Omnibus

VERSE
The Parrot and Other Poems

AUTOBIOGRAPHICAL
Wodehouse on Wodehouse (comprising
   Bring on the Girls, Over Seventy,
   Performing Flea)

Yours, Plum

THE LETTERS OF
P. G. WODEHOUSE

Edited with an Introduction by
FRANCES DONALDSON

HUTCHINSON

London Sydney Auckland Johannesburg

© The Estate of P. G. Wodehouse 1990
© Introduction 1990 Frances Donaldson

All rights reserved

This edition first published in 1990 by Hutchinson

The right of P. G. Wodehouse to be
identified as Author of this work has
been asserted by the P. G. Wodehouse
Estate in accordance with the Copyright,
Designs and Patents Act, 1988

Century Hutchinson Ltd
Random Century House, 20 Vauxhall Bridge Road, London SW1V 2SA

Century Hutchinson Australia (Pty) Ltd
20 Alfred Street, Milsons Point, NSW 2061, Australia

Century Hutchinson New Zealand Limited
PO Box 40–086, Glenfield, Auckland 10, New Zealand

Century Hutchinson South Africa (Pty) Ltd
PO Box 337, Bergvlei, 2012 South Africa

British Library Cataloguing in Publication Data
Wodehouse, P. G. (Pelham Grenville) *1881–1975*
Yours, Plum : the letters of P. G. Wodehouse.
1. Fiction in English. Wodehouse, P. G. (Pelham
Grenville), 1881–1975
I. Title
823.912

ISBN 0–09–174639–6

Set in Linotron Bembo by
Deltatype Ltd, Ellesmere Port, Cheshire

Printed and bound in Great Britain by
Mackays of Chatham PLC, Chatham, Kent

CONTENTS

ILLUSTRATIONS

First section

Leonora with Debby and Boo

Leonora as a child

Leonora and Plum

Peter Cazalet

The wedding of Peter and Leonora

The Hon. Anthony Mildmay

Ethel, Plum and Leonora at Le Touquet (two photos by permission of Topham Collection)

Low Wood

Denis Mackail (by permission of Mrs Mary Oliphant)

One of Plum's letters to Mackail

Bill Townsend's illustration (by permission of Barry Phelps Collection, Dulwich College)

Plum with his fox hound, Bill (by permission of Dulwich College)

Guy Bolton

Heather Thatcher (by permission of Hulton-Deutsch Collection)

Dorothy Dickson (by permission of Mander and Mitchenson Theatrical Collection)

George Grossmith and Norman Griffin in 'The Cabaret Girl' (by permission of Mander and Mitchenson Theatrical Collection)

The playbill of 'Sally' (by permission of Mander and Mitchenson Theatrical Collection)

Second section

'The Play's the Thing' – a scene from Molnar's comedy adapted by Plum (by permission of Mander and Mitchenson Theatrical Collection)

Ivor Novello (by permission of Hulton-Deutsch Collection)

Lorenz Hart (by permission of The Bettmann Archive)

Jerome Kern (by permission of Pictorial Press Ltd)

Cole Porter (by permission of Hulton-Deutsch Collection)

Florenz Ziegfeld (by permission of Associated Press)

George and Ira Gershwin (by permission of Popperfoto)

Plum with Ian Hay (by permission of Hulton-Deutsch Collection)

E. Phillips Oppenheim (by permission of Hulton-Deutsch Collection)

'Anything Goes' – the London Production (by permission of Mander and Mitchenson Theatrical Collection)

Plum and his foxhound, Bill

Plum and Ethel at Remsenburg

Edward Cazalet

Sheran Hornby

Plum and Ethel at Remsenburg – a selection of photos

A big stretch (by permission of Pictorial)

Plum at work till the end (by permission of Pictorial)

When otherwise unacknowledged, photos are from the P.G Wodehouse archive and reproduced by kind permission of Sir Edward Cazalet.

INTRODUCTION

When P. G. Wodehouse was young he wrote in the evenings, after his day's work at the Hong Kong and Shanghai Bank, or, later on, in the offices of the *Globe* newspaper. When he was old and following the routine he preferred, he wrote all morning; then, after walking the dogs in the afternoon, again from four to six. Until he was very old his output was phenomenal. The exact extent of his published work is not known because until he was well established he often wrote under other people's names or *noms de plume*. He appears to have written ninety-six books; written or collaborated in the writing of sixteen plays; written the lyrics, or some of the lyrics, of twenty-eight musical plays, and collaborated in the libretti of eighteen of these. It is estimated that he wrote more than three hundred short stories, much humorous verse and the scenario for half a dozen films. Between 1920 and 1930 alone he wrote the lyrics, and sometimes part of the book, of twelve musical comedies, performed in London or New York, and of two others never performed; while he wrote or adapted seven straight plays.

He had a combination of qualities seldom found in the whole history of literature, in that, while essentially a popular author – his books sold millions of copies all over the world – he excited the highest admiration in leading contemporary writers. It is well known that Hilaire Belloc described him as 'the best writer of our time: the best living writer of English' and 'the head of my profession', while Evelyn Waugh speaks of his being 'touched by the sacred flame', which 'burned with growing brilliance for half a century'. However, readers of these letters will notice that Wodehouse's gifts had been pointed out by writers of almost equal eminence to Belloc or Waugh before either had spoken.

In addition to his immense published output, Wodehouse always found time to write letters. He answered all or nearly all his fan mail himself, and wrote regularly to his family and friends – not just the ordinary formal letters of thanks or replies to questions, but long letters, often covering two or three pages of single-spaced type-script. Flaubert is quoted as saying: 'I write a love letter, to write,

1

and not because I love.' Wodehouse could not be satisfied even by the colossal output he published, and he too seems to have written letters 'to write' and not because he loved.

However, one should not assume from this that he would at any time in his life have been content merely to write. He worked strictly for publication and, even after he had achieved tremendous popularity and a most distinguished fame, would write and rewrite to please an editor. Evelyn Waugh, after saying that whereas in England 'we think of ourselves as the guardian of our own reputations . . . American editors regard themselves as employers, and many sharp misunderstandings arise when European writers publish their work in the New World,' went on: 'Mr Wodehouse has never expressed any annoyance, rather gratitude, at what in Europe would seem irksome presumption. Indeed he attributes the superiority of American magazines to this editorial interference.'

I have always believed that Wodehouse neither expected nor completely understood the reverential treatment he received from so many of his most discriminating colleagues. His letters seem to bear out this assumption and reveal him as quite exceptionally naïve in his attitude to fame and to popularity, as indeed in so many other ways.

Many hundreds of letters, hundreds of thousands of words, remain; but the idea that these should be published, although often suggested, has always been rejected on the grounds that they were written for private consumption, and in consequence are repetitious, while the very bulk of the correspondence makes selection difficult. The letters to Guy Bolton are mainly about their collaboration on what must today seem old, out-of-date musical comedies, some of which were not even produced; and his letters to William Townend chiefly give his views on the other's work. To everyone else he wrote of the latest doings of his dogs and of the horror, having just finished a Jeeves novel, of being unable to think of a plot for another. This theme occurs so often in letters that it seems to be evidence that Wodehouse chose these times to bring his correspondence up-to-date – not from love but in order to write.[1]

[1] In a letter to Denis Mackail, apologising for not having written for so long owing to pressure of work, he wrote: 'This is all wrong, of course. There is no finer starter for a morning's work than writing a letter, so really what one ought to do is to begin the day by getting one off and then plunge into one's work.' There is no evidence that he went on to follow this precept.

For all these reasons a collection of letters has never seemed a possible project. Yet I returned to the idea again and again, because, although few of the letters are quotable as a whole, there is so much that is extremely entertaining and also revealing to be found in them. I always assumed that even a selection would have to be chronological, but the interruptions to every theme seemed to break the flow even more than the repetitions. Then I had the idea that it might be done more in the form of an anthology, that is under subject headings – such as Ethel, Dogs, Work and so on, taking the best rendering of the day – so that there would be some narrative interest in the stories of his pekes, Winks and Wonder; some continuity in his account of life in Paris during the war; some connected theory on the construction of a novel in his letters to Townend. After I had decided to try out this method I discovered that it had been followed by William Hadley in a selection and arrangement of the letters of Horace Walpole – an encouraging fact. It has involved a great deal of work, but the result has seemed to me worth it, and I hope will give readers as much amusement as the selection has given me. I have done the minimum of research into such questions as the exact identity of show business characters long dead, but I have sought the originals of uncollected articles and so on, wherever it has seemed of interest to do so; and, most importantly, I have given the names of the novels and stories that Plum writes about.

In the case of Wodehouse's letters to his stepdaughter Leonora, I have abandoned the method used for the rest of the letters and, with only minor cuts to avoid repetition, have given the letters in full. These letters show him in the home and, in consequence, have an incomparable biographical value. Written to someone he trusted completely, they are free from the heartiness characteristic of much of his normal correspondence, adopted I think to cover a general unease with his fellows which caused him sometimes to doubt his understanding of how to behave. They show him not merely as affectionate, but as accepting naturally and authoritatively the position of stepfather. By the time I first met them, Leonora was already managing him, but this was the way he preferred it and it did not prevent him occasionally instructing her. (See p.11, letter of 27 September 1920: 'Oh, by the way, you must stop pinching Mummie's clothes. It worries her frightfully, and you know how nervous she is.') These letters have a genuine autobiographical flavour, far greater than that of such published works as *Performing Flea* or *Bring On the Girls*.

Although Wodehouse wrote to anyone who wrote to him, he

had four main correspondents, and, since at least three of these were, apart from Ethel, the only people for whom he seems to have felt a strong affection, it seems worth saying something of each.

First, his stepdaughter Leonora; if it was not known that she was nine years old when they first met, her personality as well as his relationship with her must have given rise to rumours that she was his own. He brought her up and she took much colour from him, but in her own right she was one of the most powerfully charming people I have ever met. I use the word 'powerful' not to convey any assertiveness or intention, but because, without apparent effort, she inspired more love than anyone I ever knew, and, while evoking something like idolatry in subordinates, was accepted by her equals as a leader. I first met her when we were at school together, and here she had already learned to be even in her treatment of other people for fear of hurting the feelings of those she liked least. Her personality is nevertheless very difficult to describe because it consisted more in an even balance of qualities than any in particular. When she was young she perhaps placed too much value on humour, which made her slightly unsympathetic to one's sadder moods; otherwise she had no perceptible faults. She was kind, generous, witty, without malice or aggression. In his biography of Wodehouse, David Jasen says she was at school in England during the First World War, but I have the impression she was in America. In any case, somewhere at school at this time her name was corrupted through Nora to S'nora and from there to Snorky or Snorkles. The final versions may not immediately please everyone, but they were seized upon by Plummie, who never called her anything else.

The second most important person in Wodehouse's life was William Townend of *Performing Flea*. This friendship began when they shared a study at Dulwich and continued for the rest of their lives. The letters in *Performing Flea* were to a great extent written at the time and for the book, but they were based on Plum's original letters, of which parts are given here. Most consist of an analysis of Townend's work and this is only of value when it throws light on Plum's own methods. But his generosity to Townend is not shown in *Performing Flea* and is in fact one of the most attractive features of his character. He had no real interest in money but he gave the impression of being rather mean because he treasured small sums. I think Ethel controlled his expenditure and kept him short. In any case I remember Leonora, whom I too called Snorky, once spoiling his day when she appropriated £10 he had won racing to give to a godchild. He was godfather to my own daughter, Rose, but only on the understanding that it did not involve present-giving. It is therefore a surprise as well as a pleasure to learn of his extraordinary generosity to Townend and also in all business dealings with Guy Bolton.

Guy was the third person to whom he was seriously devoted. He first met him when, while acting as drama critic for *Vanity Fair*, he bumped into Jerome Kern (whom he already knew) at the first night of *Very Good Eddie*, music by Kern and book by Bolton. Soon afterwards the three came together to work on musical comedy, Kern writing the music, Wodehouse the lyrics, and Wodehouse and Bolton collaborating on the libretto.

Guy Bolton was a thoroughly professional technician with a gift for musical comedy, but, apart from enthusiasts for the musicals of that date, posterity will know of him only because of his connection with Wodehouse. Yet all his life Plum treated him not merely as an equal but often as a superior. They worked together in some of the most successful musicals of the age – introducing what they called 'situation comedy' to replace the large musicals with tremendous sets and showgirls – and they continued to work often in partnership until the outbreak of war in 1939.

In 1940 Guy organized a petition signed by notable Americans requesting Plum's release from prison camp in Germany, and this was probably responsible for bringing Plum's presence there to the attention of the German authorities. Then, as Plum's letters to him show, it was because Guy had a house at Remsenburg that the Wodehouses finally settled there. Here Plum and Guy returned, if with rather less success, to their previous collaboration.

Finally there is Denis Mackail, to whom he wrote over a hundred letters, more than twenty thousand words. Mackail was a best-selling novelist in the twenties and thirties and the biographer of J. M. Barrie. The son of J. W. Mackail OM, a classical scholar and Professor of Poetry at Oxford, he was the brother of Angela Thirkell, also a best-selling novelist, and the uncle of Colin MacInnes. Plum enjoyed his society and his letters, and he liked him very much, but I am not sure that he loved him. Mackail operated on a much higher intellectual level and I think Plum was a little frightened of him. In any case, there is no doubt that in his letters to Mackail he stretched himself to please, or that in consequence these are among the best of the tremendous collection which remains. Plum once wrote to Mackail: 'I have been looking through my diary and I realize that I must be one of the world's great correspondents. This is the 43rd letter I have written this month and my monthly average for the last year has been over thirty.' Many of these letters would have been written to Bolton or Townend and all would contain versions of the same events. In almost all cases the version to Mackail has to be chosen because it is so much better done. There are, however, other letters of interest, notably to Ira Gershwin, to Leonora's children, Edward and Sheran Cazalet, of whom he became very fond, and to Thelma Cazalet, her sister-in-law.

Leonora died, tragically and unexpectedly, in 1942, and Plum's letters to her cease therefore in 1939. Putting them consecutively and more or less in full in Part I gives some chronology to this part of the book, and I have therefore added to it sections of a few personal letters to Denis Mackail, since these belong under no particular heading but add to the picture of Plum's life until 1939. For reasons which will be obvious, I have included one letter written in 1945. Again for the sake of chronology, Part II is devoted to the section headed War, which consists of excerpts from the letters Wodehouse wrote from Germany and France during or immediately after that period. Part III includes extracts from letters to all the various correspondents, but this time grouped under different subject headings.

All are presented exactly as written, only the occasional typing mistake being corrected, although dates and addresses have been presented in a standard form. Recipients and addresses are not automatically given at the head of each letter, but only when they change. I have not followed too closely my own rule for dividing the excerpts under headings, particularly in the case of the letters to Mackail. Sometimes they seem to belong equally to more than one heading, and at others there is the risk of interrupting the writer's train of thought. In these cases the letters are given as a whole or in lengthy passages. Even if not written for publication, they were written by a master of English prose, and, full of charm, humour and eccentricities, they are a valuable addition to the published work.

PART I

1 LEONORA

Leonora was born in 1904 and was sixteen when these letters begin.

☆

7 August 1920

Quinton Farm
Felixstowe
Suffolk

My darling angel Snorkles,

At last I'm able to write to you! I finished the novel yesterday, and I wish you were here to read it, as I think it's the best comic one I've done. It's not meant to be in the same class as *The Little Warrior*, but as a farce I think it's pretty well all the mustard.[1] I've done it in such a hurry, though, that there may be things wrong with it. Still, I'm going to keep it by me for at least two weeks before sending it off to America, so perhaps you'll be able to see it after all before it goes. If not, you can read the original MS.

I don't suppose it will sell as a serial in England. They want such stodgy stuff over here, most of the magazines, and the *Strand* and the *Grand* are both full up with my stuff for months to come.

I have now got three more Archie stories to do and then I shall have worked off all my present contracts. I haven't got a plot yet for the tenth Archie story, but they are using a golf story of mine in the Christmas *Strand*, which will give me a fair amount of time to think of one.[2]

Mummie went off to London yesterday, and I am all alone here and rather blue. I leave on Friday and I hope we shall soon get a flat in town.

Mummie has taken up golf and is very keen on it and is really getting quite good. You must start as soon as you can. . . .

[1] *The Girl on the Boat*, published in the USA as *Three Men and a Maid*. *The Little Warrior* was published in Britain as *Jill the Reckless*.
[2] For the solution to the tenth Archie story see the letter to Leonora dated 24 November 1920, on p. 13.

Don't you think this is a good line in the book. Chap who's always thinking himself ill says to chap who is having a row with him 'My face hurts!' Other chap says 'You can't expect a face like that not to hurt!' I thought it was not only droll, but whimsical and bizarre, but Mummie said it was obvious! No human power, however, will induce me to cut it out.[1]

I've got another good line. Chap is asked if he identifies the hero, with whom he has had a row. Hero has been found in the house late at night and they think he is a burglar. He says 'I am Sam Marlowe.' They turn to the other fellow and say 'Do you identify him?' and the other fellow says 'I suppose so. I can't imagine a man saying he was Samuel Marlowe unless he knew it could be proved against him.' Somewhat humorous and not altogether free from espièglerie, I think, or am I wrong?

A man has just written to me asking if I will dramatize his new novel, which he says he wrote in imitation of my stuff. I had read a review of his novel, and had thought it was just the sort of thing to read and pinch situations from. And so we go on, each helping the other.

As a matter of fact, I really am becoming rather a blood these days. In a review of *Wedding Bells* at the Playhouse the critic says 'So-and-so is good as a sort of P. G. Wodehouse character.' And in a review of a book in the *Times*, they say 'The author at times reverts to the P. G. Wodehouse manner.' This, I need scarcely point out to you, is jolly old Fame. Once they begin to refer to you in that casual way as if everybody must know who you are all is well. It does my old heart good.

My golf is terrific now. I seldom miss. Tom Irwin, one of your trustees for the money which I hope to find some way of pinching in the near future, was down here and has given me a new putter, which produces wonderful results. . . .

I'm glad you liked *The Little White Bird*. One of my favourite books.[2]

Georgia O'Ramey is singing 'Galahad' in Cochran's new revue. Isn't it darned cheek! I want heavy damages and all that sort of thing. What scares me is that she has probably pinched 'Cleopatra', 'Very Good Girl on Sunday', and 'Blood' from *Springtime* as well.[3] It begins to look like a pretty thin sort of world

[1] See *The Girl on the Boat*, p. 289. [2] By J. M. Barrie.
[3] 'Sir Galahad' and 'Cleopatterer' were lyrics Plum wrote for *Leave It to Jane*. 'A Very Good Girl on Sunday' and 'Burletta – The Oold Fashioned Drama' (shortened to 'Blood') came from *Miss Springtime*. All four were sung by Georgia O'Ramey in New York.

if tons of hams unfit for human consumption are going to lift one's best things out of shows and use them themselves without even a kind smile.

Well, pip pip and good-bye-ee and so forth.

Your loving
Plummie

27 September 1920   Constitutional Club
                                     Northumberland
                                     Avenue
                                     London WC

My precious darling Snorky . . .

I've been living at the club for the last two weeks, trying to do some work. Mummie has been at Chingford, which isn't a bad place in itself but is too near the East End of London to be really nice. I was out there yesterday, and the place was overrun with motor buses and picnic parties. Still, in another few days we move into the house thank goodness. I am so sick of having my meals in restaurants and at the club that I don't know what to do.

I'm writing this on a hired machine, my own having been sent to the factory for repairs. I've made up my mind I'll never get a new typewriter. I can't spell on any machine except mine. I do hope it will come back from the factory in good shape. I've done a lot of work on it since it was last fixed up.

The novel is being typed, and must also be finished by now, I should think. I'll send you on the original manuscript, and you can read it in the train. I am now trying to get a central idea for a new serial for *Collier's*. The editor keeps writing to me to say that *The Little Warrior* was the best thing that ever happened, so I feel I must do something special next shot. The trouble is, unless I write a sequel and bring Freddie Rooke in again, I don't see how I can introduce a dude character, and without a dude character where am I? Among the ribstons.

I've just had a letter from a man in California who wants me to buy an interest in a gold mine for five hundred pounds. He says 'I happened to pick up the Sept *Cosmopolitan* and on one of the front pages I see a list of authors and artists and I said to myself that bunch could put this over and I have a hunch they will and your name is in the list and I'm writing you along with the others to send me your check for twenty-five hundred dollars and write on the check that it is for a one-thirtieth interest in the eight-year lease of the Kid Gold

11

Mine and then after awhile I will send you a check for your share of a million or a letter of regret telling you I have spent the money digging through the mountain and my hunch was a bum one, but anyway I expect your check.' Sanguine sort of johnny, what? I'm going to put the letter in a story.[1]

Well, cheerio, old bean.

Lots of love
From Plummie

PS   Oh, by the way, you must stop pinching Mummie's clothes. It worries her frightfully, and you know how nervous she is.

24 November 1920   16 Walton St
                                         London SW

Darling Snorkles,

We were so glad to get your letters and to hear that you are having a good time. I thought you would like Felixstowe. I'm so glad you've started riding.

The Haileybury match was a disaster, darn it. We were without Addison, and with him we should have won easily, but still they had a couple of good men away. Still we ought to have won anyhow, only the blighters started the game scared, because Haileybury had beaten Bedford so easily, and they let them score twice in the first five minutes. It wasn't till after half time that we woke up, and then we simply put it all over them. But it was too late then, and we couldn't catch up. They scored four times and we scored three. We ought to have scored half a dozen times. Murtrie played a splendid game, and your little friend Mills, the fly-half, was brilliant at times, only he spoiled it by making one or two bad mistakes. He made one splendid run nearly the whole length of the field. On Saturday we finish up by playing Sherborne.

Great excitement last night. Mummie came into my room at half-past two and woke me out of the dreamless to say that mice had been snootering her. She said one had run across her bed. To soothe her I went to her room to spend the rest of the night, thinking that there may have been mice in the room but that she had simply imagined that they had got on the bed. We had hardly turned off the light when – zip! one ran right across the pillow!!! So then we

[1] This story appeared in modified form in *Big Money*.

hoofed it back to my room and tried to sleep there, but the bed was too small, so I gave up my room to Mummie and went back to the mice room. And for some reason or other Mister Mouse made no further demonstration, and I wasn't disturbed. But the result is that we are both very sleepy today. I have been trying to work, but can't rouse the old bean.

I am at present moulding the Archie stories into a book.[1] The publisher very wisely says that short stories don't sell, so I am hacking the things about putting the first half of one story at the beginning of the book and putting the finish of it about a hundred pages later, and the result looks very good. For instance, I blend the Sausage Chappie Story and 'Paving the Way for Mabel' rather cunningly. You remember that the blow-out of the latter takes place in the grill-room. Well, directly it has happened there is a row at the other end of the grill-room, which is the Sausage Chappie having the finish of his story. Rather ingenious, what!

I went to Harrod's for the book-week, but didn't have to do anything except autograph a few books. [Herbert] Jenkins called up just now and wants me to come round and autograph a dozen of each of my books, as this book-week has caused a big run on them.

Mummie came out of the nursing home rather tired, as it was one of those places where they wake you up for breakfast at seven-thirty. She has been resting a lot since coming out, and seems much better now. We have got Ian Hay coming to dinner tonight.

The house is very still and quiet without our Snorky. We all miss you badly, especially Winifred. I have to go for walks by myself.

We listened to the Palladium on the electrophone the night before last. The chap who sings 'Smith, Jones, Robins and Brown' had another good song, as a naval officer. Refrain as follows:

'It's wonderful the difference the Navy's made to me!
    Since first I went to sea,
I'm twice the man I used to be:
    They fixed me up with a uniform,
    And it's the uniform
    That takes the girls by storm.
I'm told that Beatty's simply crazy over me,
    And so he ought to be:
    For anyone can see
That, though I owe a lot to the Navy,
    It's nothing to what the Navy owes to me!'

[1] *The Indiscretions of Archie.*

Droll, I think, yes, no? It sounds wonderful when I sing it. You must hear me some time.

Well, cheerio, old fright. Write again soon.

Your loving
Plummie

28 November 1920

Darling Snorkles . . .

We beat Sherborne yesterday after a very hot game, so that we have wound up the season with five wins and one defeat. Pretty hot!

I forgot to tell you in my last letter the tale of the laughable imbroglio – or mix-up – which has occurred with Jerry Kern. You remember I sent my lyrics over, and then read in *Variety* that some other cove was doing the lyrics and wrote to everybody in New York to retrieve my lyrics. Then that cable came asking me if I would let them have 'Joan of Arc' and 'Church Round Corner', which, after a family council, I answered in the affir. Well, just after I had cabled saying all right, I got a furious cable from Jerry – the sort of cable the Kaiser might have sent to an underling – saying my letter withdrawing the lyrics was 'extremely offensive' and ending 'You have offended me for the last time'! Upon which, the manly spirit of the Wodehouses (descended from the sister of Anne Boleyn) boiled in my veins – when you get back I'll show you the very veins it boiled in – and I cabled over 'Cancel permission to use lyrics'. I now hear that Jerry is bringing an action against me for royalties on *Miss Springtime* and *Riviera Girl*, to which he contributed tunes. The loony seems to think that a lyricist is responsible for the composer's royalties. Of course, he hasn't an earthly, and I don't suppose the action will ever come to anything, but doesn't it show how blighted some blighters can be when they decide to be blighters. . . .

I hope the riding goes well. Also the golf.

I have just heard from Reynolds that the editress of the *Woman's Home Companion* does not like *The Girl on the Boat*. Rather a jar, but she is going to pay for it, and Reynolds will try to sell it elsewhere. What on earth is wrong with that story? I thought it was the funniest I had ever done, and you yelled over it. The editor of *Pan*, who are publishing it serially here, thinks a lot of it. Yet quite a squad of editors have turned it down. It makes me feel a bit doubtful of my new story, which I start tomorrow.

14

Well cheerio.

Mummie sends her love. She is washing her hair or something this morning.

> Your loving
> Plummie

23 March 1921   SS *Adriatic*
                                                 Southampton

Darling precious angel Snorklet,

I have written to mother about your going down. You might drop a line, too.

I think the jolly old boat is just starting. I shall mail this at Cherbourg. It begins to look like a jolly voyage, if we don't cop any rough weather. This cabin is a snorter. About the size of my den, with a lounge, a chair, two windows, and a closet and a chest of drawers. In fact, if only there was that bit of lawn and shrubbery we discussed the other day, I would settle down here for life and grow honey-coloured whiskers. As it is, I shall probably keep fowls during the voyage.

Only blot is, the table they have given me is one of those ones that sway in the breeze and wobble violently if you touch them. What it will be like out in the open ocean heaven knows. If all goes well, I ought to be able to do quite a chunk of work.

I have already been interviewed by the representative of the White Star Publicity for publication in NY, and Mummie is running round in circles breathing smoke because I didn't lug her into it. I tell her that I will feature her when the reporters arrive at NY.

We had a very jolly journey down, talking of this and that. (First this, then that). Thompson is going to be a very cheery old bean to have around on the trip, and altogether everything looks pretty well all right.[1] But I haven't managed yet to get into the George Drexel Steel class, if you know what I mean, and it's generally felt throughout the ship that I shan't work it till tomorrow.

It's wonderful what a difference it makes having a decent cabin. This one is more like a room than a cabin. All very jolly.

Mummie was saying such sweet things about you in the cab.

---

[1] Fred Thompson. English playwright, mainly of musical comedy, who collaborated with Plum on the book of *The Golden Moth* (see p. 18).

We wept in company on each other's shoulders at the thought that we had to leave you.

The engines have just started going pretty hard, so I can now tell what it will be like trying to work during the voyage. All right, I think.

I'll write and tell you how New York looks. Goodbye, my queen of all possible Snorkles.

Lots of love
Your
Plummie

2 April 1921   Hotel Biltmore
                                                                New York

Prcious (or, rather, precious) angel Snork.

Well, we blew in yesterday morning and are all feeling rather wrecks after a strenuous day yesterday. In their usual blighted fussy way they got us up at six when there was no earthly need to get up before nine or ten, and it seemed hours before we could get past the passport people. It bucked us up a bit when the photographers buzzed round us and took all sorts of pictures including some movies. The only trouble is that I can't find that any paper has printed them. Maybe they'll be in the Sunday papers. One was supposed to be for *Town and Country*, a weekly paper.

Mummie hunted all round New York for a hotel. The Astor made us sick to look at it, and we very soon gave that the go-by, after having a very bad lunch there. We finally settled on this at fourteen seeds a day, which won't do a thing to the old bank-balance. Fortunately, this morning I got a good idea for a short story, and hope to write it while I'm here. We've got a very nice room, looking down on to the roof garden and three pigeons (which are thrown in free).

Our first act was to summon a bell-boy and give him the Sinister Whisper, to which he replied with a conspiratorial nod and buzzed off, returning later with a bottle of whisky – at the nominal price of seventeen dollars!!!![1] I suppose if you tried to get champagne here you would have to throw in your Sunday trousers as well. Apparently you can still get the stuff, but you have to be darned rich.

Mummie was frightfully tired. Our cabin was on the

---

[1] Written during Prohibition.

promenade deck, and we were kept awake most of the last night by the row made by lugging trunks out of the hold just outside our window. Still, we got – or climbed – into our respective evening suits and went off to *Mary*, not being able to get seats for *Sally*, which was sold out. . . .[1]

We both keep saying what chumps we were not to have brought our Snorky with us. You must certainly come next time.

We had an awfully nice trip. Fred Thompson was a wonderful chap to have with us. Full of funny stories and a most awfully good sort. We are all tremendous pals. The journey didn't seem a bit long, though it took nine days. I sweated like blazes at the novel, and wrote and revised another 12,000 words, so that I now have about 70,000 words of good stuff, and am going to shoot it in without waiting to finish the thing. I shall finish it bit by bit while I am here. I'll keep a copy for you. The scene at the boxer's training-camp came out splendidly, though it was very hard to write. I had a wobbly table, which I had to prop up with trunks, and writing wasn't easy. I generally worked every afternoon from three to half-past six. I did a good scene for Sally and Ginger. There are some fairly difficult bits still to do, but I hope I shall polish them off all right. It ought to be easier doing them in New York. . . .[2]

Well, cheerio, old scream. We're thinking of you all the time.

Oceans of love
Your loving
Plummie

☆

In 1921 Snorky went to school at the Old Palace, Bromley, Kent, where I later joined her and where about thirty girls were taught by completely unqualified teachers. The owner was Belgian, and the school professed to specialise in French. The girls were instructed to speak French to each other all day long, which led to a good deal of '*Passez-moi* the salt, *s'il vous plaît.*' When Plum visited Snorky he hid in the shrubbery on the drive and she went out to meet him because he was frightened of meeting the headmistress.

---

[1] *Mary* was a musical comedy by Harbach and Mandel which opened at the Knickerbocker Theatre in October 1920 and ran for 219 performances. *Sally* was a musical comedy with book by Guy Bolton, music by Jerome Kern and lyrics by P. G. Wodehouse. It ran for 570 performances at the New Amsterdam Theatre, New York from 21 December 1920; and for 383 performances at the Winter Garden, London from 10 September 1921.
[2] *The Adventures of Sally*, published in the USA as *Mostly Sally*.

☆

1 May 1921   Emsworth House[1]
                                       Emsworth
                                       Hants

My darling precious angel Snorkles,

I hope this reaches you before you leave Felixstowe. I shall be up in time to see you before you biff off to school. Awful rot your having to go, is my verdict. I want you at my side as my confidential secretary and adviser.

Have you heard that we couldn't work the Sammy business this trip? We found out that you have to have a permit from the Board of Agriculture to bring a dog to England, so we shall have to leave him till I go over in the Fall. I shall be going over then – I hope with the superior four-fifths – to put on a show I am doing for Savage.[2] I wrote all the lyrics coming over on the boat, except two of which I haven't got the tunes yet. It's rather a good piece. The music is ripping.

I am now sweating away down here on the first act of the Adelphi show. I've done about half of it, but it has been an awful fag. I've now got to the point where Grossmith and Berry come on and I have to be frightfully funny. Unfortunately I feel very mirthless and my comedy will probably be blue round the edges.[3]

I'm so sorry to hear you have had a cough again. You really must buck up and get fit. I wonder if Bromley will agree with you. If it doesn't, we shall have to shift you. We mustn't have our Snorky wasting away on us. . . .

We had a rotten trip coming back, being next door to a set of blighters who made a row in their cabin till two every morning, and the partition was so thin that it was like having them in our cabin.

I crammed a frightful lot of business into my twenty days in

[1] A school run by Baldwin King-Hall which was the setting for *The Little Nugget* (1913). King-Hall's sister, Ella, who eloped with Herbert Westbrook (see p. 117) was Plum's UK literary agent for twenty years.
    [2] Colonel Henry Savage, one of the idiosyncratic theatre managers who feature largely in *Bring on the Girls*.
    [3] The Adelphi show was *The Golden Moth*, with book by Fred Thompson and P. G. Wodehouse, lyrics by P. G. Wodehouse and music by Ivor Novello. It ran for 281 performances from 5 October 1921. George Grossmith and W. H. Berry were famous in musical comedy. Grossmith was the son of the George Grossmith who, with his brother Weedon, wrote *The Diary of a Nobody*. There is no sign of the show for Savage, although according to Jasen a play with book by Bolton and Wodehouse and lyrics by Wodehouse was written in 1921 but never produced.

NY. Everybody I met wanted me to do a play. I am going to do one with Guy and Jerry, this one for Savage, and maybe another. What I would like would be to stick to lyrics, which I can do on my ear. Dialogue is too much like work.

I worked like the dickens going over and wrote twelve thousand words of the *Sally* novel. Also another chunk in NY, so that now I only have about five thousand to do, and shall polish that off directly I get free of these plays. I have to stick to the Adelphi show for a while, as I promised Fred Thompson I would work on it on the boat, and I didn't touch it. Another three days ought to see me nearly through.

This coal strike makes me spit. There's always something. If it isn't something, it's something or else something.

Did Mummie tell you about herself at the highbrow dinner in NY? Somebody asked her what she thought of the League of Nations, and she said it was a wonderful production but lacking in comedy and that the dresses were wonderful. Thinking they were talking about the *League of Notions*. Droll, what?[1]

The editor of the *Cosmopolitan* told the editor of *Collier's* who told me, that the e. of the *Cosmopolitan* had more letters from readers about the Archie stories than about the whole of the rest of the magazine put together. When I left NY a movie offer of twelve thousand dollars for the series was floating in the air. Maybe it's settled by this time.

I had one day's golf at Great Neck, but the links were in rotten shape and it rained all the time and I didn't like it much.[2] I had to drive back to NY in a pyjama jacket and carpet slippers as all my things were soaked. . . .

I am enclosing a lot of letters for you which Loretta gave me. She brought in two large boxes full of mail, which had been waiting for us there.

Cheerio. Lots of love. See you soon.

Your loving
Plummie

---

[1] *The League of Notions* was an extremely successful revue put on by C. B. Cochran with the Dolly sisters.
[2] The Sound View Golf Club at Great Neck was the setting for the Oldest Member golfing stories.

20 May 1921   8 Launceston Place
                                               Gloucester Road
                                               London W8

Darling precious angel Snorkles,

You will be thinking me a f.i.h.s. (fiend in human shape) for not having written to you before, but, gosh, ding it, four separate jobs collided and I was sunk in the whirlpool. Old Savage arrived and I had to buckle to on the Lehar piece: Fred Thompson came back and I had to pop onto the Adelphi piece: Reynolds cabled and I had to revise *The Girl on the Boat*; and he also said that Collier's wanted the rest of *Sally*. My impulse in these circumstances was to go to bed with a hot-water bottle and a book, but I decided to have a dash at tackling the jobs, so I started by cutting twenty thousand words out of *The Girl on the Boat*, after which I wrote a scene of the Lehar piece and a scene of the Adelphi piece. I haven't touched *Sally* yet. They will have to wait a bit for that.

On Wednesday afternoon I had an interview with Savage, who read and liked my lyrics and then calmly told me that, for purposes of copyright, he would have to have the remaining two lyrics by today (Friday) at four!!! I hadn't even got ideas for them. By great good luck I managed to get two good ideas, and now – at 2 o'clock – I have just finished them both. So I have now done all the lyrics, thank goodness. He wants the book completed by two weeks from tomorrow. I think I can manage it all right, but it will be a sweat, and I would like to be out in this fine weather. Still, if I *am* so much in demand it can't be helped.

Mrs Westbrook has written to say that the *Strand* have raised my price from one hundred and fifty quid to two hundred quid per short story, which, with the American rights, will make about a snappy six hundred quid per s.s. – which, as you will no doubt agree, is noticeably better than dab in the eye with a burnt stick.

Mummie has biffed off to Lingfield [races], previously touching me for two pounds.

I am so glad that you like the jolly old school. It sounds ripping – or, as you would say now, *épatant*. How do you like talking French all the time? . . .

Must stop now as the bell is ringing.★
                    Lots of love
                    Your
                    Plummie

★ Telephone-bell next door.

PS   It looks almost certain now that *Oh Lady* will be put on in London. Three managers are nibbling at it.[1]

PPS   Directly this coal strike is over I'll pop down and see you one Thursday. Of course if you could get away on a Saturday it would be better. I'll find out when the St Paul's match is – I think it's a fortnight from tomorrow – and you might come and see that. It's at Kensington not at Dulwich.

15 June 1921

My poor precious angel,

We were frightfully sorry to hear of your accident, you poor old thing. What an awful shame having this happen to you right in the middle of the summer term when you want to be playing tennis and swimming. You do have the most rotten luck. Never mind, we shall have to make up for it in the holidays.

Does it hurt very much? I hope not. Do you remember when you came such a smash bicycling near the bungalow at Bellport?

I will come down and see you the very first moment I can manage. I simply must take a day to clean up the Savage play as he wants it by Saturday. But after that down I come with bells on.

Very hot and bothered just now. Poor old Mummie rather blue at having to stop in bed, and a disturbing request from Fred Thompson to put money up for the Adelphi piece, which we aren't going to do, thus making it rather awkward, as he is very keen on it.

The other night he came to dinner, stopped till twelve, couldn't start the car and had to leave it outside in the road all night. A man came and fixed it next day, but apparently thought it belonged to us, so left it where it was, and when I came back at night it was still there and once more we left it outside. In the small hours Mummie was woken by a policeman making a fuss about it. I slept peacefully through the whole affair, plunged in the dreamless.

And, as you say, the Test matches have gone wrong too! Oh, that reminds me. Jerry Kern and the baby have both gone down with the measles!!! What a woil! What a woil!

Father came up yesterday, and he is downstairs now waiting for his bites. He looks very fit.

All sorts of exciting things have been happening. Courtneidge wants to put on the Archie play – to my acute disgust as I think it's rotten.[2] I am trying to double-cross the gang and get him to put on

[1] *Oh, Lady! Lady!* was never produced in London.
[2] Robert Courtneidge, father of the musical comedy actress Cicely Courtneidge, was one of the last London actor-managers.

21

Piccadilly Jim instead.[1] Also Dillingham has cabled to Guy asking him to rush through the play which he and I and Veczey are doing, so I have promised, as Guy is busy, to dialogue it. More work! If I can stall off this Adelphi piece, I shall win through, but I am losing weight. Quite the jolly old sylph these days, and getting sylphier all the time.

Bobby Denby has gone off to Ascot, and we have undertaken to pay one-tenth of his losses or take one-tenth of his winnings.[2] I hope the lad bets wisely! He's got a nice day for it, anyway.

Father wants to know if you would like to do a bit of Cheltenham in the holidays. How about it? If you think well of the schema we might put in a week there together. But something more in the nature of the vast rolling prairie was my idea, or the little cottage by the sea. . . .

Well, cheerio, old scream. You mustn't let this arm-breaking become a habit and take up time which might be devoted to the more serious issues of life.

Oceans of love
From your
Plummie

PS   Darling thing, your letter has just come. I'm heartbroken that you're having such pain. I'll be right down and darn the Savage play. He'll have to wait.

3 July 1921

Darling angel Snork,

How I have neglected you! I've been in a state of coma since I saw you last, unable to get up enough energy to do anything, even write a letter. The old bean went right back on me, but I'm all right again now.

I hope the arm is getting better. I wonder if you'll be able to do any swimming in August. We are still undecided where to go. Mummie speaks of Le Touquet (in France), but I have an idea it's an overcrowded sort of place, and I'd rather go somewhere where we could biff about in old clothes.

---

[1] No play on either of these themes was produced.
[2] When I asked Guy Bolton who Bobby Denby was he replied: 'Oh, one of Ethel's followers.' This does not seem to have disturbed Plum at all and Denby lived with the Wodehouses for a short time in London.

Were you all broken up about Carpentier? I bore it with fortitude, having been fed up to the gills by too much stuff about Baby Jacqueline. (By the way, if you haven't seen the papers lately, this will rather go over the top. I allude to the reams of stuff they have been printing about the Dempsey–Carpentier fight, which jolly old Carp. lost yesterday. . . .)

Mummie gets back from Folkestone tomorrow, and I shall be darned glad to see her again. I have been very sad and lonesome since she went away. But I think the change will have done her good.

I went down to Dulwich yesterday to see the Sherborne match. It was thrilling. We just won when there were only three more minutes to play. I never thought we should do it. I very nearly went about the place scattering pound-notes to the lads. Wiser counsels, however, fortunately prevailed, and I still retain doubloons in the left trouser-pocket.

Love Among the Chickens is out in the cheap edition. I'll send you a copy. Townend told me it was on sale at the Charing Cross bookstall, so I rolled round and found they had sold out. Thence to Piccadilly Circus bookstall. Sold out again. Pretty good in the first two days. Both men offered to sell me 'other Wodehouse books', but I smiled gently on them and legged it.[1]

I have got four new freckles on the top of my head. Where will this end? I think I shall buy a parasol.

Don't you wish it would rain? This dry weather is having a bad effect on my brain. I can't think up plots any more, nor even work on those I have got. I am getting very sick of London.

Well cheerio. I'll pop down and see you pretty soon.

Your loving
Plummie

21 December 1921

11 King St
St James's
London SW

Darling angel Snork,

The Wodehouse home is *en fête* and considerably above itself this p.m. Deep-throated cheers ring out in Flat 43, and every now and then I have to go out on the balcony to address the seething crowds in St James Street. And why? I'll tell you. (I'm glad you

---

[1] *Love Among the Chickens* was first published in 1906.

asked me.) This afternoon at Hurst Park dear jolly old Front Line romped home in the Hurdle Handicap in spite of having to carry about three tons weight. The handicappers crammed an extra ten pounds on him after his last win, so he had to carry thirteen stone three pounds, and it seemed so impossible that he could win that I went off and played golf instead of going to Hurst Park. It is an absolute record – the *Evening Standard* says there has never been a case before of a horse winning a good race under such a weight.

We get four hundred quid in stakes – minus fifty quid which we have to cough up to the second horse and twenty-five to the third. Rot, I call it, having to pay them, and I am in favour of seeing if they won't be satisfied with seats for *The Golden Moth* or copies of my books, but apparently it can't be done. We also have to give the trainer a present of fifty quid, and a few extra tips to various varlets and lackeys, not omitting one for two scurvy knaves. Still, with what Mummie (the well-known gambler) got on at six to one, we clear five hundred quid on the afternoon, which, as you justly remark, is not so worse.

In addition to this, Mummie's judgement in buying the horse is boosted to the skies, and everybody looks on her now as the wisest guy in town. If we sold the horse today we could make a profit of a thousand pounds probably – certainly seven hundred. But we aren't going to sell.

My first remark on hearing the news was 'Snork will expect something out of this!' It seemed to me that the thing must infallibly bring on a severe attack of the gimmes in the little darling one. Mummie says that when you come back you shall collect in the shape of a rich present. (Box of candy or a fountain-pen or something lavish like that. Or maybe a string of pearls. Maybe, on the other hand, not.)

Well, that's that. So Mummie has started her career as the Curse of the Turf in great style.

I have been spending the last two days in a rush of ideas for a new novel. It will be on the lines of *Something New* and *Piccadilly Jim*, and it is coming out amazingly.[1]

I have also played golf today and yesterday, swinging a mean spoon.

Cheerio, old cake.

Oceans of love
Your Plummie

PS No, wrong. It would fetch *two* thousand more now than when we bought it.

[1] Probably *Leave It to Psmith*, the second Blandings novel.

24 January 1922   Constitutional Club
                                                    Northumberland
                                                    Avenue
                                                    London WC2

Darling Snorky,

How's everything? Darned cold, what? So'm I.

I say, I've got out the plot of a Jeeves story where Bertie visits a girls' school and is very shy and snootered by the girls and the headmistress. Can you give me any useful details? What would be likely to happen to a chap who was seeing over a school? Do you remember – was it at Ely? – the girls used to sing a song of welcome. Can you give me the words of the song and when it would be sung? And anything else of that sort that would be likely to rattle Bertie.[1]

Mummie's away in Lincs with Mr & Mrs Moseley. She may be away another week. I've got Eric Shand staying with me till tomorrow. Very pleasant.

Must stop now, as I don't hear the bell ringing.

                                Love
                                from
                                Plummie

11 March 1922   On Board
                                                    the Cunard
                                                    RMS *Aquitania*

Darling Snorky,

Just off to lunch, there's just a time to say yoodleoo. Give Cissie & Peggy my love when you see them.[2]

You looked like the Queen of Sheba at W'loo. Very nifty!

                                Lots of love
                                from
                                Plummie

[1] This became 'Bertie Changes His Mind' in *Carry On, Jeeves*.
[2] Cissie and Peggy Marais, two South African girls, shared a room with Snorky at school.

20 September 1922   4 Onslow Square
                                     London SW7

Darling angel Snorky,

Well, Bill, maybe we didn't do a thing to the customers last p.m. Wake me up in the night and ask me! Honestly old egg, you never saw such a first night. The audience were enthusiastic all through the first and second acts, and they never stopped applauding during the cabaret scene in act three – you know, the scene with no dialogue but all music and spectacle. I knew that scene would go big, because the same thing happened at the dress rehearsal.[1]

I take it from your wire this morning that you have seen the notices. They are all very good, but I'm a bit sick that they don't even refer to the lyrics! I haven't seen the evening papers yet. I hope they will continue the good work.

Leslie Henson was up in the gallery through the show!!! It must have been rotten for him, for Griffin made a tremendous hit and there wasn't a moment when the show dropped because of him.[2] Grossmith was immense, so was Heather Thatcher. As for Dorothy Dickson, she came right out and knocked 'em cold.

This morning Mummie and I are not our usual bright selves, as we didn't get to bed till six and woke up at nine! William Boosey gave a party at the Metropole and we didn't leave till 5.30. It was rather funny – we had the Oppenheims, Justine and Walter, and Beith with us at the show, so they the Opps gave us supper at Ciro's, then went on to the Metropole at one o'clock and sat right down to another supper.[3] Even I began to feel as if I had tasted food recently when they brought on oysters and grouse just after I had surrounded a mess of lobster and lamb (with veg.) . . . There isn't any doubt that we've got an enormous hit. The libraries have taken a lot of seats for three months, the same number they took for *Sally*, and everybody was magnificent. Every number went wonderfully, especially 'Dancing Time'.

Snorky darling, isn't it a nuisance, I've got to sail for New York on Saturday. I hope I shan't be away more than about three months, but I hate being away from Mummie and you. This year I seem to have been separated from you all the time. I do hope Mummie will be able to come over and join me very soon, as I know I shall be lonely. But this Ziegfeld show is sure to be a big

[1] *The Cabaret Girl*, with book by George Grossmith and P. G. Wodehouse, lyrics by P. G. Wodehouse, music by Jerome Kern. It ran for 462 performances from 19 September 1922.
[2] Leslie Henson had been offered the part and refused it.
[3] E. Phillips Oppenheim, best-selling novelist; Justine Johnstone, one of the girls in *Bring on the Girls*, was married to the film producer Walter Wanger, and Ian Hay Beith.

26

thing and I mustn't miss it as I missed *Sally*. All these dramas go to help buy the baby new footwear. . . .

Well, angel, I must stop now, as I have a million letters to write, thanking people for their wires. I'm so glad you are having such a good time. Give my love to Front Line.

Your loving
Plummie

PS   Do write Bobby a line, precious. He wrote you such a long letter and must be feeling blue all alone at Dinard.[1]

14 November 1923

17 Beverly Road
Great Neck
Long Island
New York

Well, *ma belle*, how goes it? You like the – how is it you Americans say? – the Gay City, *hein*?

Over here, figure to yourself how it is *triste*. One gets through the time somehow, but we miss the delicately nurtured. Life has lost its savour. The world is dull and grey. The only bright spot is Jack, the Cat Supreme. Did you get to know Jack at all well while you were here? He is – with the possible exception of Mitzi – the most satisfactory cat I have ever known. A genuine comedian. He always comes in through my bedroom window at one in the morning, so I have to sit up for him. The other day at breakfast he wanted to be let out, so he tapped Bobby with his paw. Bobby took no notice. Jack gave him another tap. Still no results. So then Jack, in a perfectly calm and businesslike way, moved up a bit closer and gave Bobby a bite in the calf of the leg.

Did Mummie tell you I was working on the new novel in a new way, – viz. making a very elaborate scenario, so that when the time came to write the story it would be more like copying out and revising than actual composition. It is panning out splendidly, but is, of course, the dickens of a sweat, because I can't persuade myself that I am really accomplishing any actual work besides just mapping the story out. I have reached about half-way now, and it has taken 30 pages, each containing 600 words as they are typed close like this letter. That is to say, I have written 18,000 words of scenario, the equivalent of about three short stories!

[1] Bobby Denby.

I must say I think, when it is all finished, I shall be surprised at the speed at which I shall be able to polish off the story. There are whole scenes practically complete with dialogue and everything, and I am getting the beginnings of each chapter right, which is what always holds me up. I often spend a whole morning trying to think of the best way of starting a chapter, and now I shall be able to go right ahead.

I wish you were here to discuss the plot with. I think it is a corker. Certainly it is as good as Psmith up to the point where I have got to, and I think the rest will hold up. I have got the plot more or less complete, and am cleaning it up bit by bit.[1]

We are anxiously awaiting letters from our Bing Girls in Paris.[2] Mummie's first one arrived about a week ago. What a rotten time you must have had at first. *C'est toujours ça*, what?

Since you have left I have met a lot of people you would have liked. Donald Ogden Stewart is about the best candidate for your hand that we have dug up as yet. A very cheery bird. Very ugly, but what of that? We have also seen quite a lot of Elsie Ferguson, who is very nice. Mummie would like her. Guy is doing a play for her, and she lives about two hundred yards away in North Drive. I lunched with Benchley.[3] Very pleasant. He is awfully good in the *Music Box*. He does a sort of burlesque speech, rather like some of the things in *Love Conquers All*. It is about the finances of a boy's camp. He announces that the treasurer has a cold, so cannot appear that night; then he is called to the side and speaks to somebody and comes back and says 'I guess the laugh is on me. The treasurer has *pneumonia.*'

I am wondering if you and Mummie have decided that Paris is a good spot for the family to take up its headquarters. I must say I shouldn't mind trying it for a bit. I have got very tired of America. Great Neck seems quite different this year. Last winter, with the good old loved ones around me, I enjoyed it tremendously, but it makes me restless now. I suppose it is simply because I miss you and Mummie. This bachelor life is no good for me at all.

Oh yes, I was forgetting. I have also met Scott Fitzgerald. In fact, I met him again this morning. He was off to New York with Truex, who is doing his play, *The Vegetable*.[4] I believe those stories you hear about his drinking are exaggerated. He seems quite

---

[1] *Bill the Conqueror*.
[2] Ethel and Snorky. This is a humorous reference to the stage show *The Bing Boys*.
[3] Robert Benchley, famous and very witty journalist.
[4] Ernest Truex, American actor who played the lead in *Good Morning, Bill* in 1927.

normal, and is a very nice chap indeed. You would like him. The only thing is, he goes into New York with a scrubby chin, looking perfectly foul. I suppose he gets a shave when he arrives there, but it doesn't show him at his best in Great Neck. I would like to see more of him.

It's a funny thing, I have rather gone off golf recently. On the other hand, I am very keen about bridge, and have started to play much better, though I am still pretty bad. A man named Carrington came to lunch yesterday and Guy and I trimmed him and Bobby properly. You would have laughed to see Bobby. He was doing all sorts of scientific declarations to show that he was weak in spades, and Carrington would insist on going more and more spades till he got up to three. Then Guy went four clubs and Carrington said four spades and Guy said five clubs and Carrington said five spades and I doubled and we took five hundred off them. It made oi laff hearty. Poor old Bobby got all purple and puff-faced and looked as if he hadn't a friend in the world. Carrington's hand turned out to consist of king, knave, eight, five, and three of spades! I had the ace and queen and Guy the ten!!

Jerry Kern went to a sale of Conrad's manuscripts yesterday and paid $8100 for MS of *Victory* and $2000 for MS of *Youth*. Silly ass, what? He is simply crawling with money nowadays. The Fred Stone show is an enormous success.

Snorky darling, I'll try and get this scenario finished soon and send you a copy. Then you can give me a tip or two. Of course, I don't suppose I shall actually write it just as it is scenarioed, but it ought to be pretty close.

Well, cheerio, old sort. *Je vous embrasse.*

Your
Plummie

23 November 1923

Darling Snorkie,

I have been sweating away for the last two hours writing duty-letters and it is with relief that I take my typewriter in hand and address you.

Thanks awfully for your long and well-phrased letter, received yesterday. I'm so glad you have found a niche at last (the cry goes round the Underworld – Snorky has found a niche). It sounds great:

but, as you suggest, God help the neighbours on Mondays, Wednesdays, and Fridays. They will think Sammy has strayed over to La France (or, as some say, *la belle France*).

I will send you the books as soon as poss. I bought Dorothy Speare's book, *The Gay Year* (sequel to *Dancers in the Dark*), and am reading it now. Jolly good. She seems to me to know that type of life inside out. The scene is laid in a sort of Great Neck place an hour from Grand Central, and everybody is tight the whole time; a jolly crowd.

Yesterday I finished the scenario of *Bill the Conqueror*, my new novel. 30,000 words, laddie! I may be wrong, but it seems to be simply terrific. I will send it to you directly it comes back from the typist. Then you will have plenty of time to make suggestions. Gosh, it's full of meat and action, even more so than *Psmith*. And suspense up to the last chapter.

The two musical comedies are fizzing. Jerry is doing the music for both and is tremendously enthusiastic, especially about what used to be the Duncan Sisters show. Both ought to be going into rehearsal in about a fortnight, though Flo[1] has not yet signed our contract! Still, he has got to put on a piece for Marilyn Miller by Jan 17, so I imagine we are all right.[2]

Jack the cat is greatly exercised these days by the goldfish, which are now in their aquariums in the porch off the drawing-room. He sits and gazes at them by the hour, and if not checked by a biff on the side of the head tries to flick them out with his paw. I heard Catherine say to him the other day, 'Yack, what the matter mit you? How you get that way?' – than which, as you will readily agree, nothing could be fairer.

Gawd, Snorky, you would have laughed the other night. We went next door to play bridge, and Guy was partnered with a severe female who takes the game very seriously against Mrs Heinze and me. And in the last rubber he bid recklessly and, owing to a masterly performance by self (I made a three-hearts redoubled), we got into their ribs for a twelve-point rubber and the severe female staggered away a heavy loser – thirty points down. And the cream of the jest is this, that earlier in the evening I was her partner and owing to the heat of the room and eight females babbling in my ear-hole I got *distrait* and let her down, getting set seven tricks on one occasion. Then Guy and I played her and Mrs Heinze and trimmed them good, both playing like professors. In other words,

---

[1] Ziegfeld. [2] See p. 32, letter dated 25 December 1923.

Honble Female got it both coming and going. She had sat down at that table a child; she rose from it a woman. We couldn't have done more to her if we had used an axe.

Lyric from Duncan Sisters show:

> Put all your troubles in a great big box,
> As big as any box can be:
> Put all your troubles in a great big box
> And lock it with a great big key:
> Crying never yet got anybody anywhere,
> So just stick out your chin
> AND
> JAM all your troubles in a great big box
> And sit on the lid and grin.

Incidentally, I believe I showed you that one before. Never mind.

And now what about the Oil? I'm not sure that we can quite pass that 'Call me Ilchy' stuff.[1] I remember John Stavers. An awful ass, just the sort who would like those poisonous females.

Well, *ma belle*, this will come right on top of my last letter, so you will have lots to read. (I enclosed that one in my last letter to Mummie. I hope she gave it to you.)

Your loving
Plummie

23 December 1923
[The first page is missing.]

PS   The copies of *Psmith* have just arrived. I will send you one right along.[2]

I'll attend to that letter.

An American came over to London and was very anxious to be taken for an Englishman. So he ordered a lot of English clothes from a Savile Row tailor, also spats and an eyeglass and stayed in his room at the hotel till they were ready. Then he put them all on, spats and eyeglass and everything, and got a cane and went out for a stroll. A loafer sort of chap sheltered there, too. 'Wet day,' said the loafer. The American, not wanting to give himself away by

---

[1] The Earl of Ilchester. He and his wife stayed with the Wodehouses at Easthampton. Jasen says the Countess was a source of Bertie Wooster's Aunt Dahlia.
[2] *Leave It to Psmith*.

31

speaking, smiled and nodded. 'Nasty weather,' said the loafer. The American smiled and nodded again. There was a pause. *I've* got a cousin in New York,' said the loafer. 'Wonder if you ever met him?'

Freddie Lonsdale's play *Spring Cleaning* is an enormous hit here.[1] And *Aren't We All* is still running. He must be making a fortune. I see that Al Woods has gone over to England to talk to him about still another play which he is doing. . . .

Oh, by the way. Mummie tells me that you have taken to wine in your old age. I wish you wouldn't. I have always pointed with pride to you as the one female in the world who can subsist on water. I should preserve the record, if I were you.

We had quite a scare at the Customs when Mummie returned. The poor boobs knew that she had brought in a lot of jewellery, and they thought we still had a residence at Great Neck, especially as all her baggage was labelled for there. So a detective stopped us as we were leaving and wanted to know where we thought we got off. I told him we had sold our house in 1920, and he retired, bathed in confusion.[2]

Jack the cat has got a red ribbon round his neck today. Looks an awful ass.

That's all. Cheerio.

25 December 1923

Christmas Morning
(or, putting it another
way, Dec 25
1923)

My precious angel Snorky,

Your lovely letter (*billet le plus charmant*) arrived this morning while I was at breakfast (*déjeuner*) champing (filling *le visage avec*) about half a pound of sausages (*saussisons*). It caused great fun and laughter among both young and old. . . .

I have been working so darned hard these last weeks that I haven't even time for a letter for you. Did Mummie tell you I had sold the novel to the *Sat Eve Post* for $20,000? (Of course, they haven't actually accepted it in so many words, but they read the scenario and said it was just what they wanted and agreed to the price, so it is all OK.) I have now had a cable from England saying

---

[1] Playwright famous in the 1920s, and my father.
[2] Plum used this in *The Luck of the Bodkins*.

that the *Strand* will publish it in England and pay twelve hundred and fifty quid. So it looks like a white Christmas, what?[1]

I am enclosing the original scenario. I can't send one of the typed copies, as two are out and I have to keep the third to work with. Still, you'll be able to read this one all right. I want you to tell me frankly if it isn't a pippin. It seems to me quite as good a story as *Psmith*, though of course I shall miss Psmith when it comes to dialogue – though I think Judson will be a good comedian.

I have only written one chapter so far, as it's no good starting it seriously till I can really concentrate on it. All these last weeks I have been sweating away at the two shows. Frightfully exciting.

Old Flo Ziegfeld would *not* sign our contract – kept putting us off. Until finally I cornered him at the New Amsterdam and asked what the trouble was. He then said that he had to pay Marilyn Miller ten per cent of the gross and Royce six hundred dollars a week, so he couldn't afford to pay the authors more than he paid for *Sally*. Well, you know me. Generous to a fault and consequently beloved by all. I said, 'Flo, old man, you have touched my rugged old heart. When I think of your squalid home at Hastings with only three Rolls Royces and barely one baby elephant I can't hold out. I will reduce my royalty to one per cent, which will just make the *Sally* terms.' He fell on my neck and said he would sign the contract that day if I would send it over. So I went to John Rumsey and told him to send the contract by hand to the theatre, which was done.

But nothing happened. Flo kept putting off signing and a day or two afterwards left for Detroit with his other show, *Kid Boots* (Eddie Cantor and Mary Eaton). His last word was that he would read the contract in the train and sign it and mail it back. Still nothing happened. Then we began telegraphing. But in the meantime *Kid Boots* had opened in Detroit and appeared to be a terrific hit. This had the effect of making Flo go right up in the air. He immediately got very up-stage and began to make all sorts of conditions. Telegrams passed and re-passed, getting more crisp all the time, until finally he sent one saying 'I consider it a privilege to work for a manager like myself. I will not accept a manuscript from Bolton Wodehouse and Kern until they have shown it to me and shown that they have the goods. I had too much trouble and expense making *Sally* into a show.' Hot stuff, what? We showed the telegram to Jerry, and he went right off and sold the piece to Dillingham, who, of course, took it without a murmur.[2] We then

[1] *Bill the Conqueror.*
[2] Charles B. Dillingham, also a famous theatrical manager. This piece was *Sitting Pretty*, book by Bolton and Wodehouse, lyrics by Wodehouse, music by Jerome Kern. Opening at the Fulton Theatre on 8 April 1924, it had 95 performances.

got hold of Jack Donahue, the comedian, whom Flo was trying to get, and signed him up for our piece with Dillingham. And finally we had a talk with Marilyn Miller's lawyer and told him that we had switched our piece to Dillingham, and she instantly wrote off to Flo, breaking her contract!!! So that Flo has lost his star, his comedian, and one of the best pieces ever written. It may knock some sense into the poor fish. He always pursues that policy with authors, trying to establish an inferiority complex in them and trying to make them feel that they are lucky to have a piece put on by him at all. . . .

The scheme is to come over to Paris and settle down there for a bit. Mummie arrived quite in favour of the place, in spite of the gloom of some of her letters. I feel we should have a great time. I want to learn French and intend to pitch right in at it.

While on this subj., I hope you are plugging away at French. I wish you were speaking it all the time. Do stick to it. I don't think it ought to take long for you to be a really good French nib, if you understand that play G.G. took you to.[1]

Apropos of G.G., while admitting the resemblance to Sammy, I would enter as a more serious candidate for the post of his double a griffon which I met the other day. Sammy may be the silhouette, but the griffon was the real thing.[2]

Thanks awfully for the handkerchiefs. As nifty a lot as I have ever had. Dashed good of you to send them. Mummie is having them marked, and I shall treasure them. . . .

Fellow found a man, rather tight, on his hands and knees at a street corner, groping about. 'What are you doing there?' asked the first fellow. 'I am looking' (Second Fellow now speaking) 'I am looking for a ten dollar bill I dropped at the last corner.' 'But why, if you dropped it at the last corner,' enquired First Fellow, 'don't you look at the last corner?' 'Because there's more light here,' says Second Fellow.

And again. First Fellow: 'Your face seems very familiar. Didn't I meet you at Palm Beach?' Second Fellow: 'I have never been to Palm Beach.' First Fellow: 'Nor have I.' Second Fellow: 'We must be talking of two entirely different people.'

Well, Snorky, old lad, a million blessings. ('Peace on thy head!' 'Two pieces on yours!') I'll write again very anon.

Your loving
Plummie

[1] George Grossmith.   [2] Sammy was the bulldog.

4 February 1924

Darling angel Snorky,

Your long letter made a big hit in the home. We weren't so keen, though, on this fainting business. Where do you get that stuff? I hope your cold is all right again now, and that you are once more settled down to the gaieties of that dear Paris.

Well, say, listen, kid, lemme tell ya sumfin. I sent the first 70,000 words of *Bill the Conqueror* off to the typist (*la sténographe*) yesterday, and believe me or believe me not, it's *good*. I'm taking a day off today and tomorrow plunge into the remaining 25,000 which ought to be pie. This is certainly one swell story, as good as the old man has ever done, and, thank God, I have been able to work in that line about 'I know it's paraffin, but what have they put in it?' Judson has worked out immense, and Flick, the heroine, is so like you that the cognoscenti cannot help but be charmed.

Meanwhile, the old theatrical business has got Pop properly on the run. We were going along nicely casting *Sitting Pretty* for Ray, when Jack Donahue suddenly called up and said he thought *Pat*, the other piece, a corker and wanted to play in it. So Ray instantly switched *Sitting Pretty* and started to cast *Pat*. We've been at it three weeks. At the end of the second week we had got the thing almost set when our director, Bert French, suddenly died, poor chap. Such a nice man. Excellent at his job and a really jolly fellow to work with. It cut us all up terribly. And as for the piece it knocked it cold. We tried three other directors and couldn't get them, and now we have switched back to *Sitting Pretty* again and are trying to cast that.[1]

Three weeks absolutely wasted. Ah well, *c'est la vie*.

The nuisance is that *Pat* is complete, with all the lyrics done, and half the *Sitting Pretty* lyrics have to be written. A nice thing to happen when I am so hard at work on the novel.

I've never worked so well on a novel before. I must have done over 50,000 words in a month. Oh yes, and I forgot to say that Ray has now gone cold on *Pat*, so we shall have to try and place it elsewhere. Ziegfeld wired from Palm Beach asking if it would do for Leon Errol, but that only evoked in us a faint, sad smile. We know these Ziegfeld commissions.

Talking of Palm Beach, this place has closely resembled it this winter. Thermometer never below forty, and last Sunday up to

---

[1] *Pat* had music by Vincent Youmans, book by Wodehouse and Bolton, lyrics by Wodehouse and Billy Rose, but it was never produced.

fifty-six. Gorgeous Spring weather, in which I have revelled.

Mummie is going great guns. She has developed into a regular athlete. She comes out for long walks with me and *runs* half the way. She is the nearest thing to the untamed jack-rabbit of the Californian prairie you ever saw.

Talking of jack-rabbits, Jack the cat has fallen off badly lately. He has lost all his comedy and is now just a fat slob. *C'est toujours ça. . . .*

We loved the photographs. You looked very beautiful. Though, while on the subject of looking beautiful, you ought to see the Light of the Home in her Paris dresses. A pip, believe me. She flashed the blue one with the white fur collar on me the other day and I keeled over. Nor is the beige to be despised. Mummie simply sylph-like now, as slim as anything.

Bobby is at the Royalton. He doesn't seem to like New York much, but *que voulez-vous*? If he don't get an eddication he can't be a lawyer. In other words, if he doesn't stick around New York, how can he ever become a millionaire? Also we think his complaints of the horrors of NY are largely banana-oil, designed to get sympathy.

Morris Gest has just put on *The Miracle* over here, a stupendous production, which is playing to 50,000 dollars a week up at the Century.[1] The strain was so much that he told us yesterday he had had a nervous breakdown and had to be stopped all through one long afternoon from jumping out of the window of his seventh-floor room at his hotel. And, as I very cleverly and with a good deal of dry humour said – but not to him – who were the chumps who stopped him?

I'm reading *Poor Relations* again.

Well, cheerio. Will write again very soon, if I can take an hour off from finishing *Bill*. I must get it finished this month, as the *Post* won't start until it is complete and they have to have the stuff six weeks in advance.

Your loving
Plummie

---

[1] The famous production in which Diana Cooper played the Virgin.

12 September 1924   Harrogate
                                     Yorkshire

Darling Snorky,

We are so awfully worried about your cold, darling. You simply must make a real business of taking care of yourself, because you are evidently not any too strong – good opening for a joke here, but I can hear you saying 'Obvious'. Do please wrap up warmly, especially when you come back to England, as the climate is so rotten. There is no earthly need for anyone to keep having colds and sore throats if they take care. It means that you either don't wrap up when you get warm, or else that you get your feet wet and let them rip. So you jolly well look after yourself. See, bonehead?

Harrogate isn't such a bad old spot. I played golf today for the first time and feel fine. The waters taste quite ordinary now, though the first two times I took them it was too awful for words. Exactly like rotten eggs.

I have just finished a short story. V.G. Mummie thoroughly approved of it. The central character may lead to further stories.

Meanwhile, I have got the novel practically set. I have had a rush of great ideas since I got here and tonight I had a couple more which almost finish the thing. I am going to make a long scenario of it, and I hope to start writing as soon as we get into the house.[1]

Mummie is the belle of the hotel, and dances like a breeze. Oh, by the way, there's no holding her now. A woman wrote to the *Tatler*, asking the editor to settle a bet by telling her which was Mrs Wodehouse and which Miss Wodehouse in that photo of us. The side Mummie has been sticking on ever since has been something awful – only equalled by mine when a letter turned up the other day addressed to 'P.G. Wodehouse, London'. I am going to write to myself and address it 'P.G. Wodehouse, England' and see if it arrives. The next step will be to send one addressed simply 'P.G. Wodehouse'.

I do a lot of reading here, and have added three new Edgar Wallaces to my collection! Unfortunately, the last, which I got this morning, is a dud and not worth reading.

Cheerio.

                        Your
                        Plummie

---

[1] *Sam the Sudden*, called in the USA *Sam in the Suburbs*.

30 March 1925
Gallia Hotel
Cannes (Famous
Pleasure-Resort – Ha
Ha!)

Darling Snorkles,

I am now at last in a position to give you the low-down on the Riviera, as based on the observations of self and egg-scrambler. Two days ago, I was gloomy and pessimistic on the subject of the entire Côte d'Azur, especially featuring Cannes, and Mummie reproached me, saying that Cannes was really a delightful spot. Next day, I was all chirpiness and *joie de vivre* and went about pointing out villas which we could buy and live in for the rest of our lives, while Mummie maintained a strange silence. Today, suddenly, we both exclaimed together that we thought Cannes the most loathly hole in the known world and that, once we got out of this damned Riviera, nothing short of armed troops would induce us to return.

Of all the poisonous, foul, ghastly places, Cannes takes the biscuit with absurd ease. Until we came here, I was thinking Monte Carlo not all it might be, but now I look back to those dear old Monte Carlo days with an absolute pang.

Mummie says in her letter that we have done nothing here but stay in the hotel and walk on the front, but this, with the exception of going to the Casino, is all there is to do. The only tolerable thing about Cannes is the hotel garden, which contains ornamental water with ducks, water-rats, etc, and forms an oasis in this bloodsome desert. Mummie and I have come to the conclusion that we loathe foreign countries. We hate their ways, their architecture, their looks, their language and their food. So we must simply buckle to and get a house for you in England somewhere. I am all for the Chippenham neighbourhood. We both want dogs and cats and cows and meadow-land. Directly you get out of England you get nothing but spiky palms and other beastly shrubs. I asked someone yesterday who was recommending St Juan les Pins as a spot where you might obtain rustic comfort within reach of the gay (Ha!) Cannes life if we could buy plenty of ground there. She said Oo yes! Certainly enough for a tennis-lawn. That's their idea of a rolling estate, these poor damned souls out here. If they have a stucco villa with another stucco villa adjoining it and two more stucco villas on each side and a back yard with a potted cactus, they expand their chests and say 'Gosh! This rural solitude is the stuff!' Blast, if I may use the expression, them.

Of course, in many ways Cannes is most delightful. (I mention this because I am leaving this letter on the machine while I go down to dinner, and I think the maid can read English.)

To resume. March 31st.
Good news today. Cable from America saying that the script of *Sam in the Suburbs* had arrived safely.

On the other hand, ghastly shock. The editor of the Newnes magazine which is running *Sam* serially wants to change the title and has decided on *Sunshine Sam*!!!!![1] I have written anguished letters of protest to Mrs Westbrook and also to E. V. Lucas of Methuen. Can you imagine such a foul title? Isn't it pure Ruby M. Ayres? The only thing it could be except Ruby M. Ayres is Harold Bell Wright, in which case Sunshine Sam would be a quaint, drawling old westerner, who cheers up the other cowboys with his homely philosophy, showing that you can be happy though poor, provided you do as the good book says.

Mummie's cold doesn't seem to get any better. How can it in this plague-spot?

We are now dickering with the idea of a little flat in Paris as our official address and a country house in England for you. How long ago it seems that I was writing home roasting Paris. I hadn't seen the Riviera then.

Do you know anything about Chantilly? That might be a solution. Near Paris and on a golf-links. I went there once, and thought it fairly decent, but I don't remember it very well.

We are giving dinner tonight to the entire Oppenheim Squad. It is about time, as they have stood us about fifty meals. I have also asked Captain Harwood and wife (Tennyson Jesse), who wrote *The Pelican*. I like them.

Locke gave me a couple of his books, including *Morals of Marcus Ordeyne*. Have you read that? A great book.[2]

I have actually got the rudimentary outline of a new novel going. Still in the very preliminary stages, of course, at present, but looks good. I have got as far as the point where my hero does something, and I now want to know what? Rather a good idea. He is a very shy man who accidentally writes a best-seller. A bustling American agent comes over and insists on his returning with him to America to show himself. He hypnotizes hero, who gets as far as starting in the train for Southampton with him. But on the journey

[1] It was published in the UK as *Sam the Sudden*.
[2] W. J. Locke, probably best known for *The Beloved Vagabond*.

the agent reveals the programme he has mapped out for him, lectures, personal appearances where the movie of the book is showing, etc, and the hero is so appalled that, when the train stops to water in the middle of the country, he jumps out and lets it go on without him. He now decides that at all costs he must lie low or agent will come back and snatch him up again. So he goes into hiding. It is now that the story proper, of course, starts. What happens to him? I see him at present meeting a girl who runs a bee or chicken farm (both barred because I've used them before) and getting a job as odd-job man or something and rescuing her from perils. So the real thing to settle is the girl's previous history and circs.[1]

I've been sitting out in the garden all the afternoon, and, by Jove, Cannes doesn't seem so bad after all. I think the solution is never to go into it. I propose to spend all my time in the garden from now on.

Cheerio.

Yours
Plummie

PS *April 1* Not such a bad place, Cannes! We went to the Casino last night and I won 500 francs, which makes me feel a bit benevolent. Also, Italian musicians have been singing under our window this morning. All very jolly.

10 February 1929   Rogate Lodge
                                     Rogate
                                     Petersfield

Darling Poots,

Thanks awfully for your letter. It cheered me up. I had been feeling very weak and feeble. Have you ever had flu? It leaves you a terrible wreck. Today for the first time I am feeling pretty good again. . . .

I went down to Droitwich on Tuesday night, meaning to stay a week, but couldn't stand it and came bounding back on the one o'clock train on Thursday. I've come to the conclusion that it's impossible in winter. I found a dinner-party when I returned – The Zouches, Beiths and Col. Keppel, who looked very handsome.

Ian has finished *Baa Baa Black Sheep*, and it opens before Easter in Portsmouth and in London soon after.[2] It's an awful nuisance

---

[1] Not apparently ever written.
[2] A collaboration between Plum and Ian Hay, it ran for 115 performances in London from 22 April 1929.

that I've been so ill, as I should have liked to do a lot of work on it, if I had had the energy, but I simply couldn't face it. It's fine after the first quarter of an hour of act one, but up to there it seems very slow and govey – guvvy – to me. I may be able to do something at rehearsals.

It's extraordinary how flu seems to sap the brain. The *Strand* are clamouring for a story, to be delivered on Feb. 18th, and I can't seem to get going. All the plots I have by me seem to lack something.

I haven't read *Gen. Crack* yet. But when I was in bed I read *The Ugly Duchess*, and liked it very much. I am now heading for *Jew Süss*.[1]

Mummie is very busy interviewing an architect who seems about fifteen years old. She is planning all sorts of improvements in the house. She thinks you ought to come back and join the discussions.

We miss you at every turn. I had to send off the serial without your seeing it. But I can make any changes you want for book form. I am not quite satisfied with it, but I don't know just what is wrong. It gets by all right on its situations, but I feel it is too hurried and needs some more stuff shoved in. Did Mummie tell you of the bad time we had, when *Colliers* threatened to cancel their contract if the story started in the *Pall Mall* before they could use it? After a lot of anxiety and cabling, everything was settled, but things looked very black for a while. . . .

In re the dogs. Susan is in great form. Also Winks. Bimmy is now with the Townends, and is apparently the life and soul of the place. Townend wrote to me the other day saying that she is devoted to Rene but looks on him as potty.[2] She attacked a cow and had to be rescued. She also tries to eat up all the cat's food as well as her own. Susan loves Winks. They look perfectly ripping in the Park together. Susan keeps trying to play with Winks, but Winks will have none of it. . . .

You have missed some pretty rotten weather. By the time you get back, it ought to be better. Absolutely everybody has got flu. Mummie shook hers off much quicker than I did. She seemed full of beans directly she got up. I have been tired all the time.

Must end now darling, as I am off to dine with Ian.

Your loving
Plummie

---

[1] By Lion Feuchtwanger.   [2] Rene was William Townend's wife.

PS   I lost ten pounds in the five days I was in bed! I am quite slim and willowy now. I liked your bed. It was nice being so near to Mummie. We had the doors open occasionally and chatted.

PPS   Guy sailed for England on the *Majestic* on Saturday last.

6 November 1932   Domaine de la Fréyère
                                                  Auribeau
                                                  Alpes-Maritime

Darling Snorky,

You may well imagine (*peux bien figurer*) the excitement your letter caused in the home. Mummie was having a bath when she got it and rushed out with a towel round her shrieking for me. Winks barked, I shouted, and a scene of indescribable confusion eventuated.

It certainly was wonderful news. You know me on the subject of Peter.[1] Thumbs up, old boy. Not only a sound egg but probably *the* only sound egg left in this beastly era of young Bloomsbury novelists and Denis Freemans. He really has got something. It is wonderful that you should be marrying a man who is not only the nicest chap I know but likes exactly the sort of life you like. You are bound to be happy.

And isn't it marvellous that you're so fond of Molly and such a friend of Thelma's, so that there's no awkwardness of taking on a strange family.[2] I mean, if you are marrying – say, the Prince of Wales, there would be all that business of getting acquainted with the rest of them. Personally, I think any girl would be wise in marrying Peter simply to get Molly for a mother-in-law. . . .

What fun you're going to have. You never could have been really happy with a London life. You need the country, and I can't imagine the country under more perfect conditions. Peter, apart from being Peter, has got such an interesting job.[3] You'll love it. The only thorn in the whole thing is that we can't go yelling the news all over the place. I am so happy about it that I want to tell everyone I meet. I want to stop the French peasants on the road and say '*Figurez-vous, mon brave, ma fille est fiancée à M. Pierre Cazalet, le jeune homme le plus admirable de l'Angleterre.*'

[1] Leonora married Peter Cazalet in 1933.   [2] Molly was Peter's mother and Thelma his sister. Victor Cazalet, also sometimes referred to, was his brother.

[3] For a short time Peter worked for a chemical company, but soon gave that up and spent his life running a racing stable at Fairlawne, the Cazalets' estate.

Well, you will have gathered from all this that you have sold the idea to the old folks.

All my love, darling and tell Peter that he is just as lucky as you are, because there is no one like my Snorky.

Plummie

PGW

PS   Winks and Boo must be bridesmaids, carrying your train in their mouths.

24 August 1934   Royal Picardy Hotel
                                                     Le Touquet
                                                     Paris–Plage

Darling Snorky,

We are simply enraptured by the photographs of Sheran. I never saw such a beautiful baby. What a change from the old Chinese gangster who leered at us from your bed in April, fingering her gat under the swaddling clothes. You must have her photographed every year.

We dined the other night with Mrs Somerset Maugham. Diana Churchill was there and talked a lot about you. She is an awfully nice girl. I also liked a Miss Olivierra. Do you know her?

We are looking forward to getting into Low Wood. I think we have done wisely in only taking it for a year at first. One never knows how one will like a place. I must say, though, that it will be odd if we don't like it, as we shall be living just the sort of life we like best. It seems to me that our life will be very much the same as yours at the Grange, or as the life we led at Great Neck, which I loved.[1]

Winky and Boo have just been washed, preparatory to being exhibited with Mummie in the '*Madame de 1934 et son chien*' event in the local dog show. As far as I can gather, this is decided partly by how the *Madame* is dressed and partly by personal influence with the judges. We have one of them in our pocket and are full of confidence.[2]

Rather funny yesterday. We took the dogs on the beach and thought we would lunch at the Atlantic Hotel, for, as we agreed, it is interesting every now and then to take a meal at a simple little French inn. We had melon, roast beef, and cheese and were just about to reach for the ten francs or whatever it might be which this quaint *hostelerie* would charge, when the waiter produced a bill for 115. (We had lunched the previous day at the Casino for 93.) We paid up and changed our minds about economising by shifting to the Atlantic.

The other night I went to the Casino, had a shot at Roulette, won three *mille* in two minutes and came home. At seven a.m. Winky was restless, so I took her out, and we had been out about ten minutes when Mummie arrived, having been at the Casino all night and lost three *mille*. So we took the dogs for a walk and went in and had breakfast.

Love to all
Plummie

18 October 1934   Low Wood
                                             Le Touquet

Darling Snorky,

Thanks awfully for your letter.

This morning a lot of books arrived. I take it they are from you? (They might have been from Mummie, but I don't think so.) Thanks awfully. The selection of them was genius. They were exactly the ones I wanted, and will make all the difference to life

---

[1] When Peter Cazalet's father died, he inherited the Fairlawne house and estate. Because of death duties, this was let for a few years and Peter and Snorky lived at a house on the estate called the Grange.
[2] See 'Noblesse Oblige' in *Young Men in Spats*.

here. The great trouble about this place is that it is impossible to get books and tobacco. I have been getting along, re-reading old ones from Norfolk Street.

You never saw anything so extraordinary as the change in Boo. She is now sweet-tempered and affectionate and never growls except as comedy. She has had a splendid effect on Winky, who was getting old and stodgy and now races about all over the place. She and Boo wrestle and chase each other all day.

Boo has had all the admiration ever since we got to Le Touquet. The servants here love her, and she spends half her time in the kitchen. It's curious that she should have been so bad-tempered at the Grange. I suppose Debby's size irritated her.[1]

Life is extraordinarily like being at the Grange. One gets into a regular routine and the days whizz by. One excellent thing is that the papers have to be fetched from the town, which means a four-mile walk, so there is no temptation to shirk exercise. I do a regular forty miles a week, as I exercise the dogs and stroll about as well. I am tremendously fit.

Mummie seems to think this house won't do, and I must say it has its drawbacks, but I believe we could make ourselves awfully comfortable here. After all, one really only wants one room to sit in, and the living-room is just right, as far as I am concerned.

I'm so glad you have had Mother staying with you. I'm going to write to her today. My whole trouble about writing to her is that she insists on a hand-written letter, and I can't think nowadays with a pen in my hand. I never can see why people object to typewritten letters.

I have just finished that story I told you about, the one where the chap's soul goes into the child star's body. It has come out magnificently, after a good many anxious moments. Ma Maloney, the editress of the *NY Herald Magazine* is giving me $10,000 for it (good sugar) and is having the Paris *NY Herald* pay me, thus utterly baffling the USA tax people and making them look pretty silly.[2]

I'm glad Anthony has moved in. The Grange never seems the same without him.[3]

I must say I think wistfully of the Grange. I have to keep telling myself that I mustn't really judge this life here on its present form. It

[1] Boo had belonged to Snorky. Debby was a red setter.

[2] *Laughing Gas*, published on 25 September 1936 by Herbert Jenkins in the UK, and on 4 December 1936 by Doubleday Doran in the USA.

[3] The Hon. Anthony Mildmay, later Lord Mildmay, kept racehorses at Peter Cazalet's stables and at this time moved into the Grange. Whenever Plum refers to 'the gang', this includes Anthony.

will be quite different when I'm able to pop over to England. At the moment, one does feel a bit as if one were on a desert island.

Mummie simply raved about Sheran on the phone. She must be perfectly sweet. I hear she has the bluest eyes in the world. I do wish I could see her.

Love to the Puss etc.[1]
Your
Plummie

12 November 1934

Darling Snorky,

Just been reading your letter to Mummie. How splendid that you have taken up riding and enjoy it so much. Rather, as one might say, you than me, but I'm awfully glad you're doing it.

BOOKS. Yes, do send me the two *Claudius* books.[2] I'd love to have them.

I had a letter from Denis Mackail, laughing heartily at me for saying I liked *Goodbye, Mr Chips*. I still stick to it that it's a jolly good book. I was on the eve of getting the author's last one, *Lost Horizon*, but mercifully found out in time it was a tender, wistful story of Tibet. Gosh darn these writers who leap from one spot to another.

Have you read Evelyn Waugh's *Handful of Dust*? Excellent in spots, but he ought to have you to read over his stuff before he publishes it. You would have told him (a) that he couldn't have a sort of *Mr Mulliner* farce chapter about the man going to Brighton if he wanted the story to be taken seriously and (b) for goodness sake to keep away from Brazil.

What a snare this travelling business is to the young writer. He goes to some blasted jungle or other and imagines that everybody will be interested in it.

Also that Dickens stuff. Marvellous as a short story, but much too much dragged in.

If you have *not* read Evelyn Waugh's *Handful of Dust*, by the way, not a little of the above will be lost on you.

Big doings as regards the Wodehouse fortune last week. My *NY Herald* story has got by all right, and the Guy–P.G.W. musical comedy is not only a smash in Boston, but has been bought by

---

[1] Plum called Peter 'the Puss'.
[2] *I Claudius* and *Claudius the God*, by Robert Graves.

Cochran for London. It must be pretty good if he bought it before it opened in New York.[1]

Odd about that show. We had a ghastly cable from Freedley saying that our version was hopeless and that it was being rewritten by hirelings in NY. I naturally supposed that this would mean that we should get about twopence royalties. But no. We are getting the same as on *Oh Kay*. I can't make it out. It seems to me that there can't have been so much to change after all.

Anyway, the show is billed as by us, without mention of outside help, which is good.

Our NY lawyer cabled us that he was having a conference with the income tax people last Saturday, but we have heard nothing since.

I have nearly finished my novel, but I don't see how I am going to release it till this tax thing is settled.

Big dog fight on Mummie's bed this morning. Winks under the sheets and Boo on top of them. They fought through the blankets.

What about Wells's autobiography? I've got it and read most of it, but I don't know.

Love to all
Your
Plummie

19 December 1934

Darling Snorky,

How sweet of you to write me two such fat letters. I loved them.

I am sending you the script of my novel and also of the transmigration novelette.[2] No, on second thoughts I'll only send you the latter, as I improved the novel so enormously from this version. By the time you get this, I should think Miss Christian would have finished typing it, so will you write to Mrs Westbrook and ask her to send you a copy. Ask for my original, as that is the one that will be going to Jenkins, and there is no hurry about letting them have it.

---

[1] *Anything Goes*, with music and lyrics by Cole Porter. It opened at the Alvin Theatre, New York, on 21 November 1934, where it ran for 420 performances; and at the Palace Theatre, London, on 14 June 1935, where it ran for 250 performances.
[2] *The Luck of the Bodkins* and *Laughing Gas*.

Note that the novelette is much better in the form in which it
will be printed. I sent my own fair copy over to the *NY Herald*,
thinking I should save a week or so and get the money so much
sooner, but they didn't pay me till the arranged time, so I could
have had it typed. I asked them to send me back a copy, but they
haven't done so yet. Still, this rough version will give you a good
idea of the story. It was only at the end that I altered much.

While I was writing the above, Boo scratched at the door to be
let in. I got up and let her in, and she waited till I had sat down again
and then scratched to be let out. This is her favourite joke. I expect
in a minute or two she will be scratching to be let in again.

Boo is the most extraordinary dog. In the morning I have
breakfast in a lovely warm room with a fire, and she comes in for a
minute but always wants to go out again. When I have finished
breakfast I find her sitting in the fireplace in the drawing-room with
her back against the fire. It is not lit and all the windows are open, so
that the room is like an ice-house, but she prefers it to the breakfast
room.

I believe she reasons as follows: I sit in here after dinner and it's
warm and cosy. Therefore this is a warm, cosy room. I admit that at
the present moment I have an odd illusion that I am freezing, but
that must be mortal error or something, because it has been
definitely proved that this is a warm, cosy room. Either a room is
warm and cosy or it is not warm and cosy.

I have never seen a dog so happy as Boo is now. She loved
being with Winky. The only trouble is that Pekes do tie you down
so. I would have liked to go to Paris for a day or two, as it has been
pretty dull since Mummie left, but I simply couldn't bring myself
to leave Boo and Winks. I go for an hour's walk every afternoon,
and when I come back they fling themselves on me in a sort of
hysteria of relief, as if I had been away for years. It makes me feel
that they would simply pine away if I left them for longer than an
hour.

I must say Le Touquet in winter, if you're all alone, is a quiet
sort of spot. I would have liked it better, only I have just finished
eight months of terrific strain, what with doing the novel, the
novelette and the play and having all the income tax stuff as well,
and I couldn't settle down to anything. I felt very let-down and at a
loose end, and would have loved a couple of weeks in London. I feel
better now, and am getting ahead with some short stories. But I
shall be glad when April comes and I can come over to
England. . . .

48

I am very keen on getting the papers today, as I see that the Puss and gang were riding at Derby. I hope they had a good day.

Tell the Puss that I went down to the town to buy some stamps yesterday and tried to pay the woman at the shop with a piece of toilet paper which I thought was a fifty franc bill. She laughed heartily, looking bronzed and fit.

While Rome Burns hasn't arrived yet.[1] Are you sending it?

In your letter today you say you're sending *Panorama*. What is that? I can't place it.

Isn't it amazing what a few books there are that one wants to read. Mummie sent me a list yesterday to choose from, and the only one I could even contemplate reading was *Moss Rose* by Joseph Shearer. One of them was that book of Phyllis Bottome's – I forget the title – which is about lunatic asylums.[2] It simply beats me why anybody should want to read it.

I must say the same thing rather applies to those Claudius books. I read *I Claudius* and was interested, but I felt almost looney when I had finished. I haven't been able to bring myself to start the second one yet.

I absolutely agree with you about Wells's autobiography. I always maintain that what kills an author is complacency. I have watched Wells getting more and more complacent for years and going all to pieces as a writer. His autobiography, most of it, is simply deadening. You feel as if you had been buttonholed by an old bore to whom you had to listen politely.

Aren't writers extraordinary. I simply gasped when Wells said that the Bulpington of Blupp was as good a character as Kipps. It meant that his critical sense was absolutely dead. The Bulpington of Blupp isn't a character at all. I felt the same when Conan Doyle used to say that the later Sherlock Holmes stories were as good as the early ones. It's a relief to me to know that I've got you to tell me if I am going cuckoo in my work. I shall be interested to hear what you think of this last novel of mine. I think it's good. It certainly moves.

Do you know, laddie, I believe the only way a writer can keep himself up to the mark is by examining each story quite coldly before he starts writing it and asking himself if it is all right *as a story*. I mean, once you start saying to yourself 'This is a pretty weak plot as it stands, but I'm such a hell of a writer that my magic touch will make it all right', I believe you're done.

Did you read Denis' *Summer Leaves*? I thought it was v. good. I

---

[1] By Alexander Woollcott.   [2] *Private Worlds*.

was prepared not to like it, as I hadn't much liked *Another Part of the Wood*, but it was OK.

Have you noticed what a lot of people are dying these days? Ma B., my aunt Anne, Pinero, Dennis Bradley. . . .

Must stop now. Lunch.

Love to the gang, Puss, Sheran etc.
Your
Plummie

PS   Has Sheran got any hair yet?

1 January 1935

Darling Snorky,

Happy New Year to you and the gang, and may 1935 bring Sheran some hair and eyebrows.

You were sweet to send me such a lovely box of Christmas presents. The cigars are fine, and so of course are the apples and jam. . . .

That was a great boost Wollcott gave you. I wish there were more books like that.

✩

In *While Rome Burns*, after describing what is clearly Fairlawne, the Cazalets' house in Kent, Woollcott, leaving it with a spray of orchids in one hand and a forty-inch cutlass of sinister appearance in the other, went on:

My host had heard me innocently admiring them, and to my genuine surprise had pressed them into my hand at parting. As I drove off into the night, I made a note to remember that on my next visit I must be heard expressing my admiration of several paintings by Augustus John and the late Mr Sargent, for a small bronze head of Epstein, for the avenue of immemorial yews which glorifies the drive, for the bride of the younger son of the house, and for a small black spaniel bitch named, if memory serves, Tiny.

Plum's letter continues:

Mummie blew in on Dec 23 with a six weeks old Peke puppy!!! So now we have three Pekes and are rooted here for ever. It is an angel, a male this time, but Winks and Boo won't have anything to do with it at all. Boo sulked for four days after its arrival, but has now accepted the situation. It brings back the dear old Grosvenor Mews days very vividly. We spend all our time spreading fresh paper.

Mummie has to spend an hour and a half doctoring the dogs each morning, as Winks and Boo are both a bit off colour and the pup needs more attention than a baby. It sneaks out every now and then and eats Winky's dinner, with frightful results.

We are all in a flutter, because we are giving our first dinner party on Thursday. Two couples. It ought to be rather fun.

On Christmas Day, Mummie and I took the Pekes for what was intended to be a short saunter and got lost on the dunes and finished up with a six-mile walk, and on Boxing Day we did exactly the same thing. I think this is what laid Boo and Winky out. They were very subdued the next few days.

Love to all
Your
Plummie

3 January 1935

17 Norfolk Street
Park Street
W.1.

Darling Snorky,

So glad you liked the novelette. No need to preserve MS, as the correct version is now over here.

I wrote to Westbrook today to send you my new novel *The Luck of the Bodkins*. I want you to go over this very carefully and mark the bits you don't like. I have an uneasy feeling that I have made it too long, though I can't see that there is any deadwood, as the plot is so strong. The only thing is that I may have overwritten the dialogue in spots. Mark cuts wherever you feel needed.

The copy you will get is the one I shall send to Jenkins, so there is no hurry about it, as he will not need it for months. Also, don't be afraid of making it untidy, as I always send my stuff in to him all scrawled over and corrected.

Your
Plummie

10 March 1935   Low Wood
                                                Le Touquet

Darling Snorky,

Many h.r. of the d. I wish I could be with you to celebrate it.

You will note by the above address that I have returned from Paris. I found I couldn't work there, so I dashed back here, leaving Mummie at the hotel with Bea buzzing round so she will [be] quite happy.[1] I brought Winks back with me and took her into the kitchen, where Boo had just finished having a bath, expecting a joyful reunion, and the two silly chumps had completely forgotten one another and started a terrific fight directly they met. They were separated and told to run about and make friends, with the result that they had six more fights in the next ten minutes. The last one took place in my study in a corner of the room where I had put my typewriter case. Boo was behind it and Winks in front, so they couldn't get at each other, but they stood on their hind legs with noses touching and snarled and growled for about a quarter of an hour. Very droll. Today, so far, they have only had one fight, so I think they are settling down. . . .

My stay in Paris was absolutely spoiled by another spasm of the Awful Suspense which has been going on all these last eight months. I sent John Rumsey five short stories to sell in America, and he cabled that the *Red Book* wanted to buy them at $5000 apiece. He said he expected to clinch the deal on Feb. 25. We waited all that week and no cable arrived. Then a letter came, saying that there was a hitch. It appears that the President of the Red Book Co. also runs *McCall's* magazine, and in 1922 I had a contract with *McCall's* for six short stories at $1500 apiece and then, if you remember, Bobby got me that big Liberty contract and I never delivered the stories!

Apparently, this has rankled with the Pres. all these years, and he said that by way of making up for my dirty trick I would have to shade my price a bit. So on Monday last I cabled John to take any price he could get and cable me. We were on tenterhooks all the rest of the day, and in the evening a telegram arrived. We tore it open eagerly, and it was from Lady Dudley, thanking me for exercising her Dalmatian dog during her absence from Le Touquet. . . .[2]

I have just had the typewriting bill for *The Luck of the Bodkins*, revised version. Miss Christian has charged me for 75,000 words, so that now the damned thing is apparently much too short – for

---

[1] Bea Davis was one of Snorky's greatest friends.

[2] Gertie Millar, a famous Gaiety Girl, married first the composer Lionel Monckton, and then the 2nd Earl of Dudley.

book form, though fine for serial purposes. I shall have to shove back at least ten thousand words.

Meanwhile, I am plugging away at my play. It is a maddening thing to work at, and it is on the verge of being really good, but always some little snag crops up. I think now that I am back here I shall get it all right.

Bea says you are getting wonderful at riding. I'm so glad. She also says that Sheran is splendid and is at last getting some hair.

Jolly good the Puss riding two winners at Hawthorn Hill. I hope you had some money on.

Did you see in the papers about Cochran's row with Equity? It looks as if he would not produce *Anything Goes* after all. Still, I am getting a steady hundred pounds a week from it in New York, although there are now only two lines of mine in it.[1]

              Love to the gang
              Your
              Plummie

3 April 1935

Darling Snorky,

We were simply horrified by your account of poor old Anthony's accident.[2] What a perfectly ghastly moment it must have been for you when you saw him lying there and I can't even imagine how you must have felt at that dressing-station. Gosh! isn't it awful to think of the things that can jump out at you without warning in this life. I didn't even know A. was riding on the Saturday. I was feeling my usual feeling of relief at the National being over and the Puss and Anthony being all right.

I have written to him. Mummie also. I don't suppose he will be able to read letters yet awhile. Still, they will be there for him when he gets better.

This afternoon a boy turned up with a telegram. I thought at once 'It's all over. This is from Snorky, saying the worst has happened.' But no. Just a sweet little telegram from Heather, asking if we could put her up through Easter.[3] The first we had heard of her for eight months. . . .

[1] For reasons which are not fully explained by either of his biographers, Plum actually did very little work on *Anything Goes* and made certain financial concessions to Guy Bolton because of this.

[2] Anthony Mildmay.

[3] Heather Thatcher, actress. Appeared in several Wodehouse musical plays.

Isn't it a shame that I shan't be able to come over till June. I was so looking forward to seeing you and the gang next week. Still, it can't be helped. It will give me time to become even more fascinating. . . .

Oddly enough, the play I am writing, after looking hopeless for days, suddenly came right this morning and now looks great. So we had had a bumper day.[1]

I feel very sad, though, when I think of our poor old Ant. I wonder how this will affect his future riding. Will the Lord put his foot down and say he mustn't race again? I do hope not. What an extraordinary escape he must have had – those ribs not injuring the lung.

I'm glad the Puss is so pleased with Emancipator. It was bad luck getting spilled by being bumped. What a scramble the National is.

Mummie says you looked simply wonderful in your Court dress. I wish I could have seen you.

I loved the two books you sent me. If you remember when you are next in London, will you send me Frank Swinnerton's *The Georgian Literary Scene* (Heinemann). It is all about how good I am. There was a page review of it in the *Weekly Dispatch* the Sunday before last (enclosed).

Your loving
Plummie

☆

Hilaire Belloc is generally given the credit – in an Introduction to *Weekend Wodehouse*, published in 1939 – for having first proclaimed the literary excellence of P. G. Wodehouse. However, in 1935 Frank Swinnerton wrote that Arnold Bennett had told him that he had noticed a red streamer across the top of the *Strand* Magazine: 'NEW STORY BY P. G. WODEHOUSE', while other authors including himself had to be content with their names together in a tablet at the bottom. Swinnerton writes that Bennett went on: 'I thought "This has to be looked into." I read it. He had every right to it. I laffed like anything. It was terrific!' Thinking then for a moment, he pursed up his lips and added 'He's awfully able. Far . . . abler than any of these highbrows.' Then, after telling the story of how Lord Asquith was given the

---

[1] Probably *The Inside Stand*, which opened at the Saville Theatre, London on 21 November 1935 and ran for 50 performances.

54

latest Wodehouse by his daughter as they travelled by train from Paisley after the election defeat which ended his parliamentary career, he went on:

Those are tributes which show an author's uniqueness; and I mention them as revelations of the altogether peculiar power wielded as teacher by Wodehouse. He is not deliberately a reassuring author; he does not seek to cheer and console. He is neither prig nor buffoon. He merely creates merriment – for fun. In a period when laughter has been difficult he has made men laugh without shame. He has done it less by means of his comic invention, although it must be comic invention that carries his books into lands other than our own, than by means of his vocabulary. True, the vocabulary serves but to put briefly before us what solemner writers would say at immense length (if they could say it at all).

☆

Plum's letter continued with the following postscript:

PS   You would have laughed this morning. Boo had a regular *crise des nerfs* at breakfast time in Mummie's bedroom. All about nothing. Usually she calms down at once if put on Mummie's bed, but today she went on swearing to herself for about ten minutes. A looney, of course, but in all her moods loveable. I never saw anything so priggish as Winks was during this scene. She sat on my lap looking up in my face, and you could hear her saying '*I'm* good, aren't I?'

☆

4 June 1935

Darling Snorky,
The story arrived safely. I agree with your criticism – v. sound. But the trouble is that I believe the story in the shape in which it now is won't do and will have to be withdrawn altogether till I can find some way of fixing it. John Rumsey reports that editors in NY, while liking it themselves, dare not print it for fear of offending readers because the hero is a clergyman and is trying to swindle an insurance company![1]

Isn't the American middle-class outlook weird. Still, it's no use trying to go up against it, so I shall withdraw the story and see if I can't do something with it from another angle.

Meanwhile, I have been sweating at two more, both of which are coming out very slowly but quite well. One is a Ukridge story.[2]

[1] 'Anselm Gets His Chance' in *Eggs, Beans and Crumpets*.
[2] Probably 'Ukridge and the Home from Home' which appeared in *Lord Emsworth and Others*, published in 1937 by Herbert Jenkins.

55

I'm so glad you have come round to Ukridge.

Sensational news. Yesterday we bought Low Wood!!! We have been changing our minds every day since we got back, and as late as yesterday morning had made an offer for another house. But it was refused, and then Mummie suddenly switched back to Low Wood.

I must say I am delighted. I have grown very fond of the house and with the alterations we are going to make it will be fine. We came to the conclusion that we wanted to live in Le Touquet and that Low Wood was the best bet on account of the position.

I suppose you are down at Eton today.[1] I wonder if it is raining there, as here. I hope not.

I had my first swim on Sunday. Frightfully cold.

Armine and I went down to Bexhill and saw Mother.[2] She seemed a bit frail, but not too bad. I say, what an enormous size Armine is. I made him walk from the Dorchester to Victoria, and three times *en route* he pleaded for a cab. And when we got to Bexhill he had a fat lunch at half-past one, a big tea with some friends of his at Cooden at three-thirty, and another tea at Mother's at four-fifteen. He told me he thought he had put on a little weight in front – did I notice it? I said I thought he had a little.

Must stop now. Lunch.

> So long. Love to all.
> Your
> Plummie

PS   I can't get a glimmer of an idea for a novel. I seem to have used up all the plots. I suppose it will come some time.

8 September 1935

Darling Snorky,

Just caught boat, and found that about two thousand of the proletariat had decided to catch it, too. Was half an hour late, met by Kathleen at 8.30, and told that Mummie was giving a dinner party at 9.30 to a group of nibs. . . . I just managed to get my nose past the stick at 9.45. All very pleasant. . . . On to Casino, where Mummie, the poor sap, lost a bit but I made six *mille* and cleared out with it.

I loved my visit, as always, and wish I could have stayed

---

[1] The letter was written on 4 June.   [2] Armine was Plum's elder brother.

longer. ('The hell you do,' you mutter. 'It seemed quite long enough to *me*.') I carried away with me sentiments of the liveliest gratitude for your refined hosp.

I arrived back to find my *Daily Mail* article the talk of Le Touquet. Everybody seems to think it is my masterpiece! There's one thing about writing for the *DM* – you do get read.[1]

Mummie is very fit and longing to see Sheran.

My heart bleeds for you. I do hope you will soon be feeling better. What a shame that you should have to go through all this.

Bill and René sent their love. Poor little Bim wasn't well. V. pathetic. Winks and Boo, on the other hand, bursting with health. I got a great reception.

All my love, darling. Love to the Puss and Nanny etc.

> Your
> Plummie

☆

Edward Cazalet, whose name is the subject of much of this letter, was born in April 1936.

☆

26 February 1936   Hilbre
                                                    Le Touquet

Darling Snorky,

Your fat letter to Mummie arrived by this afternoon's post. I'm glad you're feeling better. Jolly sensible taking that three weeks in bed. Nothing like it.

Stephanie. Oke with me, though Mummie says it reminds her of the Rector of Stiffkey. I once knew a girl named Stephanie Bell. I like the name. The thing that is breaking me all up is this idea of Edward if offspring is a son. I suppose Mollie is all for it, but I can't see where it comes in. Pete can't have been old enough to have known Edward Cazalet very well, so I don't see why he and I – two of the best fellows in the world – should be exposed to the risk of being related to someone who, unless steps are taken through the proper channels, will be called Teddy. Why not William, after Mr Cazalet? Then we should have a good honest Bill, which could be great.

[1] The article appeared in the *Daily Mail* on 5 September 1935, and is given as Apprendix A.

57

Alternatives

(a) 'I see old Bill Cazalet, the rugger blue, won the Grand National yesterday.'

(b) 'They tell me Teddy Cazalet is on the Riviera with Dennis Freeman, getting brown absolutely all over.'

No comparison.

I am longing to come over for my next stay at the Grange. Expect me reasonably soon, and have the place entirely clear of your Christmas guest. I am sweating away at the moment, making *Laughing Gas* into a novel. It's coming out marvellously, and it's pretty sickening to think that there is no serial future ahead of it. I have tacked on some marvellous plot. (Note the two marvellouses. Edward – Teddy Cazalet, who was so wonderful as Richard of Bordeaux at the Gate Theatre, will talk like that.) I have got about another fifty pages to do of new stuff, and then I get back into the main stream and the rest remains aziz. So I ought to finish quite soon.

I never told you about St Moritz – The White Hell of St Moritz, as it is called. Of all the ghastly spots! I didn't think I'd be able to cope with it for a bit, but then I hit on a great scheme – viz. to stay in my room till lunch, then a quick walk from 2.30 to 3.30, then back to my room till bedtime. After that, I found Switzerland quite enjoyable, and managed to get two short stories written. If I ever have to go there again, I shall cut out the quick walk.

Old Bea would come in to lunch, all flushed and rosy from a row with Harry and a dash down Corviglia, and we would tell her just what we thought of her blighted St Moritz.

I was so glad when Bea told me that you didn't like ski-ing. I had two lessons. I didn't mind the going down, but it seemed to me that nineteen–twentieths of ski-ing was shuffling up hills. And even when you get good, you have to take a train.

The dogs are in tremendous form. They fight at least three times a day. At first we thought it was Boo who started these fights, but now we find that it is generally Winky. She raises her head and stares at Boo. Boo's back is generally turned when this begins, but gradually she feels Winky's eyes and turns and stares back and then they fly at one another.

I thought that dream of yours awfully funny.

Low Wood is progressing slowly. I think it will be a very nice house when it's finished. The new garage is up and is a great improvement. The grounds are huge – parklike and extending to fully an acre.

We spend our afternoons now walking on the dunes. We take Dick, Lady Dudley's Dalmatian with us. Boo has a great crush on him and dashes about after him up and down precipices. You ought to see her.

Didn't you love that Peke cover on the last *New Yorker*?

Love to all the lads. I was sorry to see Pop M[1] fell on Good Shot the other day. Silly ass. Tell him to stick to his saddle like a man.

Your loving
Plummie

PS   Teddy would take to ski-ing like a bird.

17 March 1936

Darling Snorky,

. . . A thousand thanks for hosp. (King-Hall always used to say 'Why a Thousand?'.) I don't know when I've enjoyed a visit to the old spot more. Pretty well the ideal week. It was such fun being busy all the time – now dashing up to London, now cleaning out the ring at Hurst Park. The only flaw was that I missed our haystack walks. I always remember those, and my heart rather bled when to the church and back was all that you could manage. Never mind, six weeks from now we'll be doing the haystack course (as your old man would say).

I found Mummie ever so much better. Full of beans. And today was like a real Cannes day. I have been feeling wonderful.

The Dalmatian, Dick, attacked a tiny terrier the day before yesterday and is in disgrace. I never can make dogs out in that way. You find the biggest of them going for small ones. They don't seem to have any sense of fair play. (Play the game, you cads. . . .)

Do you think Peter would handle my National bet for me? He probably has ways of sneaking a better price. Tell him I want a tenner each way – not, I think, SP, but consult him about this. I have an idea Emancipator will shorten. If he thinks another tenner on him to finish, oke.

Not much new. Boo was sick at lunch. . . .

[1] Mildmay.

Love to all. Take care of yourself. Kiss Sheran for me, also Deb and Tiny.

> Your loving
> Plummie

16 April 1936

My darling angel Snorky,

This is just a line to tell you how much I love you and how much I am thinking of you. I am praying that you won't have too bad a time, because you're very precious to me.

I am bucking myself up by thinking of the lovely summer you will have when it's all over. What a fuss we shall make of you.

I shall come over directly you are able to see people. What a long time ago it seems that I saw you with Sheran at the nursing home and you said she was like a Chinese gangster! And do you remember Lord Somebody's baby being brought in from next door, and we agreed that Sheran looked prettier than that, anyway.

I can't bear the thought of you being in pain. I do hope things will be as easy as last time. Thank God there won't be that awful rush and confusion. I'm glad Mummie will be with you.

It's a lovely sunshiny day, and I shall stroll about with the dogs and think of you. And tonight I shall take out all your old letters and read them.

I hope this reaches you before the great day. I want you to know how much I admire you for the way you have gone through all this beastly time of waiting. Everybody thinks you have been wonderful.

> Bless you, darling,
> Your
> Plummie

28 December 1936

> 1315 Angelo Drive
> Beverly Hills
> California

Darling Snorky,

I had just settled down to work off my correspondence – owing to my having ignored all letters for about a month in order to concentrate on work, I have quite thirty letters to write – when Mummie brought me your letter, so the rest of them will have to wait.

That's wonderful news about the stables. I remember Brian Tighe, a very respectful young man who laughed heartily at my gags in order to get in right with Pete. Pete and Anthony will have lost their form badly if they can't get his money out of trust. Though there is something grim about Anthony plotting to grab other people's dough, because I have had my eye on his for years, and am simply biding my time. . . .

Yes, I am back on *Rosalie* again, just as in the dear old days, but this time, thank goodness, it really is a solid proposition. If you remember, last time everybody felt that musicals were hopeless, so they wanted to do the thing as a straight picture. That being so, the original story had to be thrown away, and when I got round to it people were picking straws out of their hair and suggesting plots about princesses who grew to the age of twenty-one with the mistaken idea that they were boys. I am now working on the original story, as done by Ziegfeld, with Bill McGuire, who wrote the musical comedy (with Guy) as my supervisor, and everything looks very bright, as they are planning it for their big musical of 1937 and if I can pose as the saviour of the thing – the man who converted a half-million dollar loss into a five-million profit – I shall be in very strong at the studio.

The beauty of it is that Bill McGuire really understands his job. He knows musical comedy backwards, and is a top notcher at pictures. His last thing was *The Great Ziegfeld*, so that anything he approves of will get by with Sam Katz, who is the actual boss of the enterprise. And he and I work together splendidly. Altogether, things look good. *Rosalie* always was a pretty good bet, as was shown by the fact that it ran a year in New York with a score without a hit tune in it, purely on the strength of its comedy. I think we have got a good lay-out, and I have been working very hard on it, having done half of it in about three weeks.[1]

Thanks for the page from *Express* about the recent Edward. Over here, the Hearst papers, of course, took a very yelling attitude about the thing, trying to stir up feeling on the ground that wasn't a pure, sweet American girl a fitting mate for the highest in the land: but the others were all right, and Mencken wrote a very good article, putting the thing very sanely and showing what an ass Edward was.[2]

[1] For the full story of *Rosalie* as a film, see the section on Hollywood, p. 130. As a play, with music by Gershwin and lyrics by P. G. Wodehouse and Ira Gershwin, it was put on at the New Amsterdam Theatre in 1928.
[2] H. L. Mencken, influential American journalist.

A significant thing, I thought, was that when I went to the pictures the other night and Mrs Simpson came on the news reel there wasn't a sound. Nobody clapped. It shows once more how futile the Hearst papers are when it comes to influencing the public. He roasted Roosevelt day after day for months, and look what *he*'s done. What people buy the Hearst papers for is the comic strips.

I agree with you that England has come darned well out of this. By God, sir, I'm proud of the boys. Can you imagine any other country in which a king's abdication would have been received with a sort of universal 'Oh, yes?' and just left at that?

I hope Bea is now admitting that Father knows best. I told her that bird was no good.

Very exciting about my money. I'm glad Pete has taken me out of the red, but do stop him getting beaten by short heads. No percentage in that sort of thing.

In the intervals of working on the picture, I have managed to revise and sell to the *Saturday Evening Post* a couple of short stories which I wrote last year. One of them – 'All's Well With Bingo' – they tell me they think the best I have ever done. It is, too, pretty well. I can't seem to get that novel of mine finished, though. I have reached Page 205, but it is a frightfully tricky story, and I can't just dash off an odd chapter here and there. It needs concentration.[1]

We went to the Nigel Bruces for Christmas dinner. Very pleasant. Nearly all English people there. I met Ronald Colman, who is about the most difficult man to talk to I have ever encountered, and Herbert Marshall (who, it seems, is all washed up with Gloria Swanson. Isn't it extraordinary how these people have these terrific affairs and then they just go phut). I sat next to Lili Damita, who talked about nothing except you.

The rainy season has just begun. I don't like it. I had to stop swimming about a month ago, as the water got too cold. I find I can't take it as I used to.

The puppy is too sweet for words. Winky loves her, and they play together all the time. Having her as a companion has turned Winky into a young dog again, though she is much too fat.[2]

We have become very fond of this house now. Getting cushions and lamps for the sitting-room has made all the difference. One great advantage you get up in the mountains is the quiet and

---

[1] *Summer Moonshine.*

[2] This was Wonder, the most famous of the Pekes. She accompanied the Wodehouses throughout the war, in Germany and later in Paris.

the walks. The day before yesterday we took the dogs for an enormous hike all over the mountains.

We have now got an English couple, whom we like personally very much. The man is good, the wife not much. But we have discovered that when you have a party you can ring up an agency for extra cooks and waiters and so on, so I think we shall be able to get along with these two.

Mummie bought a Royal portable the other day, and was starting to write a letter to you on it last night. I don't know how far she got.

Fred Astaire's next picture is to be *A Damsel in Distress*, with music by Gershwin. Nothing much in it for me except the glory.

Must stop now. Love to you all.

Your
Plummie

10 April 1937

Darling Snorky,

Your marvellous letter arrived this morning. The best I have ever had from you. . . .

I must say the thought of another six months out here appals me a bit. It puzzles me why I should have liked it so much last time and dislike it so much now. It may be the weather. Just after I started swimming again, it has suddenly got icy. And, of course, I am having one of my in-between-books times. I finished the novel I had been working on since last May, and haven't managed to get another plot going yet. I am beginning to get glimmerings of one now, so I expect I shall be all right soon.

I think you're quite right about only coming out here for three or four months. The place isn't really fit for human habitation after that.

Helen Wills is here now, having tests at Fox.[1] What on earth they think she can do on the screen, I can't imagine. I gave her lunch yesterday. I have an idea she has more or less split up with Pop Moody. At least, she never mentioned him, and she seems to spend all her time away from him.

Your letter made me very homesick! What an ideal life you lead. We were thrilled by your hunting feats. You must be a jolly

[1] Tennis champion. Won Wimbledon eight times.

good rider now, far beyond the Mrs Dunlop stage. I am longing to get back and see you in action. One really does feel at the other end of the world here.

I do hope that idea of going to live at Fairlawne comes off. It would be perfect. I don't see how you're going to be able to put Anthony and me up at the Grange much longer with She-She wanting a room of her own soon and Edward throwing his weight about. My objective is a cosy suite at Fairlawne, with use of swimming-bath. . . .

The situation as regards the movies is as follows:- It seems to be pretty certain that I shall do a four weeks job on *Damsel in Distress* for Fred Astaire, unless some other job comes up before that. There is talk of my doing *Robin Hood* for Warner's and also a new Grace Moore picture for Columbia.[1] Meanwhile, my new novel is being shown round the studios, and that may click. I think the obstacle in the way of my getting work is the fact that my agent is demanding $2000 a week, while there seems to be a strong feeling that I'm damned lucky if I get $1750. Personally, I think I'm worth about $500. When you reflect that horny-handed directors, with dozens of successes behind them, are only getting $1500, what have I done to deserve $2000? On the other hand, I'm such a good chap that I feel my yessing alone is worth a good stiff salary.

I was sorry to hear that Denis had had a breakdown. But didn't you feel he always would? It does make one think a bit, doesn't it, when you suddenly realise that these birds you've been looking on as moderately young suddenly begin to show their age. Denis must be forty-six now, but I always think of him as a promising beginner. I must write to him. (Note: Sentence beginning 'It does make you think' very involved. What I mean is that the birds show their age and you suddenly realise the passage of time.)

☆

This letter to Peter was found in the file of Leonora's letters.

☆

[1] Grace Moore, originally a musical comedy actress, became an opera star in New York before going to Hollywood.

7 May 1937

Dear Pete,

A letter from Snorky arrived this morning, in which she said that your wrist was healing well. I'm awfully glad. Rotten luck getting crocked like that. . . .

I have been seeing a lot of Gubby Allen, who came from Australia via Hollywood. A very good chap. I met him two years ago at Le Touquet. He was extraordinarily interesting about body-line, and the picture he drew of conditions during the Jardine–Larwood tour were almost exactly like an eyewitness's description of the Spanish war.[1] Larwood, apparently, was going about saying that he did not intend to return to England without having killed at least a couple of Australian batsmen, and Jardine threatened to leave Gubby out of the team if he would not promise to start bowling at the batsmen's heads immediately he was put on.

This tour seems to have been almost as bad in a quieter way. Apparently the Australians never cease trying to slip something over on the English captain. Example:- In the New South Wales match one of the umpires, named Barlow, cheated so badly that Gubby told them that he would never play with him again. A few days passed, and the time arrived for the umpires for the Test Match to be submitted to Gubby. He had some difficulty in getting them to name them, but eventually they said they would be two men named Jones and Bartlett. 'Bartlett?' said Gubby. 'I've never heard of him.' 'Oh, very well known Australian umpire,' they replied. 'Excellent fellow, and very kind to his old mother.' 'You don't by any chance mean Barlow, do you?' said Gubby. Upon which, the Australian Board of Control slapped its forehead and said 'God bless my soul, isn't it amazing how one gets names mixed up. Yes, Barlow, of course. That's the chap's name.' The idea being that if Gubby had accepted Bartlett and agreed to Bartlett, it would have been too late for him to have done anything when he arrived on the field for the test match and found Barlow grinning at him.

Gubby struck me as a bit soured by it all. He was also sick with the rank and file of the English team, who failed enthusiastically on every occasion, so that the fast bowlers had to get the side out of the hole in practically every game. What England needs, apparently, is the sort of bowler I used to be in my prime – the sort of man who never gets a wicket but bowls six yorkers per over and can't be scored off.

[1] G. O. Allen captained the English cricket team against Australia in 1936–37. The famous body-line controversy had occurred during the 1932–33 series when Jardine was captain.

There is a big strike on in the studios now, which may quite easily develop and close down the picture industry indefinitely. I get a big laugh out of it. 'So you wouldn't take up my option, eh?' is the way I feel. 'Well, now see what's happened to you.'

In addition to this, our butler is still, at the moment of writing, soused to the gills. Over here, the domestic staff takes every Thursday off, and apparently our man went and got badly pickled. I got down this morning at nine, to find all the blinds still drawn and no preparation for breakfast. It is now nearly lunch time, and he is still sleeping it off.

I liked Snorky's description of your Coronation orgies. Free beer for the village is going to set you back a bit. I wish I could be with you. We made a bad mistake in taking this house on for a year instead of for six months.

Love to all
Yours ever
Plum

13 July 1937

Darling Snorky, . . .

That was a shocking tragedy about Gershwin, wasn't it. The gruesome thing about it is that everybody treated the thing so lightly. (I mean, at first.) We had asked him to our party, and he couldn't come and Mrs Ira Gershwin said that it was 'simply something psychological' – in other words, rather suggesting that he had had a fit of temperament because Sam Goldwyn didn't like a couple of his songs. On the night of our party, too, Mrs Edward G. Robinson (the wife of the film star) invited us to a party she was giving for George Gershwin on July 14. I said we should love to come, but wasn't he supposed to be ill? She smiled in a sort of indulgent, knowing way and said 'Oh, *he*'s all right. He'll be there,' – again suggesting that he was doing a sort of prima donna act. Then last Sunday in the paper was the news that he had been operated on for a tumor in the brain, and a few hours later he was dead.

Well, let's get on to something more cheerful!

Your account of Ascot made me very homesick. I do hope I don't get entangled into staying out here longer than my one year. I rather shudder when my agent talks to me about what he is going to do, once the *Damsel in Distress* is produced and I get a big screen credit. If I do make a hit with it and get offers at enormous salary, I shall do like Sherriff and come over here for visits of no longer than three months.[1] I wouldn't take on another salaried job like the last one for anything.

I must say it is altogether different working at RKO on a picture based on my own novel from being on salary at MGM and sweating away at *Rosalie!* I like my boss, Pandro Berman, very much.[2] He is the first really intelligent man I have come across here – bar Thalberg, whom he rather resembles. Everything is made very pleasant for me, and I like the man I am working with – a chap named Pagano. The way we work is, we map out a sequence together, then I go home and write the dialogue, merely indicated business, and he takes what I have done and puts it into screen play shape. Thus relieving me of all that 'truck shot' 'wipe dissolve' stuff!

It is also pleasant to be working on something that you know is a real live production and not something that might be produced or may be put away in a drawer for years! As far as I can gather, we are going to start shooting this picture in about a week. We have actually completed about sixty pages out of probably a hundred and fifty, but this isn't as bad as it sounds, because we can write twenty pages while they are shooting two. There is a whole sequence laid in London which will take them at least ten days to shoot, I imagine, and they can be getting on with that while we are finishing the script.

Helen Wills is getting a divorce!! I thought she would.

Did Mummie tell you that I went on the air with Hedda Hopper the other day.[3] She does a weekly talk about Hollywood, and she asked if she could interview me. I wrote a comic interview, full of good lines (which I gave mostly to her – nothing small about me) and it was a great success – in spite of the fact that she killed my gags by laughing in front of each one and putting 'Well' at the head of each line. (I find I am a real ham at heart. I go about now with my hat on the side of my head, saying 'Say, lissen, if that dame hadn't of stepped on my laffs, I'd have had 'em rolling in the aisles.')

My God! What a hell the home must be, with old Pete boiling pig's urine in the study! When I get back, you and I must get

---

[1] R. C. Sherriff, author of the theatrical hit *Journey's End* (1928), wrote several film scripts in America.

[2] Probably best known for the seven Fred Astaire films he produced.

[3] Famous gossip columnist whose work was syndicated all over America for forty years.

together and dope out a plot, using all Pete's stuff. Chemistry in the study is exactly the sort of thing Lord Emsworth would do.

Those strolls after dinner, cutting thistles, sound like heaven. I wish I could live in England, but I'm blowed if I see how it can be managed, unless Siva protects us. And I believe the new Finance Act dishes that.

Get Bill Townend's last book for Pete. It is called *They Crossed the Reef*, and is absolutely as good as *Voyage Without End*.

My new novel starts in the *Saturday Evening Post* next week.[1] It was very difficult to write, but has come out well. I have almost got out a plot for a new Jeeves novel, which I think is good, but the nuisance is that I have had to use two or three ideas which I had hoped would make a novel each.

I think Pete was very wise to sell the horses. There is no comparison between receiving four pounds a week and paying out two and a half. I wish I could have been at the auction. . . .

Did I tell you that on two successive days we found the puppy playing with enormous tarantulas in the garden? The second one was on the steps of the bathing-pool, and I should probably have trodden on it with bare feet, if I hadn't seen her gruffling at it. (Local Peke Saves Master.)

Winky is in marvellous shape. Nine years and two months old and brought up from infancy on cheese, sugar, cake, milk chocolate and ham, and the fittest dog in California!

> Love to everybody
> Your
> Plummie

13 August 1937

Darling Snorky,

How clever of you to write to me direct about that money. It would have spoiled Mummie's day. There is no need for her to know anything about it, as I have written to the Hongkong Bank to send old Pete a cheque, which you ought to get soon after you get this letter. What a damned nuisance these income tax people are. Have you noticed that there's always some sum like eighty pounds to be paid, however much you shell out.

It's much better recouping Pete on the quiet like this, as

---

[1] *The Code of the Woosters.*

Mummie is so keen to get back to what we had before we paid out that twenty thousand to the American tax people. I shan't miss it from my Hongkong account, as it was all gambling winnings, anyway, so what the hell!

I loved the snap shots. Sheran is becoming a regular beauty.

I finish my job on the *Damsel in Distress* tomorrow, after ten weeks all but two days, proceeds $15,000 minus $500. It has been splendid financially, as I only expected to get a couple of weeks polishing the existing scripts. But that script turned out so badly that they threw it away, and I and another man started doing a new picture from the bottom up, following the story of the book pretty closely. But much better is the fact that I have really come across with some good stuff, so that my name is big in the picture world. Wodehouse, the man who gets paid $1500 a week for mere charm of manner has been supplanted by Wodehouse, the fellow who delivers the goods.

It was a very pleasant job as I was working under a producer, Pandro Berman, who really has got intelligence, taste and everything. I think the picture is going to be good. They have been shooting now just three weeks. I delivered the last of my stuff yesterday.

I think I have made a big hit with my work on this picture. The other day, after they had been shooting, the director rang me up to tell me he was so enthusiastic about my stuff that he had to call me up and tell me so! And I hear in roundabout ways that it has got over.

Last Sunday Eddie Goulding turned up with a scenario he had written, which he wanted me to work on for Warner's.[1] I hear today that the deal is settled, and that I shall probably start it on Monday. And Pandro Berman told my agent definitely that he wanted me to do the next Astaire picture. So things are working out well.

Mummie is all right again now and going strong. We had a domestic upheaval a week ago, when she fired the staff. I really think the average servant here is the scum of the earth. We found out later that these two had worked for the Frank Morgans and, when thrown out, wrote dirty cracks about them on all the walls of the kitchen premises.[2] They had a Scotch terrier with them, which used their bedroom as a Gents Toilet, and it took us two days cleaning up.

[1] English playwright.
[2] Frank Morgan, an American actor, had been in the original stage version of *Rosalie* (1928).

We went to a party at the Edward G. Robinsons the night before yesterday. Very nice, but I do hate getting to bed late. Heather was there. She starts a small part in the picture today, I think. She isn't doing badly, really – three pictures this year – but I doubt if she will ever really make much of it out here. She looks too young for 'Aunt Caroline' parts and not young enough for heroines or comic sisters.

Scandal about Henry Daniell and wife.[1] Apparently they go down to Los Angeles and either (a) indulge in or (b) witness orgies – probably both. Though don't you feel there's something rather pleasantly domestic about a husband and wife sitting side by side with their eyes glued to peepholes, watching the baser element whoop it up? All it needs is the kiddies at *their* peepholes. And what I want to know is – where are these orgies? I feel I've been missing something.

We were thrilled by the book of photographs of Low Wood. How you must have worked over it. It looks as if you had made the place marvellous.

Met a rattlesnake just outside our front gate a few days ago. Fortunately the puppy wasn't with me, or she would have started playing with it.

I had a letter from Victor a couple of days ago, saying that he would be out here on Sept 7. It will be great seeing him again. What we are wondering is if he has come out to marry Helen Wills!! Do you think there is any chance of it? She is an awfully nice girl. What a mug she was to marry that man.

> Love to all
> Your
> Plummie

12 February 1938

Low Wood
Le Touquet

Darling Snorky,

Well, baby, here I am, full of gratitude to you for giving me such a wonderful time at the old home. I don't know when I have enjoyed a visit more. Everything done in slap-up style, and no complaints whatsoever. Lavish browsing and sluicing (bar the day when we got down to the fag end of the bacon) and exceptionally brilliant conversation. Read enclosed, which puts in a nutshell my views on Jack's attitude.[2]

[1] English actor.
[2] Jack (Donaldson) was not only a Socialist, but had earned both Plum's and Peter's contempt by saying he thought there would be a war. They said he loved bad news.

I think I won't come back immediately – (a) because I'm settled down here, trying to think out something to write and (b) because I had better eke out my visits a bit before April 5. If I come and stay for another longish visit, they might claim me as a resident. And I know I wouldn't be able to tear myself away under a couple of weeks. Tell Pete I have implicit faith in him as handler of my little bit of stuff. Anything he wants to put on anything for himself and Anthony will suit me.

I am in a bit of a quandary. (See Benchley's *My Ten Years in a Quandary*.) I feel that my next novel ought not to have a country house setting, and I can't see how I can get a rapid action plot except in the same. Also I must give the idea of somebody stealing something a rest for at least one book. But what else there is to write about, I can't imagine. What I would really like is a good Hollywood plot. Can you think of one? I'm afraid, though, that I've used up everything I can write about Hollywood in *Laughing Gas* and the short stories.

I do hate these in–between–novels times. I sit in front of my typewriter and feel that this time there really is nothing on earth that can be worked up into a story. My only consolation is that in 1924 I was absolutely destitute of ideas and none in sight. Since when, I have written fifteen novels and about a hundred short stories. So I suppose something will eventually emerge. But the agony is intense.

Mummie sent along my will yesterday. Or, rather, the lawyer did. The outlook seems pretty smooth for you if I trip over a shoelace and break my neck.

I got a great reception from the Pekes. But as usual, I was worrying myself about them quite unnecessarily. Madge tells me that they were perfectly happy in my absence and didn't miss me a bit. I get fooled this way every time. I conjure up pictures of Winky with haggard, hopeless eyes, saying 'He cometh not', and all the while she is at the peak of her form, without a care in the world.

The butter is now finished, but the pie is still going strong. I am just going to have my lunch now, and there the dear old thing will be, I have no doubt.

> Love to the gang
> Your
> Plummie

30 October 1938

Darling Snorky,

I got your letter just as I was starting off to catch my train and handed the pyjamas to the porter at the Splendide to send off to you. I hope they arrived all right.

I loved my sojourn at the old G.[1] I hope the atmosphere after my departure was one of gloom, not a delicious sense of relief with everybody stretching their legs out and saying 'Well, *now* we can begin to get somewhere!' I am hoping that even Edward chewed the lower lip a bit. . . .

Arriving at Ian's on the Wednesday night, I found that Mrs Ian had been operated on for appendicitis that afternoon![2] I was amazed. I thought on Sunday that I had never seen her looking fitter. Ian tells me she was very tired in the car going home. She's getting on all right, and the rest in the home will probably do her a lot of good. The doctor told Ian that she would soon be out, and he said 'Keep her there as long as you can.'

Life at Low Wood is being poisoned by the fact that there is a man living down the road whose wife is in Canada and who is at a loose end and relies on us for company. He rolled up before dinner for cocktails the day after I got back, and returned after dinner! We are dining with him tonight, and things look pretty serious. I think we shall have to clear out. We tried to shake him off by introducing him to the Briands, and he went there three nights in succession and stayed till midnight. They now turn off all the lights on the ground floor directly after dinner and go and sit in their bedrooms.

Still no news from the *Saturday Evening Post* about my serial. Isn't it extraordinary. I have been reading it through again and it seems OK, so I am hoping for good news.

Love to all the gang. See you soon.

Your
Plummie

4 January 1939

40 Berkeley Square
London W1
(Good address. *Ça fait
riche.*)

Darling Snorky,

I can't get over the awed feeling of having been lushed up at the

[1] The Grange. [2] Ian Hay and his wife.

Grange for a solid month. Nobody but the iron Cazalets could have stuck it out. But, grim though the experience may have been for you always remember that I enjoyed it. Nay, loved it. I was feeling so emotional about it yesterday that I came within an ace of buying Pete two shillings' worth of halfpenny stamps, to replace those I pinched. Wiser feelings prevailed, however, and he doesn't get them. (I have used the word 'feeling' three times in above. Flaubert would have had something to say about that.)

We are frightfully snug here. The last word in luxury.

Did Mummie tell you that I got out at Crystal Palace and walked to Berkeley Square? That's a mark for Pete to shoot at. It took me two and a half hours, so must have been about ten miles. I felt that I must do something to correct the queasiness caused by a month's gorging at the Grange.

Last night, very nice dinner at Bea's. She does things extraordinarily well. Not only pheasant etc, but all sorts of exotic fruits. She seems a bit dubious about flying over the Timor Sea, and I don't blame her.

We ran into Randolph Churchill on Sunday, and lunched with him at his flat yesterday. I have misjudged him. Very good chap.

Love to all
Yours ever
Plum

14 February 1939   Carlton Hotel
                                          Cannes

Darling Snorky,

How sweet of you to write and send me all the news from Molokai. (Your letter arrived five minutes ago, and I am now answering it. Quick service.) I'm so sorry about Pete's cartilage, though I suppose it will help him a lot having it removed. Bad luck about the children.

I finished the play yesterday, exactly three weeks from start to finish. It needs a little polishing, but is otherwise all right. I must say it looks pretty good. The great thing is that I have got terrific curtains for acts one and two. If you remember, the thing that killed *The Inside Stand* more than anything was the fact that it had no second act curtain and the laughter, after going strong for most of the act, gradually died away and the curtain fell in silence.

I would feel absolutely confident of this one, if it is not too unsophisticated for the theatre. You know what I mean – a Jeeves story is pretty damned wholesome. They may want something more adult. On the other hand, *The Code of the Woosters* did run serially in both *Saturday Evening Post* and *Daily Mail*, so it must be the sort of story a great many people like. That's my only qualm.

I'm not exactly writing it for anyone, but I told Jack Waller I was doing it and he was very interested and we had a meeting, at which he started casting the thing more or less. I told him right away that, after he had lost money on *The Inside Stand*, I didn't want him to take this one on unless he thought it had a very good chance, and so I wouldn't have anything in the nature of a commission to dramatize the book. I said I was going to dramatize it anyhow, and then we could talk.

As a matter of fact, though, there won't be any difficulty in getting it produced. What I am hoping is to get it done in America. I have written to George Abbott about it. He is about the best man out there. (By the way, have you seen *French Without Tears*? If not, I wish you would slip in to a matinee. It's a splendid show, and I am writing with a view to getting Mackenzie Ward for Bertie. Jack Waller thinks he would be right. So do I. Bertie is the really important part. Dozens of men could play Jeeves.)

I can't imagine how I thought I ever liked Cannes. It seems to me now a hole of a place. But I have been able to concentrate splendidly on my work. You would never recognise me now as the trencherman of The Grange. Today I breakfasted on rolls and tea, lunched on two oranges. I have been doing that sort of thing right along, and must have lost pounds. I weighed myself today in clothes and I was 91 kilos, and now all that remains is to find out how much a kilo is.

I lunched at Oppenheim's house up in the mountains the other day. Lord Darnley was there and spoke as if he was a pal of yours. Nice chap, but much too tall. Except for that, I have hardly seen a soul. I have worked till lunch, then gone out for a walk, come back and worked till dinner, and then dined somewhere quiet by myself. A darned good life, if you've got a job to finish.

I'm frightfully thrilled about the move to Fairlawne. It will be marvellous coming to stay there and seeing all your trees growing.

If I can get a berth on the Blue Train, I shall leave here almost immediately. Mummie has taken Northwood, opposite Gertie's for two months. It seemed to me, when I dined there, a bit poky, but perhaps it's all right, and my study at Low Wood will be habitable.

Fancy Pete becoming a Socialist.[1] I had just found a crushing retort to Jack D. Jerome K. Jerome told W. W. Jacobs that he couldn't understand why Jacobs was afraid of Socialism. He said that under Socialism all Jacobs's needs would be supplied. And Jacobs said he didn't want his needs supplied. He said 'I don't want a lot of people messing about with me and doing me good, damn their eyes.' It seemed to me to sum up just what one feels about the thing. Still, if it's OK with Pete, it must be all right.

In re Jorrocks. Apparently there's a catch about it being Cheltenham, owing to the railway arrangements of that time. Jorrocks goes down by train, and there weren't any trains to Cheltenham. One school of thought says that Silversands or whatever the name of the place was Brighton. I think the locale (French) was a mixture. Probably he took Cheltenham conditions and put them down near Tonbridge.

I say, t. does fly, doesn't it! Fancy Pete being too old for the Yeomanry. (But not for the Loel Yeomanry. Rather good, absolutely spur of moment.)[2]

Love to all

Your

Plummie

PS   When is the stable going to get some more winners?

10 March 1939   Low Wood
                                               Le Touquet

Darling Snorky,

Many happy returns. What a pity I'm not with you, to help you celebrate. I hope the ox roasted whole goes down well.

I must say it gave me a bit of a pang when I read in your letter that the dining room at the Grange had been closed.[3] I suddenly realised that I had eaten my last meal there (unless the new people come across with an invitation). There's something rather sad about the thought that the Grange days are over. Still the new era ought to be good. But we had some good times in the old tenement. You with a cold, Pete with a broken leg, Anthony with the botts and the children down with whooping cough – those were the days.

[1] Peter did not of course become a Socialist at any time.
[2] Snorky used the name Loel Yeo as a pen-name.
[3] The Cazalets were moving into Fairlawne.

Low Wood is now in an indescribable mess. They think up new things to do to it every day. One of the chimneys has now been taken down, together with the roof of my study, and the remains are littering the lawn. But I think the study ought to be fine later on. Apparently I shall have quite a bit of extra space.

The new puppy is simply marvellous. A terrific sport. It seems to have no legs, but it gallops about after us for miles, and is as good as gold at night, never uttering a sound. A trifle leaky at the moment, but I always think that makes a place homey. Do you remember at the Mews how we used to spread paper for Boo all over the floor of the sitting-room, and there would be one little space of a few inches overlooked and Boo would always make straight for it.

Loppy is wonderful too. We are devoted to him. He has a rooted idea that if he really gets down to it he can catch a sea gull, and he chases them for miles over the sands.

Life here is very quiet and pleasant. Last night we had two people in to dinner, and today the reaction made us feel quite faint. I felt as if I had been through some great public banquet.

I have been working pretty hard since I got back from Cannes at short stories. I wrote one, and then quite suddenly got a plot out for another. So I shall have finished two in about three weeks, if all goes well.

I got rheumatism in my right arm at Cannes and haven't been able to get rid of it yet. I rub it with Sloane's Liniment and the house reeks to heaven. I can't make out why this should suddenly have happened to me. The machine running down, I suppose.

I say, listen. My publisher, Derek Grimsdick, is going to be married on March 27. What steps do I take? I think I should come through with something for about a fiver, but what? And how do I get it? Are you going into London before then? Or Frankie? Or anybody? If so, I wish you or they would buy something suitable for a publisher and send it to him at 3 Duke of York Street, Saint James's, SW1. I'm blowed if I know what to get. Can you think of anything?

But of course you in person won't have a moment just now. You must be frightfully busy with the move. Still, try to shove it off on Frankie. It's no good asking Jack to do it. He would just buy a couple of bombs.[1]

We had a long letter from Heather the other day. I sat right

---

[1] Jack and Frankie Donaldson. We lived in a house on Peter's estate.

down and answered it the same evening, which is better service than she usually gets from the Wodehouse family. I gather things are pretty sticky in Hollywood. I have just heard from an outside source that my agent has gone out of business and is now a producer at RKO. He never bothered to let me know. I am now in the hands of Basil's agent, Eddington, who is supposed to be good. But I doubt if there is any chance of my going out there again. I think the whole situation has altered and they are now using the horny-handed $300 a week men to do the stuff.

I didn't like Cannes at all this visit. I don't think I shall go there again. Old Oppy was very pleasant, as usual. He is seventy-four, but if you want to keep him away from the girls you have to use a machine gun. I had one dinner with him at the Casino, when he was in great form, and then a lunch three days later at his house in the hills, when he was a bit grumpy – not with me but with wife and son-in-law. Just an off day, I imagine. At the dinner he didn't seem a bit older than when we first met him.

> Love to the lads, children, dogs etc
> Your
> Plummie

That was the last letter written by Plum to Leonora. She died in 1944, and he did not hear of her death until the liberation of Paris later in that year. The few letters to Denis Mackail follow appropriately, partly because Mackail was devoted to Leonora, but chiefly because several of them are revealing on matters, such as her talent for writing, which are not mentioned elsewhere.

2 LETTERS TO DENIS MACKAIL

13 May 1921
Constitutional Club
Northumberland
Avenue
London WC2

I feel I must write a line to say how much I enjoyed your *What Next*! It is simply terrific. If it is your first book, as I believe I read somewhere, I call it a marvellous effort.

Hoping you will produce something of the same sort every few months.

5 December 1923
17 Beverly Road
Great Neck
Long Island
New York

As you suggest, I am a swine not to have written before, especially as you gave me such a good time with *Summertime*. I finished it the third day out, and thought it was – if not the best of all – at any rate bracketed top with *Romance to the Rescue*. I'm not sure in some ways it isn't even better than that classic. It was ripping meeting David again. I always love your girls, too. That bit about the ghost of the dog is simply high water-mark. The whole book is absolutely topping, and I hope it is selling as it ought to. I saw the notice in *Punch*. Lucas, do you think? A foolish bit of writing, anyway. Didn't do the book anything like justice.

18 June 1925
23 Gilbert Street
Mayfair
London W

I started the sale of *Greenery Street* off with a bang this afternoon by rushing into Hatchard's and insisting on a copy.[1] They pretended it

[1] Mackail's most famous novel.

wasn't out. I said I had seen it mentioned among Books Received in my morning paper. They said in a superior sort of way that the papers got their copies early. I then began to scream and kick, and they at once produced it.

When I had got to page 42, I had to break off to write this letter. No longer able to hold enthusiasm in check. It is simply terrific, miles the best thing you have ever done – or anyone else, for that matter. It's so good that it makes one feel that it's the only possible way of writing a book, to take an ordinary couple and just tell the reader all about them. It's the sort of book one wishes would go on for ever. That scene where Ian comes to dinner is pure genius.

The only possible criticism I would make is that it is not the sort of book which should be put into the hands of one who ought to be working on a short story. Ethel got skinned to the bone at Ascot yesterday – myself present, incidentally, in a *grey* top hat and white spats – and I promised her I would work all day today at something that would put us square. So far I have done nothing but read *Greenery Street*.

You certainly have got the most extraordinary knack of apparently effortless character-drawing. Old Humphrey is immense, and yet you don't plug him in any way – just let him wander into the story as it goes along. It looks to me uncommonly like genius.

4 March 1927   Hotel Impney
                                                 Droitwich
                                                 Worcestershire

You can now retire from business and spend the rest of your life messing about at the Athenaeum, for you have written THE book, – the one you ought to have gradually worked up to and eventually turned out in your sixties.

I don't see how you are ever going to top *The Flower Show*. It is the last word. I thought you were going to find it hard to go one better than *Greenery Street*, but to my mind *The Flower Show* is in a different class altogether. It makes *Greenery Street* seem like just an ordinary jolly little story. If the old Wodehouse judgement is as keen as it always has been, *The Flower Show* is one of the really big books, fit to take its place in any company. Honestly, the only books I have ever enjoyed and admired as much are *The Egoist* and *Vanity Fair*.[1]

[1] There are many other letters in this vein.

12 April 1931   1005 Benedict Canyon
                                                 Drive
                                                 Beverly Hills
                                                 California

We have at last got our beloved daughter home again, after a five
months absence in New York. She is sweeter than ever, and full of
beans.

I don't know if she will want me to tell you before she does, but
she wrote a short story and sent it in to the *American Magazine*
without any name on it, so that it got no pull from the fact that I am
writing for the *American*, and each of the four editors sent it on with
enthusiastic comments, and they bought it for $300 and want lots
more. She also sold an article for $150.

She really can write like blazes, and, thank goodness, is now
very keen on it. Her stuff has a terrific amount of charm, and she has
only got to stick to it to do awfully well.

8 April 1932   Domaine de la Fréyère
                                                 Auribeau
                                                 Alpes-Maritimes

I'm so glad you liked Snorky's story. I thought it was marvellous.
It's such a pity that she writes with such difficulty. Have you ever
seen a Snorky MS? She sits in bed with a very thin-paper pad and
one of those pencils that make the faintest possible mark, and in
about four hours produces a page. Then she writes another page
next day and puts a ring round it and a hieroglyphic on page one –
that is to show that part of page two goes on page one, then you
read the rest of page one and go back to page two, in the meantime
inserting a bit of page four. All in that filthy, obscene handwriting
of hers. Still, the results are good. Do egg her on to writing some
more. I'm so afraid this beastly dress business of hers will absorb
her.

4 January 1945   Hotel Lincoln
                                                 Rue Bayard
                                                 Paris

A few days ago I got your card, which was very welcome. Peter
came to see me about a month ago, and was speaking about your
words in *The Times* about our darling Leonora, telling me how

much they had touched him. What a horrible, bleak feeling it gives one, to think that we shall never see her again. It just sets the seal on all the ghastliness of life these days.

☆

In an obituary notice, Denis Mackail wrote: 'She was wise as well as deliciously witty – that kind, brave, generous creature, with the charming voice. . . . So gay, so quick, so amusing; but with depths in her, too. . . . We are not likely to forget her. . . . Still less are we likely to light on such a union of qualities again. She was unique. . . .'

PART II

3 WAR

To William Townend   Hilbre
2 December 1935   Le Touquet

Isn't this Sanctions business the craziest thing you ever came across. All we had to do was just leave Italy and Abyssinia alone and nobody would have got hurt, because I can't imagine anything safer than being in an Italo–Abyssinian war. As far as I can make out, neither side has yet come within fifteen miles of the other.

4 September 1937   1315 Angelo Drive
                                     Beverly Hills
                                     California

Our great excitement here is waiting for the ten o'clock news bulletin. What a hell of a mess the world has got into! I suspect plots all round me, don't you? I mean, this Japan business, for instance. My idea is that Italy and Germany said to Japan 'Hey! You start trouble in the East and do something to make England mad. Then they will take their Mediterranean fleet over to Shanghai, and then we'll do a quick jump on their neck while they have no ships on this side.' I'll bet they're sick we haven't fallen for that.

     Slight embarrassment these last few days, as we had Hon'ble Japanese butler. He left yesterday.

23 April 1939   Low Wood
                                 Le Touquet

Do you know, a feeling is gradually stealing over me that the world has never been farther from a war than it is at present. It has just dawned on the civilians of all countries that the good old days of seeing the boys off in the troop ship are over and that the elderly sportsmen who used to talk about giving sons to the country will now jolly well have to give themselves. I think if Hitler really thought there was any chance of a war, he would have nervous prostration.

Incidentally, doesn't all this alliance-forming remind you of the form matches at school, when you used to say to yourself that the Upper Fifth had a couple of first fifteen forwards, but you'd got the fly half of the second, the full back of the third and three forwards who would get their colours before the season was over. I can't realise that all this is affecting millions of men. I think of Hitler and Mussolini as two halves, and Stalin as a useful wing forward.

Anyway, no war in our lifetime is my feeling. I don't think wars start with months of preparation in the way of slanging matches. When you get a sort of brooding peace, as in 1914, when a spark lights the p. magazine that's when you get a war. Nowadays, I feel that the nations just take it out in blowing off steam. (I shall look silly if war starts on Saturday, after Hitler's speech!)

The ghastly thing is that it's all so frightfully funny. I mean, Hitler asking the little nations if they think they are in danger of being attacked. I wish one of them would come right out and say 'Yes, we jolly well do!'

3 October 1939

When this war started, I suddenly found myself totally unable to write letters. I don't know why. I suppose I had the feeling that they would never get to their destination. But now the post does seem to be working, if a bit spasmodically. I expect you'll get this in about ten days.

I'm wondering a lot how you are getting on. They all say that there is going to be a big boom in books, and I suppose that will include magazines, so maybe we shall be all right. I should think a book like *And Now England* – what a pity they didn't call it *The Hun*, as they were thinking of doing – ought to take on new life if it is pushed properly.

Are you doing any war work? Mine is confined to running a doss house for French officers. We have three, though the only one I see anything of is the one actually in our part of the house. Owing to the war catching Low Wood half furnished, we had only one guest room and the others have had to sleep in the staff wing. (Which sounds as if L.W. were about the size of Blandings Castle!)

When was your silver wedding? Weren't you married just before me? Ours was last Saturday, and we gave a party for the whole of Le Touquet, including fifteen non-English-speaking French officers, who of course arrived early, before we could

Leonora, with the Red Setter Debby and her Peke, Boo (see page 45).

Leonora at the age when Plum first met her.

Leonora and Plum.

r and Leonora's
ding, as reported
contemporary
spaper.

P. G. WODEHOUSE'S DAUGHTER WEDS.—Mr. Peter Cazalet, brother of Captain Victor and
Miss Thelma Cazalet, who are both M.P.s. and Miss Leonora Wodehouse, daughter of Mr. P. G.
Wodehouse, the writer, had a quiet wedding at 9.30 a.m. at the village of Shipbourne, Kent. The
bride and bridegroom are in the small picture. In the large picture are Mr. and Mrs.
Wodehouse (left) and the two M.P.s.

Above Peter Cazalet with Tiny, the
black spaniel coveted by Alexander
Woolcott (see page 50).

Left The Hon. Anthony Mildmay,
later Lord Mildmay of Flete, one of
'the gang' (see p 45).

Le Touquet, 1926. *Left* Ethel (on the left), Plum and Leonora go for a stroll.
Above After tennis, Leonora relaxes with Plum (note her odd shoes).

Low Wood, where Plum and Ethel lived from 1935 until their capture by the Germans.

nis Mackail, to whom Plum
te over a hundred letters. 'In
etters to Mackail he stretched
self to please . . .'

of Plum's more informal
rs to Mackail.

13

TELEPHONE,
MAYFAIR 2503.

Jan 27-1927

17, NORFOLK STREET,
PARK LANE. W.1.

Dear Denis.

What do you mean about your story in the supreme strand? Barring the one like Bradmuth it's absolutely in Class A. One of your very best. I thought the stuff about the two surgeons in the van terrific.

I say, when do we meet? Next week some time? I want to spend the early this week sweating away at a couple of half finished stories.

Do you think that article was all right? It makes me feel definitely the Kindly Old Buffer.

Yours ever
Plum

P.S. We have a new Peke. Frightfully timid, as it had been ill-treated before it came to us. We are trying to win its confidence with the suavity of our manner.

Left Bill Townend, Plum's close friend from the time they shared study at Dulwich, was also the illustrator of Plum's early children's book, *The White Feath* The picture is from this book.

Right Heather Thatcher relaxing, golf club in hand, at Le Touquet when visiting Plum. She was a friend who appeared in several of Plum's plays.

Below Guy Bolton, Plum's close friend and collaborator. Guy and Plum worked together in some c the most successful musicals of th age, and they introduced 'situatic comedy' to replace the large musicals with tremendous sets an showgirls.

Left 'Bill and me.' Plum called his foxhound Bill after Townend.

Right Dorothy Dickson in 'The Cabaret Girl' (see next page).

THE PLAY

With which are incorporated "THE PLAY," "THE PLAY SOUVENIR," "THE STAGE SOUVENIR"

PICTORIAL

NO.
249

VOL.
XLI

1 S.
NET

MONTHLY

"THE CABARET GIRL."

George Grossmith and Norman Griffin in 'The Cabaret Girl', Plum's hit collaboration with George Grossmith and Jerome Kern.

The playbill of 'Sally', starring George Grossmith, Dorothy Dickson and Leslie Hanson.

muster our linguists. Still, after a rather sticky ten minutes, everything went triumphantly. The officers lined up in front of us and sang an old Flemish chant, which involved two of them holding a towel over our heads. Rather impressive.

How is your part of the world for living in these days? Le Touquet is fine. One slight drawback is that the war has caused almost all the villas to be occupied, so that I don't get that desert island feeling which I love. Still, if we are going to be marooned here for three years, perhaps a few neighbours will be a good thing.

We black out, of course, which is a nuisance. But the worst nuisance is that we are not allowed to 'circulate'. That is to say, the only place we can go is Paris Plage. Ethel was talking airily about running in to Boulogne for a bite of lunch today, and we found it couldn't be done even with fifty-five passes and cards of identity. I don't mind very much, as I never do want to go anywhere. . . .

Didn't you think that was a fine speech of Churchill's on the wireless? Just what was needed, I thought. I can't help feeling that we're being a bit too gentlemanly. Someone ought to get up in Parliament and call Hitler a swine.

Must stop now, as our only link with the post office is leaving and I must get this off.

8 December 1939

Long time since I wrote. Sorry. How is everything with you? . . .

I have been reading all Churchill's books – i.e. the World Crisis series. Have you read them? They are terrific. What strikes me most about them is what mugs the Germans were to take us on again. You would have thought they must have known that we should wipe them out at sea and that there never has been a war that hasn't been won by sea power. It's very curious to see how the same old thing is happening all over again, with the difference that we are avoiding all the mistakes we made last time. I never realised before I read Churchill that the French started off in 1914 by losing four hundred thousand men in the first two weeks. Also, what perfect asses the Germans made of themselves. There was a moment when all they had to do was strike East and they needn't have worried about the blockade. Instead of which, they went for Verdun, which wouldn't have done them any good if they had got it.

23 January 1940

I agree with you about the weariness of war. I find the only thing to do is to get into a routine and live entirely by the day. I work in the morning, take the dogs out before tea, do a bit of mild work after tea, and then read after dinner. It is wonderful how the days pass. One nuisance of living here is that we get today's papers tomorrow, and not always then. The Continental *Daily Mail* is regular enough, but a touch of fog in the Channel is often enough to stop the English paper. . . .

I liked Churchill's speech the other night, didn't you? When he had finished, we switched off the radio and discussed it, not knowing that the next item on the programme was a Ukridge story. Still, I don't imagine I missed much. . . .

I can't make out what is going to happen. Do you think everything will break loose in the spring? I don't see how it can, as surely by that time we shall be too strong. My only fear is that Germany will be able to go on for years on their present rations. Apparently a German is able to live on stinging nettles and wood fibre indefinitely.

6 April 1940

We alternate here between a sort of cook-general life and a staff of servants such as you would find at Blenheim or somewhere. This is due to the fact that all the men we have ever employed come and work for us when they get leave. This last week we have had a marvellous butler (husband of the cook) and two extra gardeners. In a day or two they will have disappeared. I do think the French are marvellous. They just take a war in their stride. They toddle off and fight and come back and work and then go and fight again.

☆

Wodehouse and his wife were still in Le Touquet when the Germans over-ran and occupied it. They, like many others, had not expected the speed of the advance, and when they tried to leave, their car broke down and it was then too late to get out. On 21 July 1940 Wodehouse, aged fifty-eight, was committed to an internment camp, together with twelve other male aliens in Le Touquet. They were transported in stages by train in cattle trucks to their final destination, a lunatic asylum in Upper Silesia.

Wodehouse remained there until he was released on 21 June 1941. He was then taken, under guard and for reasons not known to him, to the Adlon Hotel in Berlin. There, almost immediately on arrival, he ran into an old friend whom he had known in Hollywood. This friend was in the company of a second man who suggested to him that he should give some broadcast talks to America, not yet in the war. Wodehouse – seeing, he was later to say, a chance to thank the many Americans who had written to him whilst in internment – seized the opportunity without further thought.

Shortly afterwards, he recorded five talks of a humorous kind, describing his experiences in camp and based on talks he had already given to the other prisoners there. At the time he failed to appreciate the implications; it was only later that he came to realise that this had been an enormously ill- considered thing to have done. Unknown to Wodehouse the recorded broadcasts, which had been intended for the Americans, were repeated over the German wavelengths to England.

Owing chiefly to the vicious charges then made in a broadcast by Cassandra (William Connor), but also to the many letters to newspapers, which assumed without any evidence that Wodehouse must have broadcast propaganda for the Germans, some people immediately believed that he had betrayed his country. It is therefore important to state what he did *not* do.

He did not willingly stay in Le Touquet after the Germans occupied it, nor did he entertain any Germans while he was there. He did not receive a proposal to leave camp and go to the Adlon in exchange for agreeing to broadcast; he went there because he was taken under guard. There was no deal of any kind. He broadcast five talks to America of a purely humorous kind, but he spoke no word of propaganda for the Germans.

The BBC made reparation for the Cassandra broadcast through a broadcast made by Evelyn Waugh as a tribute to Wodehouse on his eightieth birthday, and in 1975 he was created Knight Commander of the British Empire.

Plum remained in Germany, where Ethel joined him – bringing with her the peke, Wonder – until September 1943. The letters which follow tell the rest of the story.

☆

To William Townend   Berlin
11 May 1942

At last I am able to write to you!! This is being taken to Lisbon by
my Hollywood friend, Werner Plack. . . . He will mail it and I
hope it will eventually arrive.

You really have been wonderful, Bill, writing to me so
regularly. I got all your letters and loved them. . . .

Camp was really great fun. Those letters in the *Daily Telegraph*
about my having found internment so awful that I bought my
release by making a bargain with the German Government made
me laugh. I was released because I was on the verge of sixty. The
Germans don't intern people after sixty. When I was in Loos Prison
the first week, a dozen of us were released because they were sixty,
including my cellmate William Cartmell, the Etaples piano tuner.
Of course, he may have made a bargain with the German
Government by offering, if set free, to tune its piano half price, but I
don't think so. And even if he did, what about the other
eleven? . . . No, I think all these men were released for the reason
stated, because they were sixty, and so was I. Though I admit it
doesn't make nearly such a good story.

Camp was fine. The first few weeks, at Loos Prison, Liège
Barracks and the Citadel of Huy, were on the tough side, but once
we got to Tost everything was great. I played cricket again after
twenty-seven years, and played havoc with the opposition with
slow leg-breaks. I was in the middle of an over when they came and
told me to pack. (What happens in a cricket match when the bowler
is suddenly snatched away in the middle of an over? Can you play a
sub? And, if so, is he allowed to bowl?) We used to play with a
string ball (string wound round a nut) which our sailors
manufactured.

I remember you saying to me once how much you liked the
men in the last war. It was the same with me. I really do think that
there is nothing on earth to compare with the Englishman in the
cloth cap and muffler. I had friends at Tost in every imaginable walk
of life, from Calais dock touts upwards, and there wasn't one I
didn't like. The War Graves Commission gardeners are the salt of
the earth.

I got very religious in camp. There was a Salvation Army
colonel there who held services every Sunday. There is something

about the atmosphere of a camp which does something to you in
that way.

☆

The Wodehouses were sent to Paris in the autumn of 1943 and
were there at the time of the Liberation, after which Plum wrote
letters to all his friends.

☆

30 December 1944   Hotel Lincoln
                                          Rue Bayard
                                          Paris

I agree with your suggestion of a book about my life these last
years, and have already written my camp experiences, but in a very
humorous vein. I shall rewrite the whole thing and add my French
chapters. The nuisance is that when I get to the two years I spent in
Germany after leaving the camp there is really nothing to write
about. I was in the depths of the country most of the time, and when
I was in Berlin I did nothing but write and take Wonder for walks.
It's extraordinarily hard to describe my life there. I suppose I was in
the middle of all sorts of interesting things, but they didn't touch
me. We had a few friends, English and American women married
to or the widows of Germans, and we saw them, but apart from
that I lived the life of a hermit, plugging away at my writing. . . .

☆

This is the first of many references to the Camp Book. It was
never published, and no manuscript was found after Plum's
death.

☆

I wish there was some means of getting to know just how I
stand now in England. I had resigned myself to being an outcast
with no friends except you and René, but since the liberation we
have had the nicest possible cards from all our friends in England,
and now you say that Christison, Rees, Paddy Miller etc have been
asking after me. It gives me the pleasant feeling that I have lost none

of my friends, and I am hoping that eventually things will straighten themselves out. The unfortunate thing was not being able to contradict lies told about me at the time. It's hopeless to do it three or four years later. Flannery's book, for example.[1] Not a word of truth in it. Nobody ever came down to the camp to talk to me about being released and making talks on the radio. And all the conversations he reports as taking place between himself and me were non-existent. I only saw the man three times, once when I got me to do that talk with him on the radio, another time when I came up to Berlin and ran into him having dinner at the Adlon, when I stopped at his table and said about a dozen words, and the third time when Ethel arrived. From his book you would think that we were always together. I wish, by the way, when people invent scenes with one, that they wouldn't give one such rotten dialogue. Can you imagine me saying some of the things he puts into my mouth? But I suppose there is nothing to be done about it now.

☆

In the autumn of 1944 Plum and Ethel were arrested and taken to the Palais de Justice where they sat for seventeen hours on two wooden chairs before they were interrogated. They were rescued by Malcolm Muggeridge, who gave the following account of what happened:

I located them at a police station on the Quai d'Orléans. No one seemed to know why M. and Madame Wodehorse (as they appeared on their warrant) were there, and I had no difficulty in arranging for Ethel's immediate release. It appeared that, using her highly individual French at its shrillest, she had reduced the whole station to a condition of panic: aided and abetted by her peke, Wonder, whom she had insisted on taking with her when she was arrested. By the time I arrived on the scene, the police, I could see, were desperately anxious to get Ethel and Wonder off the premises as soon as possible.

Major Muggeridge had more difficulty over Plum, and the only way in which he could secure his release was on health grounds. Plum was transferred to a clinic, from where the following letter to Townend was written.

☆

[1] *Assignment to Berlin*. Harry Flannery's account has been discredited.

My arrest by the French came as a complete surprise! I had gone to bed at about twelve on the night of November the twenty-first, and at one o'clock woke to find two inspectors in my room. They took Ethel and me to the Palais de Justice, and we spent sixteen hours without food in a draughty corridor. Next day they released Ethel, and I spent four days in the inspectors' office. I was then brought to this hospital, where I have been ever since.

The original idea was to put me in the camp at Drancy but thank goodness that was changed. I believe Drancy is very tough, not at all like my beloved Tost, where life was one long round of cricket, lectures, entertainments and Red Cross parcels. Here in the hospital I am sitting pretty, though naturally it is pretty foul to be cooped up. I have a room to myself, quite good food, plenty of tobacco and drinks, and Ethel is allowed to come and see me. I also had a marvellous five days' visit from Peter.[1] He used to bring champagne every day and we had great times.

I generally wake up at four a.m., lie in bed till six, then get up and boil water on a boiler lent me by one of these *inspecteurs* who are excellent chaps, and we are great friends.

15 February 1945   Paris

I was in the clinic when I wrote to you last. (I hope you got the letter all right.) I spent eight weeks there, and then Malcolm Muggeridge drove Ethel and Wonder and me down to Barbizon, about thirty miles from Paris, in the most awful blizzard. We lunched at a marvellous restaurant in Fontainebleau forest in front of a great log fire and thought things were going to be wonderful. But when we got to the hotel at Barbizon, we found it was a strictly summer hotel, no carpets, no heating and no running water owing to the frost freezing the pipes. However, we settled down and had a very good time for three weeks, and then the hotel was requisitioned, so now we are back in Paris. I think eventually we shall go to Ethel's friends the De Rocquignys at their house near Hesdin, but in the meantime Paris is very pleasant, though living conditions are getting tougher every day and I don't like the look of the Seine, which may burst its banks at any moment. Still, Paris is always Paris, and we are quite happy. . . .

[1] Peter Cazalet.

15 February 1945

I wonder how I am regarded at Dulwich. Have you any means of finding out? Perhaps Slacker[1] could give you some ideas. Mine is a curious position, as I meet nobody but friends and keep getting encouraging letters, so that I sometimes get the illusion that everything is all right. I have to remind myself that there must still be an enormous body of public opinion which is against me. (I was just writing this, when an air raid warning sounded. I thought all that sort of thing was over in Paris. I can't imagine the Germans having planes to spare to send here. Still, there it is. I will let you know how the matter develops.) Where was I? Oh, yes. Enormous body of public opinion. Or is there? It's so difficult to find out. I meet English and American soldiers, and when they discover who I am they are perfectly friendly. And yet unpleasant things still appear from time to time in the papers. By the way, what was it that *The Times* said about me – you referred to it in your last card – which you said was nice? It's fine if the papers are beginning to change their attitude. But I'm afraid there is a long way to go before things can come right, but I haven't a twinge of self-pity. I made an ass of myself, and must pay the penalty. One thing these troubles have driven home to me and that is what wonderful friends I have. When everything goes right, one rather tends to take one's friends for granted, but being in a position like mine makes one realise how splendid they are. (Hon'ble air raid still apparently in progress, as there has been no All Clear, but nothing seems to be happening. We got a scare one night at Barbizon when terrific explosions suddenly shook the hotel. I believe it was some Allied plane which had to jettison its bombs in the neighbourhood.)

I have been plugging away at my latest novel. I managed to get a hundred pages done while in the clinic, in spite of constant interruptions. I would start writing at nine in the morning and would get a paragraph done when the nurse would come in and sluice water all over the floor. Then the *concierge* arrived with the morning paper, then the nurse with bread for lunch, then another nurse with wine, then a doctor and finally a couple of *inspecteurs*. It was the same thing in camp, where I used to sit on my typewriter case with the machine balanced on a suitcase and work away with two German soldiers standing behind me with guns, breathing down the back of my neck. They seemed fascinated by this glimpse into the life literary.

---

[1] S. 'Slacker' Christison, Secretary to the Old Alleynians for over forty years.

To Denis Mackail
16 February 1945

Hotel Lincoln
Rue Bayard
Paris

When not working, I re-read *Life with Topsy* and enjoy it even more than at a first reading. I wish I could get hold of your recent novels. Perhaps when Smith and Brentano reopen in Paris, I shall be able to. Already things are much better in Paris as regards reading, as we now get the London papers a day after publication, and I have been able to resume my *Times* crossword puzzles. (What is 'Exclaim when the twine gives out' in ten letters?)[1]

We are now back in Paris (the above address will always find me) after three weeks at Barbizon, which Robert Louis Stevenson used to like so much. We wanted to stay there, but the Army took the whole village over. It must be a pretty good place in summer, but we didn't see it at its best. For more than half our stay the roads were a mass of ice and Ethel had rather a bad fall, but is better now. I like being back in Paris, and I think we shall stay here till the spring and then go to some friends in the country. The only catch is that it is so difficult to work here, as we have to go out for all our meals, such as they are, and whenever I really get going Ethel comes in and says that Wonder has to go for a walk *immediately*. Wonder, by the way, is in terrific form. She is now eight, and everybody we meet asks us if she isn't a puppy. I hope your new Peke is going strong.

I spent December and January in a clinic, where I was very comfortable, as we had heat (unknown now in Paris except in clinics and the hotels where the diplomats live). I managed to do a lot of writing, though a bit hampered by the *inspecteurs*, who would keep popping in and asking how I was getting on. There were always two of them in residence, changing every three hours, so I now number quite a lot of *inspecteurs* among my friends. I was great pals with all of them, even the two whose corkscrews I broke. They were always delighted to nip out and buy me bread and wine and to open the bottles when bought. It is rather nice to think that I could walk into the Palais de Justice at any moment and be warmly greeted as an old buddy by at least twenty *inspecteurs*. I spent three days and nights in their *bureau* at the Palais de Justice. They work like beavers there till ten at night, and then haul down the beds from the walls and you all turn in. They used to tell me all about their home lives.

Ethel has just been in to say that Wonder has to go for a walk *immediately*, so I must end.

[1] Stringendo ('with increasing speed' –O.E.D)

To William Townend   78 Avenue Paul Doumer
22 April 1945   Paris

The above is now my official residence. By an absolute miracle we
have been able to get a furnished flat and move in tomorrow. Ethel
made friends with the French wife of an Englishman at the Lincoln,
who had found a flat and was moving in immediately, and then her
plans were all changed by her having to go to the country, so she
said we could have the place. I went to see it yesterday and it is just
what we want. Plenty of room, two bathrooms, nothing unpleasant in the way of furniture or pictures. We ought to be very
snug there, and we can have it for as long as we want on a series of
three month leases. It is almost impossible to get a flat in Paris now,
even people at the Embassy can't do it, so you can imagine how
thankful we are. Ethel managed to keep on her room at the Lincoln,
but we never knew when she might not have to move, and there
was absolutely nowhere I could go except to this Danish friend of
mine, and I felt that he must be getting fed up after five weeks of
me. So now we are all right.

22 May 1945

Like you, we have no help and Ethel has to do all the cooking. It is a
lot of work for her, but I really think it has improved her health. We
go out and buy vegetables and she makes delicious soup every day.
With that and cheese, when we can get it, we manage all right. By
the way, I don't quite know how long we shall be here. We have
taken the flat for three months and can take it on again for as long as
we like, so I imagine we shall renew our lease, for while life is pretty
tough in Paris it seems to be worse elsewhere, and the great thing
about Paris is that we have the American Library. Anyway, the
point is – you can address letters here till the end of July, but if you
address them to the Lincoln they reach me next day, so perhaps it is
safer to go on writing to the Lincoln.

I wish I could get hold of some of Chandler's stuff.[1] It sounds
from what you say just the kind of thing I like. An occasional new
book creeps through to Paris, but it is very difficult to get hold of
anything except pre-war books. I have just got the new Peter
Cheyney and it makes one realise there has been a war on to look at
it. It is about an inch thick and printed on a sort of brown paper and

[1] Raymond Chandler, thriller writer, also had fond memories of Dulwich, which he
entered the term after Plum left.

the price is nine and six. Before the war no publishers would have put out a shilling edition like that. I think the paper shortage is worse than the food shortage. Here in Paris the papers don't come out on Monday, which must be maddening for them if something big happens on the previous day. One week the non-appearance day was shifted to Wednesday for some reason, with the result that the papers were not able to report the death of Hitler!

To Denis Mackail
22 May 1945

I have finally and definitely given up the *Times* crossword puzzles. The humiliation of only being able to fill in about three words each day was too much for me. I am hoping that what has happened is that they have got much more difficult, but I have a gloomy feeling that it is my brain that has gone back.

Did you ever read Du Maurier's *Peter Ibbetson*? I am living in the spot where Peter spent his childhood, and it is still like a village. The thing I like about Paris is that you can go about in any sort of clothes. I go out to buy the bread in the morning in a sport shirt and a red cardigan, but no one stares. The bread in Paris now is really wonderful, much better than I ever remember it in peace time. The catch comes in when you try to get butter. It costs in English money something like thirty shillings a pound. Of course, our real trouble is that while Ethel and I are perfectly content to be vegetarians Wonder won't look at anything except meat, so we have to get it for her somehow. Luckily when you pay in francs it doesn't seem like spending real money. The tobacco situation, after many anxious moments, is now excellent owing to the munificence of a series of American officers who have loaded me up with Prince Albert etc. Matches are the great difficulty, but here again our gallant allies have come out strong. One of them gave Ethel seven boxes yesterday, so we are all right again for a bit.

To Guy Bolton
30 May 1945

I have been working steadily all through these troubled years, and now have four novels and ten short stories in my drawer. When my agent wrote from New York last September, he told me that

American magazine editors were inclined to fight shy of my stuff, but perhaps the passage of time will improve the situation. I have had no new book published in England since 1939, but my London agent tells me that half a million copies of my cheap editions have sold over there in the last three years, so that the feeling against me can't be so very solid. From the fact that without exception all the English and Americans I have met in Paris – about a hundred in all – have been friendly I imagine that the anti party is principally made up of newspaper people. Anyway, my friends have been wonderful, thank God. Every one of the people whose friendship I value has written to me sympathising. You can imagine how glad I was to get your letter, and I can only hope that my reply reached you, as I wouldn't want you to think I had ignored a letter like that.

10 July 1945

I am finding life very pleasant just now. The charm of Paris has suddenly gripped me, and I enjoy living here. It is a precarious sort of life, as you never know if you will get anything to eat (except bread, which is excellent). But up to the present the supply of manna in the wilderness has held up and we have done very well. Occasional parcels arrive from England containing Oxo and beef cubes, which added to vegetable soup make a perfect meal. The great shadow that hangs over one is the prospect of the Winter. Last year it was awful – no heating whatsoever and several very cold snaps. And it doesn't look as if it were going to be any better this winter. The cagey thing to do is to get arrested by the French. They shove you in a hospital, where you get constant heat and hot water and meat every day!

17 July 1945

Life here continues very pleasant, but gosh how expensive. The smallest extra bit of food like a piece of cheese or a pound of butter costs hundreds of francs. We shall be all right if we can get money over from England, and when I saw my bank manager today he said that all money paid in England after March 29 of this year can now be transferred to Paris. If this is so, we can manage. But we are wondering what is going to happen this winter, as another fuel shortage seems certain. Meanwhile, everything in Paris seems bright enough. The weather is wonderful, and everyone seems cheerful.

To Denis Mackail
7 August 1945

The thing to be in France now is a British Officer. They have a club at Maurice Rothschild's house, which has an enormous garden, and when Anthony Mildmay took us to dinner there on Sunday the bill – for three of us, four courses and a bottle of champagne – came to 275 francs. Anywhere else in Paris now a bot. of champagne would cost a minimum of 400 francs. This house of Maurice R's was built by him purely for purposes of entertainment. It has *one* bedroom. That's the way to do things. Wouldn't you love to have one house to live in and one to entertain in.

To Guy Bolton
1 September 1945

I was awfully pleased and grateful for what you said in your letter about getting up that petition for me. How sweet of Virginia to sweat round with it. You say it did no earthly good, but I'm not sure. I think it was that and the agitation made by the *Saturday Evening Post* that induced the Germans to release me three months before I was sixty. Certainly something happened to make them do it, and it certainly wasn't anything to do with my broadcasting, because the idea of broadcasting did not come up till after I had been released. Isn't it the damnedest thing how Fate lurks to sock you with the stuffed eelskin. After I was released and taken to Berlin, (this was on June 21, 1941) I was dumped down at the Adlon and there I ran into a man name Barnikow, one of my oldest friends. I wonder if you ever met him in Hollywood? He was always around, and was at one time engaged to Kay Francis. I had never looked on him as a German at all, as he was so entirely American. Well, we got talking about my camp experiences, and a friend of Barnikow's, who joined us, said Why didn't I broadcast these experiences to my readers in America. It never occurred to me that there could be any harm in doing this, and I particularly wanted to do something in acknowledgement of all the letters I had had from American readers, so I jumped at it. And that is what started this global howl

99

that has been going on ever since. How right the man was who said 'If you ever get a good impulse, stifle it'. That was absolutely all there was to it, and from the way people have carried on you would think that I had been a sort of William Joyce.[1]

3 September 1945

Tear the insides out of the blighters, laddie. (I am all full of vim and venom just now, as I am in the middle of the chapter of my camp reminiscences in which I reply to my critics, notably Mr Harry W. Flannery, whom I propose to reduce to a spot of grease. I am living on raw meat, and human life is not safe within a mile of me.)

To William Townend
13 September 1945

The clippings were invaluable. I was particularly glad to have the letter from 'Disinterested'. I think I have made out a very solid case – it is simply an elaboration of that letter in the *Alleynian*, giving the facts and supporting them with a lot of documents – and I hope it will get across. My trouble has been to get the right tone. You know how one's moods change from day to day. I go for a walk and work up a spirit of defiance and come home and write a belligerent page or two indicating that I don't give a damn whether the public takes a more favourable view or not, because all my friends have stuck to me and it's only friends I care about. Then I sleep on it and wonder if this is quite judicious! Also, comedy will keep creeping in at the most solemn moments. I wrote this yesterday:-

> The global howl which went up as the result of my indiscretion exceeded in volume and intensity anything I had experienced since the time in my boyhood when I broke the curate's umbrella and my aunts started writing letters to one another about it.

I showed the script to Ethel, making sure that she would swoon on reading the above and insist on it coming out, and she thought it marvellous and said that whatever I cut it mustn't be that. What do you think? Will the reaction be 'Ha, ha. I don't care what this chap has done. He makes me laugh' or 'Mr Wodehouse appears to

[1] Better remembered as 'Lord Haw-Haw', the Englishman who broadcast propaganda for the Germans throughout the war.

imagine that his abominable action is a subject for flippancy'. You see. It might go either way, and I can't tell in advance. . . .

I don't know why it is, but I am enjoying life amazingly these days. Thunder clouds fill the sky in every direction, including a demand for $120,000 from the US income tax people (case starts on Monday unless they settle it in advance), but I continue to be happy. After all, there has been a distinct improvement since a year ago. Today, a year ago, I was in the middle of the most vital part of my statement to a flinty-eyed Home Office official, not knowing if he believed a word of it and wondering, even if he did, whether I hadn't been technically guilty of crimes punishable by death. Since then, both England and France seem to have dropped the idea of a criminal charge, and it appears to be a straight issue of the social end of the matter.

To Guy Bolton
21 October 1945

We are having a hell of a time in Paris now. Owing to the drought electricity has to be economised, and the way they are doing it is by cutting off the light for half an hour intervals. I sit down to work at five, and at five thirty out go all the lights and I have to sit and think till six, when they go on again. At six thirty another black-out, lasting till seven, and at seven thirty another which last till eight and finally kills my work.

I think we shall be moving from here at the end of November to a luxurious apartment on the Blvd Suchet next door to the Duke of Windsor! Oddly enough, it is only two thousand francs a month more than this hovel we are in, so if we can get it we shall be on velvet. It is right on the Bois, so that exercising the Peke will be greatly simplified. By the way, your Dumbo is an absolute angel. I loved the photographs, and am longing to meet him.

To Denis Mackail   36 Boulevard Suchet
7 November 1945   Paris (16)

First of all, observe and jot down in your tablets the above address. It is a new flat into which we move as soon as we can get our packing done. Very posh, being right on the Bois (wonderful facilities for Peke exercising) and two doors from neighbour Windsor, who lives at No 24 and will no doubt be dropping in all the time. We got it through Bea Davis, the owner being a friend of hers, and the price is almost the same as we are paying for the Paul Doumer hovel. I think we shall have a good time there, as it is beautifully light and, as I say, with vastly superior facilities for promenading the *petit chien*. If we feel in sporting mood, Auteuil race course is only a hundred yards away. One excellent feature is that I have a very good work room. The only drawback, which can easily be remedied by taking the damn thing down and hiding it in a spare room, is an enormous picture of a nude which dominates the living-room. I have already expressed to you my views on nudes. I want no piece of them.

To William Townend
8 November 1945

Note above address. We move out of this flat in a day or two and go to this other one, a very ornate joint belonging to Lady Deterding, two doors off the Duke of Windsor. Oddly enough, the price is practically the same as that of the hovel we have been living in for the last seven months, in which everything you touch falls to pieces. Bea Davis got the new place for us, and I think we shall be very comfortable. We have a store of wood, and there are fire-places, and also a number of electric heaters. So, always provided that electricity is not severely rationed, we shall be all right. About the only drawback to the place is that it is rather a long way from the shops. In peace time this would not have mattered, as goods would have been delivered, but nowadays everything has to be fetched. By the way, the relief of having got rid of bread tickets is tremendous. I have always been OC Bread, going out in the morning before breakfast for it and being responsible for seeing that the tickets lasted out, and it was always a very near thing and a great anxiety. One month I had to borrow half a loaf from the *concierge* on the last day.

To Denis Mackail
27 November 1945

The new flat is a stupendous success. It is like living in the country with all the conveniences of town. We are right on the edge of the Bois, and every morning I put on plus fours and a sweater and go and do my Daily Dozen under the trees before breakfast. The improvement in my health has been immediate. I am now very fit, and my eyes, which had been troubling me owing to the bad lighting at 78 Paul Doumer, are now all right again. One thing I love about the French is that they are not hicks – I mean that if they see anything unusual they accept it politely and don't guffaw. Not a single pedestrian who has passed me during morning exercises has even turned his head. They see a man in a white sweater and golf bags bending and stretching and they say to themselves 'Ah, a man in a white sweater and golf bags bending and stretching. No doubt he has excellent motives, and in any case it has nothing to do with me.' This sort of attitude reconciles one to some of the things they don't do better in France. On November 17, for instance, I went to the post office and filled in a form notifying them that I had changed my address and wished all mail to be sent to 36 Blvd Suchet. It still goes regularly to 78 Paul Doumer.

To Guy Bolton
5 December 1945

They are still pushing us around in Paris. The food situation is ever so much better, but owing to the drought they have had to economize on electricity, so we shall spend a good deal of our time until it really rains in darkness. I am writing this in the morning, as it is hopeless to try to do anything after dark. Just as one is settling down to write, out go all the lights. It is ironical to reflect that this time last year everyone was in a dither because there had been so much rain and the Seine was expected to overflow any moment and flood the city.

To Denis Mackail
23 December 1945

The last words in your second letter struck home. Though, as a matter of fact, I haven't anything much against Christmas day itself. The time to keep cool is about a week before, when you realize that you can't postpone the buying of presents another day. Ethel and I had our purgatory about three days ago, when we went down to the Rue de Rivoli and I waited interminably outside the Metro where Wonder was nearly squashed. Anything that happens now seems all right in comparison. We gave a dinner last night, and we go out three times next week. After that things will get normal again. Thank God Ethel had the courage to refuse an invitation which would have involved dancing, of all ghastly things. But who am I to talk to a man with a wedding looming up on the horizon?

To Ira Gershwin
23 December 1945

I am longing to get over to America and see you all and try to do some work. What would you say my standing was over there now? I hope people realize that my unfortunate performance on the German radio was merely a well-intentioned attempt to do something in return for all the letters I had had from America during my internment. I thought it a good idea at the time, but have since changed my mind. I suppose I was in an unbalanced mental condition after a year behind barbed wire, but that was all I actually did – give five short descriptions of life in camp, purely designed as entertainment for the boys in the USA.

To William Townend
11 January 1946

Life here continues very pleasant. I am getting fonder and fonder of Paris. It was a blow when they started rationing bread again, but in actual practice it doesn't affect us much. We now have a cook who buys the stuff and there always seems enough. There is some sort of row on just now between the wholesale and retail butchers, which has resulted in no meat for the populace for about two weeks. But something always seems to turn up. There is a mysterious Arab gentleman who calls from time to time with offerings. He has just come and fixed us up with a great chunk of mutton.[1] Also a Dane (unknown to me) has sent us an enormous parcel, the only trouble being that all the contents are labelled in Danish, so we don't know what they are. There are three large tins which I hold contain bacon, but Ethel, who is in a pessimistic mood today owing to a bad night, says that they are stuff for cleaning floors. But surely even the most erratic Dane wouldn't send us stuff for cleaning floors. The only

[1] Text in margin: 'And a rabbit!'

way I can think of of solving the mystery is to ring up our Danish friend at Neuilly and spell the labels over the phone to him and ask him to translate. (NB   We did very well at Christmas, managing to buy two chickens and a turkey, and our ex-lodger of the Low Wood 1939 days, who is in the fish business, sent us a large box of fish.)

5 March 1946

We aren't doing badly just now. The Pole still sticks by us and we now have an English-speaking cook as well, but unfortunately only part-time. Still, between them they take a lot of the work off Ethel and we are really quite comfortable. Food is still very scarce, but somehow we always seem to get some just when the larder is getting empty. Denby tells me there are some nice parcels on the way over. One of them is from a former agent of mine who embezzled about £15,000 of mine during those years when the first income tax case was on and I was helpless. What is the procedure? Do I write him a fawning letter of thanks or do I merely say 'Okay, laddie. Now you only owe me £14,900'? Isn't it extraordinary, in passing, that literary agents are nearly always rigidly honest but theatrical agents nearly always crooked.

To Denis Mackail
28 March 1946

PARIS. The Queen of Cities now that that blasted winter is over. I could write you one of those Nature things they tuck away in odd corners of the daily press about the view from my open window as I write this. These last few days have really made one feel that there is a faint hope for the human race. As you would put it in your epigrammatic way, 'optimism reigns'. My only trouble is that spring seems to make my feet swell, so that none of my shoes fit me.

To Ira Gershwin
5 April 1946

The other day I received a letter from the Police Commissaire of this district asking me to call at his office, as he had 'documents to give me'. Naturally I thought first of all the unpleasant possibilities, such as a peremptory order to leave France in twenty-four hours. What it was was a courteous notification by the French Government that I was now considered by them absolutely cleared – in a word, that they were my pals and I was their pal and that from now on we would start the new life together. Rather a relief, what? It seems to me that if France, the most jumpy and suspicious country on earth, has come to the conclusion that I am all right, there can't be much wrong with me.

To Guy Bolton
6 April 1946

I was thrilled to the core to learn that you and Va both like the Camp Book so much. The question of publication (immediate) or postponement has been turning my three remaining hairs whiter than ever, but I now agree with you that it will be better to wait. Before they had read it, all my advisers in America were against publishing. Then they read it and were all for it. Then Doubleday, my publisher, brooded on it and reached the conclusion that the novel ought to come first, and he seems so certain that the public has no prejudice against me and that the novel will sell well that I am content to let him go ahead on his own lines. He assures me that he has made exhaustive enquiries all over the country and everything is all right. Bobby Denby reports the same after talking to a number of people in Chicago and elsewhere.

To William Townend
3 June 1946

My pleasure in reading your kind words about *Money in the Bank* was slightly marred by the sudden entry of a spectacled Frenchman with a bill for thirteen *mille* (£26 to you) for electric light, this including nine *mille* penalty for overindulgency during the winter. Ethel nearly fainted, and I, though a strong man, was shaken. I always knew we were for it, as we went in freely for hot water and heaters during those cold months, but I had supposed that they would just shake a playful finger at us and fine us about a quid. Still, it's better than being cold. I have had to reread your letter to recover my composure.

To Guy Bolton
5 July 1946

This pessimistic outlook about my being able to visit America is due to a growing conviction that I am being given the good old run around. It seems impossible to get action. The Vice-Consul in Paris assures me that what is holding things up is the apparent un-willingness of the British authorities to give them what they call 'the facts'. I now have several people, including Willie Wiseman, working at that end while Washburn and his crowd worries Washington, so something may break shortly.[1] But I confess I am doubtful.

You see, I imagine the Brit. authorities are feeling that they had better watch their step. In 1941 the BBC, which I suppose is part of the British Government, specifically called me a traitor. If now they inform the US Embassy that there was nothing in the charge and that they have no grounds for accusing me of traitorous conduct, they probably feel that they will lay themselves open to a terrific counter-attack on my part and will have to pay up heavily in libel damages. So they are acting cagey and stalling along.

That is the only explanation I can think of which makes their actions intelligible. As the Vice-Consul here said to me, the whole thing could be cleared up in a couple of days, if they wanted to clear it up.

30 August 1946

I simply must write and tell you the good news. This morning there arrived from a newspaper friend in Virginia a review of *Joy in the Morning* from the *New York Times Book Review*, Sunday last, raving about the book and concluding with this:-

> Maybe Wodehouse uses the same plot over and over again. Whatever he does, it's moderately wonderful, a ray of pale English sunshine in a gray world. . . . There is, of course, the question of Mr Wodehouse's 'war guilt'. Upon mature post-war reflection, it turned out to be about equal to the war guilt of the dachshunds which were stoned by super-heated patriots during World War I.

[1] Watson Washburn looked after Plum's legal affairs in America for many years.

Terrific, isn't it? The one paper that matters is the *NY Times*.

I sent you a copy of *Joy in the Morning* yesterday. I hope you will like it. I don't think it's bad, considering that it was written during the German occupation of Le Touquet, with German soldiers prowling about under my window, plus necessity of having to walk to Paris Plage every morning to report to a German Kommandant with a glass eye, which made him even more formidable than the ordinary German Kommandant.

11 September 1946

We have to move from here early in October, and then what? I feel that I ought to go to America and make some money, but against this is the fact that I would be separated from Ethel, added to the fact that I should have to doss in with three or four other men on the boat and probably have a trying time with the reporters on landing. As you say, when you get to 65, you want sleeping accommodation to yourself. Here's an odd thing, though. When I was in camp, I slept in a dormitory with sixty-six other men and loved it, yet when I left the camp in company with one other man and had to share a room with him at the Adlon for a couple of nights, I could hardly get through it. I don't think I would mind mucking in with twenty or thirty men on board a liner. Though the trouble would be, where to get a place to write in? Incidentally, when I first went to America in 1903, I travelled second class with three other men in the cabin, so the wheel has come full circle, as you might say.

2 October 1946

That is most excellent news that you have a room for me in both your houses. God knows, though, if I'll be able to get over. That shipping strike seems to have made travelling impossible. I have been besieging the United States Line for months, and it was all set that I should get a berth on a Liberty ship. Then Liberty ships ceased to run. My name is down – whatever that implies – for the *America* on Oct 26 and they want me to look in about Oct 12 to find out if they can take me. I hear there is now another strike, so maybe the America won't sail. I nerved myself to go and apply for a seat on a plane, but was told that there would be nothing till the end of the year. I'm afraid prospects don't look too good.

What hell life is these days, as you say. We have got to give up this apartment two weeks from now, and it seems impossible to get another or to get into a hotel, except the ones that charge the earth. The bitter part is that we keep finding nice little hotels where there are rooms, but they won't take dogs! I'm beginning to agree with the lawyer in the *New Yorker* – that picture where his client is being led off to the penitentiary and he says 'Look on the bright side. After all, it's three squares a day and a roof over your head.'

PART III

4 ETHEL

To Denis Mackail   23 Gilbert Street
4 December 1924   Mayfair
                                London W1

I should love to see *Patricia* next week.[1] The only thing is that the Boss insists on seeing it, too, which rather dishes the Athenaeum dinner. I think the best plan would be for you to come and dine here. We can then discuss all sorts of matters before going on. By this system you get a glass (or more) of the Wodehouse port, which you would otherwise miss.

To William Townend   17 Norfolk Street
12 February 1927   Park Lane
                                London W1

This house is still in an awful mess, with workmen all over the place, and Ethel says she loathes it. As a matter of fact, when it is finished I think she will like it. It's going to be pretty hot. My library is magnificent, if a bit too much like 'Mr Wodehouse among his books'. It is lined from floor to ceiling with old books and it is only on closer inspection that you find that these are absolutely unreadable. They are what is known in the trade as 'book furniture' – i.e. old encyclopaedias etc. bunged in to act as background. To think that I, who always swore that I would never have a book in the house which was not one of my favourites, should have sunk to this!

17 May 1927

This is the god-darndest house you ever saw. Ethel has spent a fortune on it, going on the principle of buying things that are really valuable and will always have the same value if we want to sell

[1] *Patricia*, written by Mackail, ran for 160 performances from 31 October 1924 at His Majesty's Theatre.

113

them. She paid twelve hundred and fifty quid for a carpet the other day, and has already been offered a hundred and fifty quid more for it, so maybe the system isn't so looney as it might seem at first. But still she and Leonora moan that the place looks awful! As a matter of fact, everything is all right bar the drawing-room, which has still to be furnished. The main trouble with my library is that it *is* a ruddy library and not a cosy study. We can't seem to get that formal note out of it. It's a big room, with book-lined walls – the books unfortunately consisting of old second-hand volumes known in the trade as 'book furniture'. That is to say, they are just to furnish the room and aren't supposed to be read. Of course, everyone who comes in utters an admiring cry and says 'Ah, you collect old books?', but I know all the time what fakes they are and it oppresses me a little, so that I do most of my work in my bedroom, which is really jolly and where we'll have tea when you come. All my own books are up there.

25 February 1931   MGM
                                                  Culver City
                                                  California

I say laddie, don't mention this cheque when you write. I am not supposed to have so much in the Hongkong bank.* You understand.

     *PS   To make sure you've got this letter, when you write say you got my letter of Feb 25th.

To Denis Mackail   1005 Benedict Canyon
12 April 1931   Drive
                                     Beverly Hills
                                     California

Ethel has been entertaining largely lately. She starts by asking two people to lunch, then 'Who can we get to meet them?'. This gets it up to four. Then come all the people who would be hurt at being left out, and eventually the thing becomes a Hollywood orgy. This afternoon we had fifty people to lunch! It's not as bad as it sounds, because in this lovely climate you feed out of doors. We had bridge tables spotted about the garden and patio and a large table with cold food in the dining room, so that people simply helped themselves. As usual, Ethel feels it was a frost, but it wasn't really. It went off splendidly.

To William Townend   Carlton Hotel
6 February 1932   Cannes

Will you take £100 of enclosed and pay the rest into my a/c at
   Hongkong & Shanghai Bk.
   9 Gracechurch St
   EC4.
When you write, don't mention a word of this. Just say you got my
letter of Feb 6.

6 March 1932   Domaine de la Fréyère
                                      Auribeau
                                      Alpes-Maritimes
I have been having rather a rotten time with my work. The
American Magazine editor did not like my last two stories, and
played me rather a dirty trick by going and seeing Ethel in NY and
asking her to make me change them. The result is that she keeps
after me about them, and I can't change the damned things – it
means inventing entirely different plots. So whenever I try to start a
new story Ethel comes up and asks me what I have done about these
two, which puts me right off my stroke.

23 April 1932

Ethel came back from Cannes yesterday, raving about a Peke she
had seen. Winky sat and listened with rather a nasty look.
     Thank goodness, I think Ethel has had enough of living out of
England. She now seems resolved to open Norfolk St in March
next, when we get it back. I'm delighted, as I hate living abroad. I
loved Hollywood, but I am not so keen on this place.

1 December 1932   Dorchester Hotel
                                      London W1
I won a thousand quid gambling at Cannes. I am going to open an
account for seven hundred quid at your bank and tell the manager
that it is security for you to overdraw against if you want to. So that
will make things all right for you, as you can always feel that you
have that behind you.
     WHEN WRITING DON'T SAY A WORD ABOUT EITHER OF THESE
TWO NEWS ITEMS.   I think Ethel wants

to keep the first dark, and the second is naturally a dead secret between you and me. Don't refer to any of this in your letter, as the fools downstairs keep taking my letters to Ethel's suite. I am in suite 440, she is in 717, and I can't get them to separate our letters.
VITALLY IMPORTANT.

9 February 1933   Domaine de la Fréyère
                                         Auribeau
                                         Alpes-Maritimes
I want to have a talk with you about money matters when I return. The outlook is dashed good. Even after a disastrous visit to the Casino last Saturday, I am two thousand quid ahead on my year's gambling, so I'll be able to ease the situation a bit at Fairlawn.[1] My idea is to guarantee an overdraft, so that you will feel safe. If you don't need it, then it's still there. But if you want to take six months off to write a novel, that will be at the back of you.

15 March 1933   No address given

I have just signed a form at lunch guaranteeing your overdraft of £1000. The money to meet it is in Fixed Deposit at Barclay's, Strand. I also have £500 there in current a/c. (The £1000 is made out to you *and* René.)
    Now, I think the best plan is for you to look on the money as a legacy. Don't touch it if you can help it as long as I'm alive. If you get hard up tell me and I can always rally round with a hundred or so. I want to feel that if I pop off before you do you will have the £1000.
    Don't answer this, or if you do don't allude to the money. It's a dead secret between us and the good old bank mgr.

16 January 1938   Low Wood
                                         Le Touquet
By the way, the most rigid secrecy, of course, about that money. I don't suppose for a moment that Ethel will say anything but remember to warn René that E. knows nothing about it and I don't want her to. Absolute dead secrecy. (E. is a bit worried about

[1] The Townends' house, not to be confused with Fairlawne, the Cazalets' house.

money just now, for no real reason except that we are having to spend a lot getting this house into shape.) But of course you understand, don't you?

7 September 1938

Listen, Bill. More money shortly, when I see you again. I had an experience last Saturday night at the Casino which I've often dreamed of but never brought off. Playing at big table – put up five *mille* for my bank – Ethel put in another five – won eight *coups*, each of over a hundred quid – when the bank finally went down, Ethel and I divided a hundred and sixty *mille* – i.e. close on a thousand quid!!! so I shall have some tucked away for you. *(Don't refer to this when you write.)*

This is the first bit of gambling luck I've had this year, and I shan't go again. I must say it's a terrific thrill. What happens is that when your bank gets up to twenty *mille* (about a hundred quid) and you win the next *coup*, twenty *mille* is put aside and you don't have to go on risking it. And so on – i.e. each time you play and win another twenty *mille* is put aside, so that after the first twenty *mille* is put aside you aren't risking your own money, because whatever happens that – plus a lot more – is safe. I've never yet succeeded before in getting to the stage where it is pure velvet. Always before, I've gone down on the vital *coup*.

2 August 1939

Ethel went to the Casino last night and Lady Dudley (G. Millar) betted against her bank and lost more than she had on her person. She – Lady D. – was rising to go to the cashier to get some money, when Ethel, not wanting her to have the trouble, said she would go. Ethel wrote a cheque, went back to the table, and gave the money to Lady D. who paid her, thus concluding the transaction to everybody's satisfaction. It was only at lunch today that she suddenly realized that she had been paid with her own money. Equivalent to old Brook owing you a fiver, borrowing the money from you, and then paying you.[1] The worst of it is, it's going to be a darned tough job getting it back.

[1] H. W. Westbrook, an eccentric friend who was married to Plum's UK literary agent. His habit of borrowing his friends' clothes and personal possessions and his ingenious schemes for raising money gave Plum the background for the Ukridge stories.

☆

This was the last letter to Denis Mackail written before the war.

☆

To Denis Mackail   Hotel Lincoln
16 February 1945   Rue Bayard
                                                    Paris

Ethel likes the novel I am now finishing, and she is about as tough a critic as there is. The trouble is that while I read my output with considerable pleasure, the chances of anyone else doing so are at present remote.

7 August 1945   78 Avenue Paul Doumer*
                                                    Paris
                                    (* Pre-war French premier, no?)[1]

Did Ethel really omit a parrot bulletin from her letter? Her handling of the parrot situation was really the high spot of her 1940 achievements. She got it away from Low Wood in the teeth of the German army and left it with the people who own the château where she stayed. There it has been ever since, flourishing even when it couldn't get parrot seed. Apparently it gets along splendidly on bread dipped in coffee and has learned to sing 'God Save the King'. At a later date there were 200 German soldiers quartered at the château, and the parrot was apparently popular with them in spite of its choice of songs.

To Guy Bolton   36 Boulevard Suchet
11 December 1945   Paris

By the way, Ethel says Tell Guy to tell Va that she will be writing to her very soon. Up to now, what with the move and having to do all the household work — we having had no maid — she hasn't had a moment. But she is merely crouching for the spring. When she does write, Va will know she has been in a fight, as a normal Ethel letter runs to about twelve pages of single-spaced typescript.

[1] Paul Doumer became President of France in 1931 and was assassinated by a Russian fanatic the following year.

118

To Denis Mackail   Remsenburg
7 June 1952   Long Island
                                                    New York

Note new address. Ethel has gone and bought a house down here, and we are now in the process of moving in (though for the present keeping on the New York apartment). Ethel has had an awful job of it and is at present in one of her depressed moods when she says 'Why did I do it? Why DID I do it?'. But I think this will wear off. Credit side:- Lovely grounds of about four acres, including a wood through which one walks down to the water. Also everything like heating system, gadgets and so on perfect. Debit side:- House is at present a bit too small. We shall have to build a guest house by the garage. Further to the credit side:- Lovely air and comparative coolness even in the hottest weather. Yesterday it was ninety-three degrees in New York but down here quite all right.

Our great problem is locomotion. All letters have to be fetched from a post office two miles away, and supplies from Westhampton four miles away. So somebody has to drive the car. Ethel used to be a fine driver, but feels dubious about her ability to cope with present day American traffic. Our maid Peggy had some lessons in NY but Ethel wanted her down here so she had to break them off. I suppose we shall manage somehow. I myself intend to bicycle.

25 July 1953

Ethel has got a watering jag on. Ever since we came down here she has never ceased watering the garden. She put in four hours at it the day before yesterday, finishing at midnight, and at five a.m. it started to rain, breaking a record for the last eighty-one years . . . four inches or something like that.

To Jack Donaldson   1000 Park Avenue
12 December 1953   New York

Ethel and I lead a very quiet – almost unconscious – life with our Peke Squeaky and our foxhound Bill. We have taken on this flat for another two years. It is expensive, but worth it, I think, because it is nice to have a place in New York. But we are tending to live more and more down at Remsenburg. Ethel has made great changes in the Remsenburg house, and it is now quite a show place. Think of

Knole or Blenheim and you will get the general idea. You know, large sun parlours protruding in all directions and the sitting-room enlarged to about the size of the Albert Hall. There is a rumour that we can knock some of the cost off our income tax – we pay American income tax – and I hope it is correct.

Love to you both from us both.

To Denis Mackail
10 February 1954

Squeaky is eight and experts seem to think Bill must be ten. Distressing episode yesterday. Ethel in her energetic way was cleaning our terrace, shovelling the snow and slush through the door on to the main roof, not knowing that the maid had let Squeaky out of the kitchen door on to the main roof. So S. came trotting round the corner full of beans and got a shovelful of slush right in the face. Ethel had to do a lot of comforting and chocolate-giving before she was restored.

1 May 1954

I am actually writing this at Remsenburg, we return to NY the day after tomorrow. I shall be sorry to leave, as there are signs of better weather after the chilliest and most miserable spring I remember in America. Wood fires every night, three blankets on bed and overcoat and gloves when walking. Ethel has been buying trees like a drunken sailor – if drunken sailors do buy trees – and though we shall have to go on the dole very soon the result is rather wonderful. The garden is beginning to look like something, and as I write hammering comes from the next room, where a squad of workers are putting mirrors on the walls as first step to turning room into a bar, if you'll believe it. I know quite well that when we have our bar Ethel will continue to make the cocktails in the kitchen. But I think the idea is to be prepared in case the Quality come pouring in. Ethel, who loathes seeing a soul except me and the dogs, can't shake off those dreams of being the centre of a rapid social circle. (Good line in my forthcoming Jeeves novel about Bertie's Uncle Tom. 'His face wore the strained, haggard look it wears when he hears that guests are expected for the week end'. Don't you hate having people about the place?)

24 June 1956   Remsenburg
                                                Long Island
                                                New York

We are at Remsenburg for the rest of the year. Ethel wants to give
up the Park Ave apartment, which we have till September 1955,
and I am all for it. This house really is fine now. Ethel's new sun
parlour is terrific. Huge windows on every side and a great view of
the estate. This morning they are putting in the bar in a small room
on the other side of the house. God knows why we want a bar, but
E. thought it a good idea. What is supposed to happen is that the
County saunter in for a drink, and we mix it at the bar. The County
little know that if they come within a mile of us we shall take to the
hills. But that's Ethel. She really loves solitude as much as you and I
do, but she has occasional yearnings to be the Society hostess and go
in for all that 'Act Two, The Terrace at Meadowsweet Manor'
stuff.

15 October 1954

Life has become slightly hectic now because Ethel makes me rake
up the leaves. It strains all sorts of unexpected muscles. Wonderful
exercise, of course. Yesterday I worked for two hours and got
every lawn and the drive cleaned up. Today lawns and drive are a
mass of leaves, and all the weary work to do again. That's life, of
course.

18 April 1956

Ethel is planning vast alterations in the house, which, if they
fructuate – is that the word? – will mean shifting to the apartment
which we rent in Westhampton, which is six miles from here. I am
not looking forward to the move, as I shall miss my fairly luxurious
study and shall . . . Bill just started to moan, so must break off . . .
have to work in a bedroom.

10 September 1956

We have at last got the workmen out of the house and the place is
really looking fine now. At last I have a really spacious workroom

with plenty of light. The only trouble is that they have built book shelves to hold about a thousand more books than I possess, so that part of the room looks a bit bare.

To Guy Bolton
24 September 1961

By the way, please don't say anything to Ethel about that £300 and tell Va not to mention it if she writes to E. I'll explain when I see you. This is the most marvellous pen. Ethel pinched it from the manager at [Bohack's].

To Edward Cazalet
26 April 1968

The Colonel sends her best. She is slacking in bed today with two cats and Jed the dachshund on her bed.

☆

Edward Cazalet (whose name had caused Plum such pain, see p. 57) had stayed with the Wodehouses when he was doing National Service and had nicknamed Ethel the Colonel, a joke much appreciated by Plum, who afterwards always referred to her in this way.

☆

12 December 1968

The Colonel has found the Shelter a great interest. She goes there every day and feeds the cats and dogs.

☆

Ethel had persuaded Plum to give $35,000 to an institution for sheltering stray dogs and cats called Bide-a-Wee. This was a great pleasure to her until a new manager introduced a rule that no one except staff was to feed the animals. Virginia Bolton told me that by this rule he lost $300,000 which Plum had intended to leave to the Shelter. The letter to Edward continues:

☆

The heat is on concerning Debbie, who, the vet says, is too fat, and the Colonel has given strict orders that she is not to be given bits. I went up to say good morning to the Colonel just now, and there she was handing out toast and egg to Debbie. And so it goes on. . . .

To Ethel Wodehouse
30 September 1973

My precious angel Bunny, whom I love so dear.

Another anniversary! Isn't it wonderful to think we have been married for 59 years and still love each other as much as ever except when I spill my tobacco on the floor, which I'll never do again.

It was a miracle finding one another. I know I could never have been happy with anyone else. What a lucky day for me when you agreed with me when I said 'Let's get married'!

The only thing that makes me sad is your health. How I wish there was something I could do. What is so extraordinary is that you come to me in pain and not having slept, and you look just as beautiful as you did fifty-nine years ago. But how I wish that you could get a good sleep. I wish I could say all the things I would like to say, but really they can all be said in one sentence. I LOVE YOU.

Bless you
Your Plummie

5 HOLLYWOOD

To Denis Mackail
26 June 1930

Metro-Goldwyn-Mayer
Studios
Culver City
California

This is the weirdest place. We have taken Elsie Janis's house.[1] It has a small but very pretty garden, with a big pool. I have arranged with the studio to work at home, so I sometimes don't go out of the garden for three or four days on end. If you asked me, I would say I loved Hollywood. Then I would reflect and have to admit that Hollywood is about the most loathsome place on the map but that, never going near it, I enjoy being out here.

My days follow each other in a regular procession. I get up, swim, breakfast, work till two, swim again, work till seven, swim for the third time, then dinner and the day is over. When I get a summons from the studio, I motor over there, stay there a couple of hours and come back. Add incessant sunshine, and it's really rather jolly. It is only occasionally that one feels as if one were serving a term on Devil's Island.

We go out very little. Just an occasional dinner at the house of some other exile – e.g. some New York theatrical friend. Except for one party at Marion Davies's place, I have not met any movie stars.

The second day out on the liner I developed a terrific attack of neuritis, and spent the rest of the voyage in bed. I managed to get rid of it about two weeks later. One of the rules, when you have neuritis, is that you must knock off drink, so I got a flying start with that two weeks and kept on the wagon for another six. Then I had to go to a party and I couldn't go through it without cocktails. They have a damnable practice here of inviting you to dine at seven-fifteen. You then stand round drinking cocktails till nine-thirty, when the last guest arrives. Then you go in to dinner. At Marion Davies's I refused all drinks and it nearly killed me. By dinner time I

[1] Elsie Janis appeared in the Bolton/Gershwin/Wodehouse shows *Miss 1917* and *Oh Kay*.

was dying on my feet. Poor old Snorky had to talk to the same man from seven-fifteen till 9.30 and then found she was sitting next to him at dinner!! Fortunately, it was such a big party that we were able to sneak off without saying goodbye directly dinner was over. Gosh, what an experience.

On the other hand, teetotalism certainly makes one frightfully fit. Also slim. I have become a lean-jawed, keen-eyed exhibit, like something out of Sapper.

The actual work is negligible. They set me on to dialogue for a picture for Jack Buchanan. I altered all the characters to Earls and butlers, with such success that, when I finished, they called a conference and changed the entire plot, starring the earl and the butler. So I am still working on it. So far, I have had eight collaborators. The system is that A. gets the original idea, B. comes in to work with him on it, C. makes a scenario, D. does preliminary dialogue, and then they send for me to insert Class and what-not. Then E. and F., scenario writers, alter the plot and off we go again.

I could have done all my part of it in a morning, but they took it for granted I should need six weeks. The latest news is that they are going to start shooting quite soon. In fact, there are ugly rumours that I am to be set to work soon on something else. I resent this, as it will cut into my short-story-writing. It's odd how soon one comes to look on every minute as wasted that is given to earning one's salary. (Now, don't go making a comic article out of this and queering me with the bosses!!)

Let's have a line soon. Tell me all the news. I hear nothing out here. Have you resigned from the pest hole yet?[1]

To Guy Bolton   724 Linden Drive
19 July 1930   Beverly Hills
                                         California

I shan't have any difficulty in finishing my version of acts two and three. I find that I work marvellously here. I just want to sit at my desk and work all the time. I fear I shall not be able to string out the dear old picture I've been tied up with ever since I arrived much longer, as they really do seem to be starting the shooting on Monday, and they may give me something tougher to do next time. Still, I shall always have lots of time for other work.

I really believe I must have had the softest job on record. A horde of scenarioists have constructed the picture, even to the

[1] The pest hole was the Garrick Club.

125

extent of writing the dialogue. All I have had to do is revise and adapt their dialogue. And they never expect me to go near the studio unless there is a conference. . . .

What a curious place this is. Directly I get outside my garden and see those miles of beastly mining-camp houses, my heart sinks. But as long as I am in the garden I love it. Thank heaven I don't have to go to the studio much.

There's no doubt about it, this is the abode of the damned. Every now and then I get very homesick. Still, the garden is lovely.

To William Townend   Metro-Goldwyn-Mayer
16 August 1930   Studios
                                       Culver City
                                       California

I have had another barren spell as regards ideas. Isn't it the devil, how you get these brilliant periods when nothing seems easier that to plot out stories, and then comes the blank. Oddly enough, Hollywood hasn't inspired me in the least. I feel as if everything that could be written about it has already been done.

As a matter of fact, I don't think there is much to be written about this place. What it was like in the early days, I don't know, but nowadays the studio life is all perfectly normal, not a bit crazy. I haven't seen any swooning directors or temperamental stars. They seem just to do their job and to be quite ordinary people, especially the directors, who are quiet, unemotional men who just work and don't throw fits. Same with the stars. I don't believe I shall get a single story out of my stay here.

Did you find the climate here monotonous? I must say I would welcome an English shower just now.

To Denis Mackail   1005 Benedict Canyon
28 December 1930   Drive
                                       Beverly Hills
                                       California

I feel an awful worm, not having written to you for so long, but a genuine pressure of work stopped me. The studio wished an awful job on me – viz. they made me write a perfectly rotten picture *as a novel*!! Exactly eight times as much sweat as doing an ordinary picture. What the idea was, I don't know, unless they thought that, writing it in that form, I would put in a lot of business which they could use. It ran to 45,000 words, and I was writing a little thing on my own at the same time against the clock. It shows what a great climate this is, that I didn't succumb.

Asked to what he attributed his success, Mr Wodehouse replied that he thought, on the whole, that it could be attributed to cold water. Have you ever taken a cold bath? I bet you haven't. Well, listen. Every morning before breakfast – and I mean every morning, not once a month – I put on a bathing suit, do my exercises, and then plunge into our swimming pool, the water of which is now exactly fifty degrees. And, what is more, I like it. I can't think what has come over me since I've been here. I used to loathe anything but the hottest water, and now, even if I do have a hot bath, I take a cold shower after it. The result is that I have lost seven pounds in weight and am almost unbelievably beautiful.

The great advantage of this place is that it is so loathsome the moment you get outside the garden that there is no temptation to do anything but sit at home and work. I am turning out incredible quantities. I don't get any more ideas than I used to, but – give me an idea – and I can deliver in a couple of days. . . .

Candle-Light has been bought by Metro-Goldwyn. My share is five hundred quid – gross overpayment for what I did on it. But I simply can't induce the blighters to buy anything of mine. Thalberg, the head man, told me that *Leave It to Psmith* was his favourite novel, but when I suggested that he should come across with money for the movie rights he merely smiled sheepishly and the matter dropped. . . .

PS   The maddening thing about this place is that I haven't been able to get a single story out of it yet. I suppose there are plots to be found in Hollywood, but I can't see them. For the moment, then, our old line of Dukes and Earls will continue as in the past.

To William Townend
14 March 1931

I am doing a picture version of *Candle-Light* now for John Gilbert. This looks as if it might really come to something. Everything else I have done so far has been scrapped – not my fault, mostly.

But I doubt if they give me another contract. The enclosed par from *Variety* can only refer to me, and it looks to me darned sinister. My only hope is that I have made myself so pleasant to everyone here that by now I may count as a relative. The studio is full of relatives of the big bosses who do no work and draw enormous salaries.

I must stop now, as I have to go out to dinner. (Corinne Griffith, as a matter of fact. She is a ripper.)

To Denis Mackail
10 May 1931

My contract with MGM ended yesterday, and they have shown no sign of wanting to renew it. My plans are to stay out here till September and then dash over to England if only for a short visit. . . .

I haven't been able to get much out of Hollywood so far, but then I have been restraining myself from satire out of love and loyalty for dear old MGM. Now that the pay envelope has ceased, maybe I shall be able to write some stuff knocking them good.

This place has certain definite advantages which make up for it being so far from home. I love breakfasting in the garden in a dressing-gown after a swim in the pool. There's no doubt that perpetual sunshine has its points. I've never been able to stay more than a few months in one place before, let alone a year. And the people here are quite fun. I find I enjoy going out to dinner. . . .

The movies are getting hard up and the spirit of economy is rife. I was lucky to get mine while the going was good. It is rather like having tolerated some awful bounder for his good dinners to go to his house and find the menu cut down to nothing and no drinks. The only thing that excused the existence of the Talkies was a sort of bounderish openhandedness.

☆

In June 1931 Plum gave an interview to June Alma Whitaker of the *Los Angeles Times* in which he said:

It dazes me. They paid $2000 a week – and I cannot see what they engaged me for. They were extremely nice to me, but I feel as if I have cheated them. You see, I understood I was engaged to write stories for the screen. After all I have twenty novels, a score of successful plays and countless magazine stories to my credit. Yet apparently they had the greatest difficulty in finding anything for me to do. Twice during the year they brought me completed scenarios of other people's stories and asked me to do some dialogue. Fifteen or sixteen people had tinkered with those stories. The dialogue was really quite adequate.

Then they set me to work on a story called *Rosalie*, which was to have some musical numbers. When it was finished, they thanked me politely and remarked that as musicals didn't seem to be going so well they guessed they would not use it. That about sums up what I was called upon to do for my $104,000. Isn't it amazing?

This interview was quoted in full in the *New York Times* and *New York Herald Tribune* and other newspapers all over the country. At the time it was widely believed and it has now become part of the Hollywood legend that, single-handed, Plum galvanized the bankers who supported the film industry into action to ensure reform. In fact after the Wall Street crash of 1929 reform of the industry could not have been long delayed.

☆

To William Townend
29 June 1931

Metro-Goldwyn-Mayer
Studios
Culver City
California

The movies are in a hell of a state. They say that July will mark a sort of general collapse of them. Incidentally, that interview of mine seems to have had something of the effect of the late assassination at Sarajevo (which, if you remember, led to a nasty disturbance). I can't quite understand why, seeing that I only said what everybody has been saying for years, but apparently the fact that I gave figures and mentioned a definite studio in print has caused a sensation all over the world. One of the bosses at Paramount said I had done as much damage as if a hundred picture houses had been closed.

The trouble is, you see, all these Jews out here have been having a gorgeous time for years, fooling about with the share-holders money and giving all their relations fat jobs, and this gives the bankers an excuse for demanding a showdown. Well, if it results in Mr Louis B. Mayer having to cut his salary (which at present is a snappy eight hundred thousand dollars a year), I shall feel I have done my bit.

129

26 August 1931   1005 Benedict Canyon
                                                  Drive
                                                  Beverly Hills
                                                  California

Of course, my career as a movie-writer has been killed dead by that interview. I am a sort of Ogre to the studios now. I don't care personally, as I don't think I could ever do picture writing. It needs a definitely unoriginal mind. Apparently all pictures have to be cast in a mould.

☆

Plum returned to Hollywood in 1937, to work on the musical *Rosalie*, which was where he had left off in 1931. He had no better luck this time.

☆

To Guy Bolton   1315 Angelo Drive
8 March 1937   Beverly Hills
                                                  California

An odd business, this *Rosalie*. Bill McGuire was the producer and I was supposed to write it under his supervision. But by degrees I found that I was being quietly frozen out. Everything I turned in he rewrote, keeping the substance of my stuff but changing it enough so that he could tell the men higher up that it was his work. Eventually it got so that I couldn't make any progress, and now the thing has poofed out and Bill is writing it by himself.

It's exactly the same mechanism he employed with you on the original piece. He went around saying that you hadn't written a line. Also the same as with *The Three Musketeers*. He had Flo's ear and simply edged poor Gee-Gee[1] out of it. It's the old business of the man on the spot, who has time to go about with the boss, freezing out the man who stays away. I'm convinced that that is what happened with *Anything Goes*. Howard Lindsay meant all along to swipe the piece, and he poisoned the minds of Vinton and the stars.

To William Townend
24 March 1937

Metro-Goldwyn-Mayer are not taking up my option, which

[1] George Grossmith

expires in another two weeks. I have had another frost with them. I started gaily in working on a picture with Bill McGuire, an old friend of mine, as producer, and I gradually found myself being edged out. Eventually they came out into the open and said that they had wanted McGuire to write the thing by himself all along! (It was a musical comedy, of which he had been the author of the stage version.) There seems to be a curse over MGM, as far as I am concerned.

Since then, I have had a number of offers from other studios for one picture apiece. It seems pretty certain that in about two weeks I shall be working on my *Damsel in Distress*, which RKO bought for Fred Astaire, but it will only be a short publishing job. Then Selznick wants me to do a thing called *The Earl of Chicago*.

Oddly enough, after what you said in your letter, Walter Wanger asked me to go round, as he had something right in my line, and it turned out to be Kelland's *Stand-In*! I turned it down. I got myself in bad enough last time by criticising Hollywood, and I didn't want to do a picture which would have been an indictment of the studios.

6 May 1937

I wish we had taken this house for six months instead of a year. There seems to be a probability that I shall do a four weeks job on Fred Astaire's next picture, based on *A Damsel in Distress*, but except for that nothing is stirring. I was told that I was going to do *The Earl of Chicago*, but I see that Ben Hecht is doing it. The fact is, I'm not worth the money my agent insists on asking for me. After all, my record here is eighteen months at a huge salary, with only small bits of pictures to show for it.

I would be perfectly happy if I could just be left alone to write stories, as I hate picture work. The only thing is that one doesn't want to come out here and get stuck out here, with no picture work.

24 June 1937

As I said above, I am sweating away at a picture. It is for Fred Astaire, and is from my novel *A Damsel in Distress*. When they bought it, they gave it to an ex-drugstore clerk to adapt, and he

131

turned out a frightful script all about crooks – no resemblance to the novel. Then it struck them that it might be a good thing to stick to the story of the novel, so they chucked away the other script and called me in. I think it is going to make a good picture. But what uncongenial work picture-writing is. It makes one feel as if one were working with one's hands tied.

30 July 1937

Awfully sorry I haven't written before, but Hell's foundations have been quivering. We started shooting the Fred Astaire picture ten days ago, and I still have about half of it to write!! I'm afraid this letter will have to be short and scrappy. More later.

4 September 1937

Bill, I hate this place! Not the place itself, mind you, though I feel such miles away from you and all the things – like Dulwich matches – that I'm really fond of, but the people. If I don't have to go out to parties, it's fine. I work up to lunch, then go for a walk and have a swim, work till dinner, and up to my room at 8.30 to read and listen to radio. I enjoy that. But I get so bored by the people I have to meet, especially at big parties. I would like to be an absolute hermit.

6 WORK

The letters that Plum wrote to Townend and others on the subject of writing have been the most difficult to select – partly because there are so many of them, but also because those to Townend form the basis for the book *Performing Flea*. Possibly, however, those who already know *Performing Flea* may be interested to note the differences between the published letters and the originals; and, in any case, since writing was the most important part of Plum's life, this selection would be incorrectly emphasized if it lacked a collection of his letters on the subject.

☆

To William Townend   Great Neck
28 February 1920   Long Island
                                        New York

(1) I now write short stories at a terrific speed. I've started a habit of rushing them through and then copying them out carefully, instead of trying to get the first draft exactly right. I have just finished an eight thousand word golf story in two days!!! Darned good, too. It just came pouring out. I think this is a record that will stand for a long time, though. It nearly slew me. As a rule, I find the inside of a week long enough, if I have got the plot well thought out.

(2) On a novel I generally average about eight pages a day, i.e. about 2500 words. On the other hand, I've just done 100,000 words of a new novel in exactly two months. But I don't know what's come over me lately. I've been simply churning out the stuff. I think it was due to knocking off stories for a year or so and doing plays.

27 June 1922   4 Onslow Square
                                        London SW7

Listen, laddie. Any more humorous plots you can think out will be heartily welcomed. I've got to start another damn series in the *Strand* Feb number, and haven't any ideas except that I think I'll do a series about Ukridge this time. I have a good plot, where he steals a chap's trousers in order to go to a garden party and all that sort of thing.[1] At the date of the series he is still unmarried and you can make him always in love with girls, like Bingo, if necessary. The keynote of the series is that he and all his pals are devilish hard-up – sort of Leonard Merrick Bohemian stuff, only London – and a plot which has as a punch Ukridge just missing touching a man for two bob would be quite in order. . . .

I am now contracted to finish a novel, 28 short stories, and a musical show by the end of October. I have no ideas and don't expect to get any. All right, what!

23 May 1923   Easthampton
                                               Long Island
                                               New York

Another thing is, what you want to put your stuff over is ACTION. . . . The more I write, the more I am convinced that the only way to write a popular story is to split it up into scenes, and have as little stuff in between the scenes as possible. See what I mean? Well, look here. I did a story the other day, the only thing that was arrived at in the first fifteen hundred words was that I met Battling Billson down in the East End and told him Ukridge's address, which he had lost. But by having me go into a pub and get a drink and lose my money and be chucked out by the barman and picked up by Billson, who happened to be passing, and then having Billson go in and clean up the pub and manhandle the barman I got some darned good stuff which, I think, absolutely concealed the fact that nothing had really happened except my giving him the address.[2]

4 November 1923   c/o Guaranty Trust Co.
                                               14th St and 5th Ave
                                               New York

Just one more thing. I think you have made a mistake in starting interesting stuff and then dropping it. The beachcomber in chapter one is so intriguing and novel that it is a dull shock to find that he only makes that one appearance. Also, Chick's mother. The

[1] Probably 'First Aid for Dora' in *Ukridge*, published on 3 June 1924.
[2] 'The Return of Battling Billson' in *Ukridge*.

principle I always go on in writing a long story is to think of the characters in terms of actors in a play. I say to myself, when I invent a good character for an early scene, 'If this were a play, we should have to get somebody darned good to play this part, and if he found he had only a short scene in act one he would walk out. How therefore can I twist the story about so as to give him more to do and keep him alive till the fall of the curtain?'

This generally works well and improves the story. A good instance of this was Baxter in *Leave It to Psmith*. It became plain to me as I constructed the story that Baxter was such an important character that he simply had to have a good scene somewhere in what would correspond to the latter part of act two.

23 September 1924   Grand Hotel
                                                         Harrogate
                                                         Yorkshire

I say, do you like the title:-

Sam in the Suburbs

I have got a good central idea. Hero takes semi–detached house at Dulwich next door to heroine, who has told him she never wants to see him again, and they scrap across the wall. Hero's dog assaults heroine's kitten and so on. Meanwhile, crooks are trying to get at stolen bonds which a former crook has buried somewhere in hero's house. See? It's working out fine.[1]

1 October 1924

The short story I've just finished, entitled 'Honeysuckle Cottage', is the damnedest funniest idea I've ever had. A young writer of detective stories gets left five thousand quid and a house by aunt, who was Leila May Pinckney, the famous writer of sentimental stories. He finds that her vibrations have set up a sort of miasma of sentimentalism in the place, so that all who come within its radius get soppy and maudlin. He then finds to his horror that he is . . . but it will be simpler to send you the story, so I am doing so. I polished it up a good bit in typing it out.

---

[1] *Sam the Sudden*, published in 1925. In the USA it was called *Sam in the Suburbs*.

28 October 1924   23 Gilbert St
                                                   Mayfair
                                                   London W
I believe I told you once before that I classed all my characters as if
they were living salaried actors, and I'm convinced that this is a
rough but very good way of looking at them.

The one thing actors won't stand is being brought on to play in
a scene which is of no value to them in order that they may feed
some less important character, and I believe this isn't merely vanity
but is based on an instinctive knowledge of stage craft.

22 December 1924

I'm awfully glad you liked *Sally*. I don't remember the *Times*
review of it, but they seem to loathe my stuff. They gave *Bill the
Conqueror* a rotten notice. However, it doesn't seem to make much
difference.

Do you find you work easily these days? I've been having a
deuce of a job on my new story. The stuff, when I've done it, is all
right but I don't seem able to write more than about three or four
pages a day. I found that over *Sally*, which I wrote in London, so I
suppose it's something to do with being in London. Of course, I
have had a lot of interruptions in the shape of dinners and things. I
don't know why it should affect my work if I am going out to
dinner, but it does. It always makes me stop an hour before I need.

17 May 1927   17 Norfolk St
                                                   Park Lane
                                                   London W1
I've had frightfully good notices for the *S. Bachelor*, including a
leading article – no less! – in the *Morning Post*.[1] How it's selling, I
don't know. Hatchard's told me that nothing was selling these
days, but Times Library said it was going very strong.

1 April 1928   Hotel Impney
                                                   Droitwich
                                                   Worcestershire
So sorry not to have written before. I have been much tied up with a

[1] *Morning Post,* 10 May 1927

very difficult story. I wish to goodness you were here to help me with it. It's one of those maddening yarns where you've got beginning and end and only want a bit in the middle. The idea is that Lord Emsworth has been landed with a niece at the castle, niece having got engaged to man her family disapproves of. Freddie has seen a film where the same thing happened and the man disguised himself with false whiskers, went and sucked up to the family, and then, when they all loved him, tore off the whiskers and asked for their blessing.

So he sends this young man to stay at Blandings, telling Lord E he is a pal of his named Robinson. He tells the young man to strain every nerve to ingratiate himself with Lord E.

Now, you see what happens. The young man spends his whole time hanging round Lord E helping him up out of chairs, asking him questions about the garden etc etc, and it simply maddens Lord E, who feels he has never loathed a young man more.

See the idea? Well, what is bothering me is the getting of the cumulative details which lead up to Lord E loathing the young man. Can you think of any? What *would* a young man in that position do, thinking he was making a big hit with the old man and really driving him off his head? It all leads up to my big scene, where Lord E, having at last, as he thinks, eluded the young man, goes and bathes in the lake and is so delighted at being away from him that he starts to sing and kick his feet from sheer joy. Which causes the young man, who is lurking in the bushes, to think he is drowning and dive in and save him.[1]

4 July 1928

17 Norfolk St
Park Lane
London W1

I wish we could get together. I should like to have your help on a novel I'm trying to think out. It's coming darned slowly – or, putting it another way, slowly.

I've just finished and sent in to Pop Grimsdick what I think is a great introduction to the book. I was baffled at first, as I didn't want to do the ordinary stodgy introduction. I wanted what would practically be a funny article, and I think I have got it. I've got one bit which I like about meeting you and saying 'That man has been

[1] 'Company for Gertrude', a short story in *Blandings Castle*.

137

sorting lemons', and then a long bit about lemon-sorting, very funny, and warning readers not to mind if the lemon-motive creeps into your stories. I can't explain it very well, but it's the goods. The whole thing has come out well, and will, I think, help the book. It runs to about 1700 words.[1]

26 July 1928   Hotel Impney
                                               Droitwich
                                               Worcestershire

Also, very important. Cut out nearly all the exclamation marks. They are death to a story, and the printers who work for Jenkins seem to have a passion for them. I've just been re-reading my *Damsel in Distress*, of which I did not correct the proofs, and it is terrible. Also *Piccadilly Jim*. Specimen sentence – 'But wait a minute! I don't get this!'

28 September 1928   Rogate Lodge
                                               Rogate
                                               Petersfield
                                               Hants

Have you any short story plots you want to dispose of? I need a Lord Emsworth plot and also a Ukridge. I am planning a vast campaign. I want to write six short stories simultaneously. I have three plots to begin with and I want three more. Don't you feel, when writing a story, that if only it were some other story you could write it in your head? I do. I'm sure the best way is to have two or three going at the same time, so that when you get sick of the characters of one you can switch to another.

11 November 1929   17 Norfolk St
                                               Park Lane
                                               London W1

I'm longing to come down and see you all, but I'm in the middle of a story, which I must finish before I can make any move. I've gone and let myself in for one of those stories which lead up to a big comic scene and now I'm faced with writing the scene and it looks as if it is going to be hard to make it funny. It's a village Rugger

[1] The Wodehouse Introduction to *The Ship in the Swamp* by William Townend is given in Appendix B.

match, where everybody tries to slay everybody else, described by Bertie Wooster who, of course, knows nothing about Rugger. It's damned hard to describe a game you know backwards through the eyes of somebody who doesn't know it. However, I suppose it will come. These things always do. But it isn't easy to get comic high spots.[1]

9 December 1929

I can use all the stuff you sent, as I have made the hero's late father a prospector and he presumably told the hero stories when he was a kid, which the hero uses later. It is working fine.[2]

To Denis Mackail
26 June 1930

Metro-Goldwyn-Mayer
Culver City
California

Frightfully sorry I haven't written before. I have been in a whirl of work. After three months absolute deadness, my brain began to whirr like a dynamo. So you see one does recover from these blank periods. I hope yours is gone. I have written three short stories, an act of a play, and the dialogue for a picture in three weeks, and have got six brand new plots for short stories!!! I believe our rotten brains have to go through those ghastly periods of inertness before getting a second wind.

10 May 1931

A nasty jar the other day. A man, prefacing his remarks by saying he loved my stuff, wrote that he thought I had overwritten *Big Money*, and he sent me the book with his cuts!! The poor ass had cut out practically everything, including all the really funny bits which the critics had praised. And he obviously meant so well and was so genuinely trying to be friendly and helpful that I can't savage him. But the result has been to make me distrustful of my work.

　　Why is it that a single slam from even the most patent imbecile can undo all the praise of a hundred critics? If he had gushed about the story, I wouldn't have been a bit pleased. But just because this

---

[1] 'The Ordeal of Young Tuppy', a short story in *Very Good, Jeeves*.
[2] *Big Money*. Plum eventually made the hero an orphan, but he used Townend's information to describe the life he wanted to lead.

one man found faults in it, I find myself against all my reason becoming diffident.

8 April 1932   Domaine de la Fréyère
                                                Auribeau
                                                Alpes-Maritimes

Yes, I did start a letter to you, but lost it. And I didn't write again because for the last four weeks I've been sweating at a new novel. I've just finished 110 pages, all revised and rewritten about three times, and I'm very pleased with it. It's a Jeeves novel and ought to be easy to write, but so far has proved a ghastly fag. That first person stuff cuts both ways. It gives you speed, but you're up against the fact that nothing can happen except through the eyes of the hero.[1]

10 September 1933   Hunstanton Hall
                                                Norfolk

Sorry I haven't written before. You know how it is. One's Art. I was on the 1st chapters and couldn't leave them. Finished yesterday, making three novels and 10 short stories in 18 months, which, as *Variety* would say, is nice sugar.

To William Townend   Low Wood
23 January 1935   Le Touquet

I am contemplating writing a stinker to Ivor Nicholson, cursing his reader – who, I imagine, is a novelist of sorts, probably someone like William Plomer. By the way, how does a publisher ever accept a novel on a reader's report? If you told the story of any book as this man has done, it would sound awful.

    Reader's report of *Henry Fourth*, *part one*, by W. Shakespeare:- 'This is the story of life in London, but it has no background. The plot is improbable and does not carry conviction, as it deals with a Prince of Wales who apparently visits public houses. There are

---

[1] The first Jeeves novel was called *Thank You, Jeeves* and was published in 1934.

literally dozens of characters in the story, but they are not living people set in a scene. There is a fat man named Falstaff.'

I am writing a farce. Ethel has been after me for years to write a play all on my own, so I said I would. It's the most ghastly sweat. But it does teach one a tremendous lot about construction.

10 March 1935

I agree about synonyms of 'said', but I am very much in favour of using 'he said' very seldom, especially in a duologue, when the reader knows who is speaking. It trips up the eye a bit as one reads. I much prefer a chunk of dialogue as in a play.

18 September 1935

You remember that Crupper story you gave me, about the woman telling lies about the girl's relations, so that she could marry the humble suitor?[1] It comes out in Christmas *Strand* – called 'Uncle Fred Flits By'. Now, in Uncle Fred I'm sure that I have got a great character, but at the moment I simply can't think of another plot for him. I'm just waiting and hoping one will come.

It's different if you have got a man with a definite job – S. Holmes or Raffles. Then you can think of things for him to do. But I couldn't sit down and do a series of Adventures of Psmith, because there is no definite line that he would take.

2 December 1935   Hilbre
                                      Le Touquet

I'm glad you liked Uncle Fred. Yes, a fine character, but unless you give me another story as good as that one I can't think of anything for him to do. He is really a sort of Psmith, and I can see in a vague way that he ought to go about helping people – and at the same time getting Pongo into trouble – but it's the details that are hard to think of.

I have now got a new system for writing short stories. I take a *Saturday Evening Post* story and say 'Now, how can I write exactly the same story but entirely different?'

---

[1] Townend specialized in sea stories, and Captain Crupper was one of his favourites.

See what I mean? Here was one which I expect you read. Girl lands man with a Peke, Man wants to sell millionaire a radio programme, but can't get at him – Millionaire and man meet and fraternize over their dislike of Pekes and Man gets the job.

It ought to be easy to think of some equivalent for that, but I've been at it a year now and it hasn't come. What comic thing is there that a man could get landed with besides a Peke?

Still, I have faith in the method. It at least does this – it sets one thinking, and then some other plot on quite different lines emerges.

Here's a rummy thing, too. For six months I have been hammering away at a plot, trying to make it come out, with no success. Last night I suddenly said 'Could this be a Ukridge story?' Ten minutes later I had the plot complete. It's the treatment that matters, isn't it.

5 May 1936

What a terrific pace you have written it at. I expect it is that that makes you think it isn't good. I have just finished mine about three weeks quicker than usual, and it is only now that I have put it away for a week and then looked at it again that I feel it's all right. I think quick writing tires the brain and makes one sick of a book, and it is only when one has recovered that one realizes how good it is.

When I was in London, I went to see the movie of *Tale of Two Cities*, and it struck me how well you could adapt that – I mean, the central idea of the waster in love with the girl sacrificing himself to save her husband and (b) the idea of the Revolutionists getting the hero's tutor to try to save himself by writing to the hero to come over and plead for him, their motive being to get the hero back to France so that they could slosh him. I can see that in one of your settings – sea captain who has got into trouble in some South American republic gets an SOS from pal who is in prison there and goes over and is caught and condemned to death. Then your big character, a sort of Captain Shuffley, takes his place and gets executed. (If you haven't seen the movie, go and see it. It is about the only one I have ever seen that seemed a real work of art. It is tremendous, and Ronald Colman terrific. I believe, if you saw it, it would give you an idea for a book, and nobody would recognize it in a modern setting.)

13 May 1936

In writing a novel, I always imagine I am writing for a cast of actors. Some actors are natural minor actors and some are natural major actors. It is a matter of personality. Same in a book. Psmith, for instance, is a major character. If I am going to have Psmith in a story, he must be in the big situations.

6 May 1937

Your query about Marquand's plot touched a tender spot.[1] I have long had my eye on the man myself. I find nowadays that the only way I can get plots is by reading somebody else's stuff and working from there, and Marquand is a man whose stories are very suggestive. I was reading a book of his the other day, called *No Hero*, where the fatal paper is hidden in a man's flask, and the man, who has always been a ready drinker, suddenly decides to reform and so does not touch the flask. If I can't get something out of that, I'm not the man I was.[2]

I don't think there is any objection to basing one's stuff on somebody else's, providing you alter it enough. After all, all one wants is motives. I think you could safely use the plot you suggest.

I'll tell you what's a maddening thing – when a fellow frankly imitates one's work and does it badly but has incidents which one could use oneself. A bloke whose name I can't remember wrote a story called *What Price Gloria*, with a typical P.G.W. Anglo-American plot and a lot of my characters under different names, and he had a sequence about a couple of vases, one belonging to an American millionaire and the other to a Lord Emsworth type which would have suited me down to the ground. It leads to the Lord Emsworth coming over to New York. What makes me sick is that if I ever do a story about two vases, the man will probably sue me, whereas I can't touch him for having an absent-minded English peer who has a valet like Jeeves and a son like Bertie.

30 June 1938   Low Wood
                                               Le Touquet
I find it so hard to write in the afternoons. If I go for an exercise

[1] J. P. Marquand, author of *H. M. Pulham, Esq.*   [2] See *Full Moon* (1947).

walk, I'm too tired to write, and if I don't get any exercise, my brain won't work!

I am v. interested in what you say about Jill the Reckless. It's what I always feel about my work – viz. that I go off the rails unless I stay all the time in a sort of artificial world of my own creation. A real character in one of my books sticks out like a sore thumb. You're absolutely right about Freddie Rooke. Just a stage dude – as Bertie Wooster was when I started writing him. If you look at the early Jeeves stories, you'll find Bertie quite a different character now.

6 June 1939   Golf Hotel
                                               Le Touquet

For just a month I have been trying to get out a plot for a novel, and have now got two in a shadowy form. One of them is fine as regards the comic part, but I haven't got the love interest yet, and it's no good without it. If it gets cooler, I will write down what I've got and send it to you. The other one, though not so far advanced, looks promising. Uncle Fred pinches a villa on the Riviera and the Duke of Dunstable gets into trouble with the police at this Riviera town and has to lie low, so Uncle Fred makes him shave off his moustache and takes him on as a butler, in which capacity he falls in love with the cook, who turns him down because in her opinion he isn't quite a gentleman. The whole thing is very vague at present, but with a start like that I ought to get something. Presumably, Uncle Fred is befriending a girl who wants something out of the Duke. I suppose the real owner of the villa turns up, and for some reason can't seize the villa – and probably has to sign on as a footman. I might even make it a yacht, and make the Duke a steward. But this might be awkward, as a yacht would have a crew, captain etc, whereas a villa would be empty.

To Guy Bolton   Low Wood
23 December 1939   Le Touquet

Your letter was like the beat of the bugle to the old war-horse. I'm frightfully keen to come over and work with you. Can you get me a commission? If so, cable and I'll be over on the next Italian boat. Would Vinton want me for the price you speak of?

From your letter I gathered that you were on the eve of a New York production (*The Gibson Girls?*), and then finishing up another for Alex. So I imagine you wouldn't need me at once. If, however, a Vinton show is being prepared and you could work me in and would like me to start on it, I can sail at a moment's notice. . . .

I am very sick of being cooped up in Le Touquet and pine for America. It is very pleasant here, but I feel my brain needs artificial stimulation

Do strain every nerve to get me a *definite commission*. Personally, I would come over like a shot on the chance of something doing, but Ethel is hard to move unless there is something definite in prospect. So get busy, and rely on me to spring to the task the moment you cable.

To William Townend   Berlin
11 May 1942

I'm so glad you liked *Money in the Bank*. It was written at the rate of about a page a day in a room with fifty other men playing darts and ping-pong and talking and singing. It just shows how one can concentrate when one has to. After I had finished it, I started a Blandings Castle novel called *Full Moon* and had done about a third of it when I was released. Ethel then joined me in the country, bringing with her about two thirds of a Jeeves novel called *Joy in the Morning*, which I had been writing at Le Touquet during the occupation. I finished this, and then I tackled *Full Moon* and finished that. I have also written a book about life in camp – very funny, but a bit on the short side. I shall not publish that till after the war.

5 April 1945   Hotel Linoln
                                           Rue Bayard
                                           Paris

I finished my novel last Sunday and immediately got what I think must have been an attack of *grippe*. All right again now. What with one thing and another, this novel took me exactly a year to write, but it has come out very well. It was one of those difficult stories where you get an apparently inextricable tangle ingeniously straightened out in the last chapter, and all the way through I was saying to myself 'Well, it's all right so far, but that last chapter is going to let the whole thing down.' But, thank goodness, the last chapter came out just right. I now have the following books shuffling their feet nervously in the ante-room, wondering if they will ever get taken on:– *Money in the Bank*, *Joy in the Morning* (a Jeeves story), *Full Moon* (Blandings Castle story), *Spring Fever* and this new one, *Uncle Dynamite*. Also ten short stories.

I am now going to settle down seriously to that book which you have been talking about in your letters, and which of *course* must be the first thing of mine to appear after the war.[1] I can't understand how Watt can think any differently.[2] It's going to be terribly difficult, though. The camp part of it is fine. I was reading it again last night, and with a few small changes it can stand. I then come to the section dealing with my life in Germany, and how on earth I am going to make that run to more than two or three very dull pages I can't think. The Paris section should be easier. Of course, the fundamental difficulty is that in that section I shall be writing about unpleasant experiences that happened to me without having the sympathy of the audience, and trying to make the reader laugh when he is drawing himself up coldly and saying 'We are not amused'.

To Denis Mackail   Hotel Lincoln
16 April 1945   Rue Bayard
                                           Paris

I was interested by what you said about writing slowly now. I have just the same trouble. I used to do my eight pages at a sitting, but now I consider two good. And I have to rewrite all the time. I don't think it's age or the war so much as one's growing sensitiveness as a critic of one's stuff. Though probably age has something to do with it. I find the actual physical job of writing takes it out of me so much now.

To Bill Townend   78 Avenue Paul Doumer
22 April 1945   Paris

I had a long letter from Watt the other day, the contents of which were quite encouraging. I couldn't gather whether Jenkins still wanted to publish me, but he said he had been making enquiries and

---

[1] The Camp Book. See p. 91.
[2] A. P. Watt, Plum's literary agent.

Collins was very keen on getting my books and was prepared to make a big campaign to put me back on the map. Also Chatto and Windus. And the Jenkins people in their letter said that my books were all in good demand and all in print. So things look bright. I do think public opinion must have changed a good deal in the last year, because my cheap editions have suddenly taken a tremendous jump, starting from about a year ago. The bad period was at the end of 1942, when the sales dropped to about 6 copies of each book. In the first half of 1943 they rose to about 100 per book, and in the first half of 1944 they were up to as much as 900. I haven't had the returns for the last half of 1944. But in all the cheap editions seem to have sold about half a million in three years, which looks as if people had had a change of heart. Of course, they may be buying my books with one hand and hating my insides with the other, but I hope not.

30 June 1945   Paris

I wrote a novel called *Spring Fever* in 1943, and the other day, not being able to get a plot for a novel, decided to make a play of it. It is coming out very well, but as always the agony of telling a story purely in dialogue and having to compress it and keep the action in spot is frightful. I have written the first scene of act one half a dozen times and it isn't right yet. Act One, Scene Two, though, is fine. The curse of a play is that you can't give people's thoughts. In the novel it was simple. I started with the Earl looking worried and then explained that he was worried because he wanted to marry the cook and he had as a rival his butler, a man of extraordinary attraction. In the play it has to be done in the dialogue. Still, it's a lot of fun.

8 November 1945   36 Boulevard Suchet
                                         Paris

I'll tell you what makes life a hell for writers, and that is that you meet someone who tells you a story as having happened to himself or a friend and you work it up and publish it, only to find that the gentleman read the thing in a magazine somewhere. But listen. What *is* plagiarism? Did you ever see a play by Freddie Lonsdale called *The Last of Mrs Cheyney*? It was about a Society woman who was one of a band of crooks, and this is revealed to the audience at the end of act one. An exactly similar situation was in an American play called *Cheating Cheaters*. And, worse than that, the big scene of Act Two was where the hero gets Mrs Cheyney into his room at night and holds her up for something by saying he is going to keep her there till they are found, which is exactly the same as Pinero's *Gay Lord Quex*. And yet nobody has ever breathed a word against Freddie for plagiarising.

7 December 1945

The good news is that the Jenkins people seem confident that *Money in the Bank*, which they are bringing out in May, will be all right. They are printing a first edition of 20,000 and say that the Trade is sanguine. If I can get by with that one, the others ought to be all right. I am beginning to feel that it won't matter that they are about conditions and a life which has ceased to exist. I don't believe people care a damn, so long as the story is funny. . . .

I had a letter from Denis Mackail the other day, drawing a very gloomy picture of the short story situation in England. He says there is now practically no market, and if you do write a short story it mustn't be over 2000 words. Bobby Denby, writing from America, says that over there you mustn't exceed 5000. This dishes me completely, as I can't keep under 7000.

To Denis Mackail
11 December 1945

What you tell me about the state of the shot story – by which I mean short story – market seems to me to come under the head of a nice bit of box fruit. I suppose there are people who can write a short story in 2000 words, but not me. As you rightly say, my 5000-word stories always ran to 7000 and even then I felt they were too short. An expert in the USA tells me that over there you must not exceed 17 or 18 pages. I now have ten in my drawer, the shortest of which runs to 30 pages of typescript – and when I say pages I mean foolscap-size pages at least a third larger than what my expert obviously means by pages, so there you are. It is a comfort to feel that there is no need to try to hack them down to an obscene length like 2000 words, for as you justly say there are no magazines to publish them, even if one did. The British short story can go to hell, as far as I'm concerned. (Incidentally, on another subject, have you ever noticed that if you strike a wrong letter on the typewriter it always comes out very clear and firm and black, while with the right letters you have to go back and hammer them twice to make them show at all?) George Abbot, the American theatrical manager, has refused my play – on the ground, as I feared, that the plot isn't right. I can never get a funny plot without having somebody pretend to be somebody else, and apparently that is poison to the New York audience.

23 December 1945

You're quite right about my books being early Edwardian. I look on myself as a historical novelist. I read a book about Dickens the other day which pointed out that D. was still writing gaily about stage coaches etc long after railways had come in. I don't believe it matters and I intend to go on hewing to the butler line, let the chips fall where they may. By the way, I was vastly encouraged, when reading in the paper about Viscount Selby and his lady friend to see that at one point 'the butler' entered and spoke a line or two. So they still exist.

To Ira Gershwin
24 January 1946

My war history has been a simple one. I have just sat in my chair and written all the time. When the Germans occupied Le Touquet I was in the middle of a Jeeves novel, *Joy in the Morning*. I continued plugging away at this for exactly two months, when they took us all off in a van to internment. After a few weeks spent in prisons, barracks etc we were dumped down at the lunatic asylum at Tost in Upper Silesia, where it was possible to resume writing and I started a new novel called *Money in the Bank*, which appeared serially in the *Saturday Evening Post* in 1941. I had to write in pencil in a room full of men playing darts and ping-pong, which made it a slow job. After my release my wife joined me, bringing me what I had done of *Joy in the Morning*. I finished this, then wrote a book about my camp experiences. Then I did another novel called *Full Moon*, then ten short stories, then a novel called *Spring Fever*, and finally a novel called *Uncle Dynamite*. So I have four novels and ten short stories waiting to be published in America. I heard from Doubleday, my publisher, yesterday that he was bringing out *Joy in the Morning* in the early fall. My trouble is that when I last heard the American magazines were a bit dubious about running my stuff, but I am hoping that they will do so soon. Of course, it's quite likely that they will think my sort of story out of date nowadays. I shall know better where I am when I see how *Joy in the Morning* sells.

To William Townend   Paris
7 March 1946

I am wondering, with some mild amusement, what the result is going to be of the impact of a book like *Money in the Bank* on the world of 1946! It is so absolutely archaic. It assumes a state of affairs which is as out of date as *Three Men in a Boat*. It will be very interesting to see how it goes. I believe that people will jump at something that takes them away from modern conditions. The same applies to the impending publication of my Jeeves novel in America. But of course my stuff has been out of date since 1914, and nobody has seemed to mind.

To Denis Mackail
4 July 1946

I find I can't do anything in the writing line these days except write letters. I don't seem to get any ideas for stories. It's true that I have a Jeeves novel mapped out, but I would like to get something else going, so that I could be brooding on it in my spare time. The actual writing of a story always gives me a guilty feeling, as if I were wasting my time. The only thing that matters is thinking the stuff out.

To William Townend
29 April 1946

Did you ever read Kipling's autobiography? In that he maintains that the principal thing in writing is to cut. Somerset Maugham says the same, and I agree with them. Kipling says it's rather like raking a slag out of a fire to make the fire burn brighter. I know just what he means. You can skip as you read, but if the superfluous stuff is there it affects you just the same. The trouble is to know what to cut. I generally find with my own stuff that it's the superfluous lines in the dialogue that are wrong, but then my books are principally dialogue. . . .

To Guy Bolton
13 July 1946

To refresh the old memory, I wrote *Leave It to Psmith* in 1924 and you let me incorporate a good bit of your stuff from the dramatization of *Piccadilly Jim* (Greg. Kelly and Ruth Gordon, tried out in Des Moines but never reached NY). There was a scene in an employment agency where I drew very largely on the Bolton genius.

20 November 1946   Pavillon Henri Quatre
                                                 St Germain-en-Laye

Joy in the Morning is doing fine. At date of publication on August 22 the advance sales were 15,000. On September 15 the total was 16,500. And by the middle of October it had got up to 19,950. Doubledays say they expect a big sale at Christmas, so things look pretty good. Nothing of mine in the last ten years has sold more than 14,000. I have seen the reviews, and they are excellent. There seems to be a feeling among the critics that Jeeves is a bit *vieux jeu* – in fact, the *New Yorker* flatly says he has become a bore. But it is now about forty years since I learned that the critics don't matter a damn. So long as the public wants Jeeves, to hell with the critics.

What you said about laughing immoderately over the prize-giving scene in *Right Ho, Jeeves*, made me wince a bit, as I am headed for a similar scene in the one I'm doing now, and I am haunted with an awful feeling that it is going to fall flat. The set-up is that Bertie has got to recite A. A. Milne's Christopher Robin poems at a village concert, and I shall have to try to make the village concert a big scene.[1] And at the moment I can't see how I am going to make it funny. Still, I suppose it will be all right when I get to it. It generally happens that after you have got momentum on in a story the various hurdles come easily. I haven't got down to thinking of

[1] *The Mating Season.*

151

the scene yet. Meanwhile, the story is coming out very well, though, as I told you in my last letter, slowly. But I'm afraid one doesn't often get a real smash like that prizegiving chapter.

24 December 1946

My publisher is not so dotty as yours, but I, too, have had my troubles. In *Joy in the Morning* Bertie speaks of himself as eating a steak and Boko is described as having fried eggs for breakfast, and Grimsdick of Jenkins is very agitated about this, because he says the English public is so touchy about food nowadays that stuff like this will probably cause an uproar. I have changed the fried egg to a sardine and cut out the steak, so I hope all will now be well. But I was reading Agatha Christie's *The Hollow* just now, and the people in it simply gorge roast duck and soufflés and caramel cream and so on, besides having a butler, several parlourmaids, a kitchen maid and a cook. I must say it encouraged me to read *The Hollow* and to see that Agatha was ignoring present conditions in England.

☆

After William Townend died, Plum's letters about his work were written almost entirely to Guy Bolton. In these he shows his essential modesty, since he and Guy continued to write plays and musical comedies, although they seldom got a production. Plum enjoyed writing lyrics and he enjoyed working with Guy, and he continued to do so almost to the end of his life. It has been difficult to make an illustrative selection, because the correspondence about plays which were not produced is apt to be obscure. I have chosen letters which I think give the best picture of Plum's life, and where there is evidence of a production I have given it.

☆

To Guy Bolton   1000 Park Avenue
2 March 1948   New York

Meanwhile, in intervals of going to the dentist, I have been sweating like nobody's business at the Guitry play and have finished the first two acts. The third is quite short, so I shall have the whole thing ready for you on your return. I think I have done some pretty good stuff, but it needs the master hand to polish it. It's a great play and I hope to heaven John's cable asking for an option will produce results. But, anyway, I felt it was a good thing to get the adaptation down on paper, even if some manager gets in ahead of us (which I don't suppose for a moment will happen, as nobody knows about the play) he would welcome the chance of using an adaptation by two geniuses like us. A bright idea occurred to me last night – Monty Woolley for the Guitry part. . . .

News on the Wodehouse front is good. Ethel did not have sinus and is returning tomorrow or next day. Wonder went through her operation splendidly. And *The Play's the Thing* goes into rehearsal on Monday with a splendid cast.[1] Arthur Margetson ought to be wonderful in Reginald Owen's part. He and Claude Allister (the 'Mell' of 1926) arrive on the *Queen Mary* at the end of this week. I must say that after a prolonged session with Hunt and Bill it is rather a comfort to work with Gilbert.[2] He just waves a wand and a perfect cast is complete in a couple of days.

16 August 1948   2 East 86th St
                                    New York

Gosh, I wish that everything that's cooking would come to the boil. The contents of my drawer are now as follows:-

A play with Melchior Lengyel (a louse. Not Lengyel, but the play. Not a hope for this one, I fear).

Two adaptations of plays by Molnar. (Russo and Ellis would like to produce one of them, but Molnar, the fathead, sold the movie rights to RKO some time ago and this is holding the thing up.)

Don't Listen, Ladies.[3] (Obviously the best bet of the lot.)

Two adaptations of novels of mine. (These are okay as regards a manager, but the manager who has taken them hasn't any money. All depends on how he makes out in this direction.)

The Milton Shubert Puccini musical. (Fine, if it comes off, but will it?)

[1] Plum adapted *The Play's the Thing* from a Molnar play. It did well in New York in 1929 and ran for 244 performances in 1948.
[2] Gilbert Miller
[3] *Don't Listen, Ladies* ran for 219 performances at the St James's Theatre, London in 1948.

The Dick Myers show.

The Hans Bartsch show.

If all these came off, I would have a share in eight shows on Broadway, which would satisfy me. I'm no hog. But, gosh, how sceptical one gets these days. I've come to the conclusion that until we corral our tame millionaire we can't count on anything.

In the above list I forgot to include my *Spring Fever* play. I don't know if I told you about this in previous letters, but I rewote it for the third time, getting it into one set and making the setting and characters American, and it didn't look at all bad. I sent it to Johnny Golden, who of course turned it down, to Milton Shubert, who hasn't answered yet, and to George Abbot. George Abbot was very encouraging and I think would have taken it if he hadn't been too busy with *Charley's Aunt* etc. to do any work on it. I have an idea he may take it for next season. Meanwhile Dick Myers is reading it. It still needs a lot of work, but it is gradually shaping.

12 May 1949   1000 Park Avenue
                                               New York

I am very busy now, making a 25,000 novelette (which will later become a full length novel) out of that play of mine, *Joy in the Morning* which Klift and Rea have in their office. I wish you would get hold of it and read it and, if possible, give me some plot suggestions. I can see that the start of the play is wrong. It needs a Prologue. In the novel I start in New York and gradually edge into the stuff in the play. I should imagine that when I really get down to the novel, I can write at least 15,000 words before the action of the play starts. The story, now that I am handling it in novel form, is darned good.[1]

24 May 1949

In re *Joy in the Morning*. I am now writing it as a novelette preparatory to doing it as a novel, in the hope of landing with one of the magazines. I see what's wrong with it. It needs a Prologue. I start my novelette with a scene showing the heroine turning down

[1] This does not appear to relate to the novel of that name but to the plot of a play which, never produced, turned into the novel *The Old Reliable*.

the hero because he's too crazy, then go to Hollywood, where 'Bill' (whom I have now turned into a woman of the Marie Dressler type) springs on the hero a scheme for buying a literary agency (so that he and she will both be involved in the venture). I think it is an improvement. At present the venture on which getting the money depends is too casually introduced. I think I can make an adequate book of the thing, but I am doubtful if it is strong enough for a play.

15 April 1950   1000 Park Avenue
                                                   New York
Yours of 27th March. Disturbing. I know those blank periods when the idea of writing seems just silly and you wonder why you ever started the thing. I do hope that by this time the old urge has begun to function again. After all, there's nothing else to do in this world. You and I were mugs not to go in for huntin' and fishin' in our youth or at least to have developed a fondness for Bridge, like S. Maugham. The only thing we both did that was smart was to take up Pekes. I find that with Wonder and Squeaky in the home I never want to go out or see anyone. . . .

5 February 1951

I know just what is wrong with my stuff for the American stage. American audiences want plays about the relationship of men and women, while I write about some kind of venture like finding a diary or smuggling jewels and so on. It's all right in novel form, because I can nurse the thing along with a lot of in-between stuff, giving them the old personality, as it were, but for a stage play I doubt if you can get by with a story which doesn't deal primarily with sex relations. My type of story is apt to be thin on the stage. So why don't we try to get something sexy for a Jeeves play?

11 May 1951

Do you remember *The Butter and Egg Man* by Kaufman? (Circ 1925.) I am making a novel of it and have got a fine start. The trouble about novelizing a play is that you have to have so much more stuff in a book and I have had to invent a lot of fresh situations. Another trouble is that I can't use the plot Kaufman wrote of the play the hero puts his money into, as in his version it was a play for a female star and in mine the star has to be a man. In K's play the manager lets hero have 49 per cent of the show for $20,000. Next time you write tell me if you think I can get away with this today. I don't want to have hero inherit – say forty thousand unless it is absolutely necessary, as it is so much funnier if he has something reasonably small. I hope I shan't strike any snags, but one has to be very watchful, handling a story twenty-five years old.[1]

(letter marked 'early fifties')   No address

I am having the devil of a time trying to make my *Butter and Egg Man* novel long enough. It will be all right for serial form – 60,000 words – but for the novel I shall somehow have to bump it up to 75,000 words and it's going to be difficult. I have some ideas for further twists to the plot, but I feel too lazy to do them. It's curious what little substance there is in any play. I thought there were so many scenes in *B and Egg Man* that it would be simple, but when you come to write it, they evaporate.

29 June 1951   1000 Park Avenue
                               New York

Just got statements from my publishers. My books have sold five million in England and four million over here. And presumably another million in the European countries, including Japan. Not so bad, what? It cheered me up. I am going deaf in the left ear, blast it.

To Denis Mackail
7 February 1952

Frightfully sorry about my long silence. Due to preoccupation with new novel. For some reason, probably old age, it has been the most ghastly sweat. I have plugged along, doing about two pages a day, for what seems like years but is really only two months. The odd thing is that the stuff reads as if it had all been written at a sitting. I have come to the conclusion that the only pleasant part of writing is

[1] Plum turned Kaufman's play into *Barmy in Wonderland*.

the fussing about with it and fixing it up when you have got something down on paper.

This is a Blandings Castle story, supposed to take place the year after *Heavy Weather*, which was published in 1933, so I am up against the old problem of how to avoid seeming to be writing of 1952. I shall have to do a Preface, I suppose, explaining that the story is supposed to be taking place in 1927.[1]

8 July 1952

We have finished the farce, and it looks very good. As usual what happened was that I sweated my guts out writing acts one and two and handed them to Guy and he wrote a completely different script, so that practically all of it is now his. I don't know why it is, but I can't write plays. Guy's stuff is a hundred times better than mine. He has that knack of construction which I can't get in a play, though I'm all right when it's a novel. Jeeves is the star of the play, but Bertie Wooster doesn't appear. . . .[2]

14 December 1952

GALAHAD. Of course you are entitled to your view of him, but if you think him a swine, how do you feel about Falstaff and Mr Micawber and, for the matter of that, Fred Barfield in *Bradsmith Was Right*? Do you consider Falstaff a drunken lout, Micawber a petty swindler and Barfield a selfish hound? Don't you make *any* allowances for the fact that a character is supposed to be funny?

WODEHOUSE. DOES ANYONE READ HIM NOW? You said in one of your letters that some BBC man had suggested they didn't but thank God we still sell a copy or two in England and also in Sweden – Sweden is booming. Last cheque for six months' sales, after deducting Watt's rake off, £683.6.11 – France, Germany, Norway, Holland, Italy and other nations too numerous to mention, including Japan.

BUT of America I cannot speak so highly. My last book sold seven thousand odd and lost money, and Doubleday – spokesman Ken McCormick – write to say that they will be obliged to reduce my advance. To which I have replied Like hell you'll reduce my

---

[1] *Pigs Have Wings.*
[2] The play was *Come On, Jeeves*; rewritten as the novel *Ring for Jeeves.*

157

advance, adding that I consider them lousy publishers who never do a thing to push an author and am going elsewhere with my next. Curse and blast them! In the course of the years they have sold a million and a half of my books, and now this!

To hell with them, anyway. I can't write the sort of dull drip the American book public wants. But, oddly enough, I can write what the American magazine public wants – three of my last four having been serialized. If I can get $25,000 for a serial, what does the book matter? I write primarily to have something to read in the long winter evenings, and the heart of England is still sound. Let America (its book public) eat cake.

All the same there are moments when I feel not so sure that you haven't got the right idea in stopping writing.

10 February 1954

I am feeling that I was a mug ever to let myself in for writing articles. I have now done eight for *Punch*, one for *Time and Tide* and one for a paper here called *Parade*, and am beginning to feel the strain. It's pie if you get a good idea, but how few good ideas there are.

24 June 1954   Remsenburg
                                               Long Island
                                               New York

About my hating the stage. I suppose I do, really. That is to say, I used to love the preliminary stuff, the actual writing, but rehearsals and tours gave me the pip. I have followed your lead to this extent, that nothing will ever induce me to write for the theatre again. Not that I suppose I could now. . . .

I'm awfully glad you liked the Earls article. I enjoy writing these *Punch* things. What a comfort it is to feel that when you've done a thousand words, you're through! The only thing that buoys me up when writing a long novel is remembering what you said in *Topsy* about coming to a dead stop in the Morning-Night book and not being able to go on, and then coming back to it and finishing it so that the break couldn't be detected. It makes me feel that somehow the thing will get finished.

☆

The following letters refer to *French Leave*, the central idea of which Guy had used in a play, afterwards a film.

☆

To Guy Bolton
30 June 1954

Remsenburg
New York

Anyway, what we have to do now is to bump the thing up to novel length. It ought not to be too difficult with all those good characters. You will see that I have put my name on the story. I think you felt that that would be the wise thing to do in view of a movie sale. I thought that if your name was on it it would put the studio that bought it originally on the track. Even with my name on it alone I have misgivings! It is such a distinctive central idea. Possible line of defence if the deception is spotted:-

Paramount (flushed with anger): Hey, Wodehouse!
P.G.W. (nervous but fairly calm): Yes, sir?
Paramount: What the hell is all this? You've sold MGM a story that we bought from Guy Bolton (now Lord Bolton of Remsenburg) twenty years ago.
P.G.W.: Surely not?
Paramount: What do you mean, surely not? It's about three girls who–
P.G.W.: Good Lord! You don't mean to tell me Guy ever *wrote* that story? He told it me one night when in his cups and I pinched it, knowing he would have forgotten all about it when he sobered up next day.

It might work.

To Denis Mackail
18 May 1955

. . . I'm glad you like my *Punch* stuff. I went into it gaily and now find it's a hell of a sweat. Still, it's all good practice in technique and what not, and I must say it's rather nice starting a bit of writing and knowing you've only got to do a thousand words.

I have a wonderful idea for a novel. Don't you think that's always fatal? What I like is to get a scene from which I can work backward and forward. So far I haven't been able to tack anything like a plot on to the idea.

22 July 1955

I have just finished a sort of autobiography.[1] It is really a peg on which to hang my *Punch* articles. But what I am leading up to is what infernally dull reading an author's life makes. It's all right as long as you are struggling, but once you have become financially sound there is nothing to say.

21 June 1956

Thanks awfully for sending me those two things about me. They cheered my up a lot. Grimsdick tells me he saw Peter Schwed, and Peter asked him what sort of a sale he expected from a Wodehouse book.[2] Grimsdick, bless him, said that he would be very disappointed if such a book did not sell 40,000 soon after publication, which must have jarred Peter, whose figure is 7000. But even so, G. says, Peter seemed determined to continue his stand about *French Leave*. He's crazy. Actually *F.L.* has done over 20,000 and is still selling briskly. I think we shall have to take a firm line and publish it with some other firm. It's such rot – the story is more or less the same as the one which was a hit on the stage and was done three times successfully in the movies, so it can't be without appeal.

3 June 1958

I wrote a short story in 1947 for the *Cosmopolitan*. Subsequently writing a Jeeves novel, I needed what we call in the tayarter a block comedy scene, so I took out the middle part of the short story and bunged it into the book. A month or so ago I thought up a new middle and sold the new-middle story with the old beginning and

[1] *Over Seventy*.
[2] Peter Schwed worked for his US publishers, Simon and Schuster.

end in England. And I have now devised a new beginning and end for the new-middle story and sold it over here. Quite a feat, don't you think?

28 February 1960

French Leave. I wrote this four or five years ago, and Peter Schwed of Simon and Schuster broke the news to me at lunch one day that he didn't like it. He said they would publish it if I insisted, but of course I said No, don't if you don't want to. And then suddenly last year with no warning I got a contract and an advance, and no explanation has ever been given.

I've just finished my new novel. Fairly good, I think but what does it *prove*? I sometimes wish I wrote that powerful stuff the reviewers like so much, all about incest and homosexualism.

To Guy Bolton
1 June 1961

I have been sweating away, rewriting *Performing Flea* for America. It has involved doing an almost completely new book, but I think it's going to be good. I have just passed the halfway mark.

24 July 1961

I finished an American version of *Performing Flea* and got the advance from Peter Schwed, which was good. But he seems to want some fixing done – notably cutting out all the stuff I lifted from *America I Like You.*

1 August 1961

I am still trying with no success to get a plot for a new novel going. I suppose it will come in time, and anyway I have about twenty months before I shall need to deliver a new book. But this impotent feeling is rather nerve-wracking. I keep getting good ideas for scenes and so on, but what I want is the core of the story. Oh, well.

6 July 1962

We now come to a moot point. Do we *coyly reveal the fact that your play on which the book was founded has already been made into a picture three times*? I strongly advise not. As far as I know, nobody except you and me and Watt knows that *French Leave* is not my own unaided work. And in any case the novel – what with Old Nick, Clutterbuck, etc. – deviates so much from your original that I don't think it is necessary to say anything. It's a pity the hen stuff at the beginning is almost word for word from your play, but that's the only thing anyone could spot. So secrecy and silence, I think, don't you? All moneys will be paid to me as apparently the sole author, and I will slip yours – in pounds, if you are still in England when the advance comes in, or in dollars if you are over here.

23 July 1963

I have got the scenario of my novel out fairly well, but I am stumped for the end. There is a woman with a child staying at Blandings Castle and Lord Emsworth wants to get her out of the place. The kid does something to Lord E's pig which rouses the fiend in Lord E and he more or less chucks her out in a fit of wrath. But what does the kid do? Tell Virginia to use some of her spare time thinking out something that will do.[1]

17 July 1969

The novel is coming out wonderfully, though slowly. I am up to the girls in safe scene, or rather Ada Cootes in the safe. I found it worked better to have Jill not in it, as it left her free to do scenes. (I make it quite plausible why she is not in safe.)[2]

31 July 1967

I have also got rather a neat bit of construction. When Horace phones Mike, Mike can't remember the combination but says it is

---

[1] *Galahad at Blandings* (US title *The Brinkmanship of Galahad Threepwood*).
[2] *Do Butlers Burgle Banks?*

in a notebook in the small safe, which of course Ferdie has opened, thus tying in the Jimmy Valentine bit.

It really is working out like clockwork. I have a good scene where Mike is talking to the old lady when Horace phones. Mike assumes that H is tight and he and the old lady are funny about it. (Horace says he is burgling the bank. Mike thinks he is tight and hangs up. Then, after M and the old lady have had their funny dialog, Horace rings up again and this time tells about Ada being in safe.)

31 August 1969

What a nuisance old age is. I find it so difficult nowadays to sit down at the typewriter and do an honest day's work. My tendency is more and more to sink into the arm chair and put my feet up and try to get some writing done with a pen and pad. It doesn't work badly. I did four pages in the arm chair yesterday, and can always improve them when I type. The novel is coming out fine so far, and I think it will be all right to the end, but the blood sweat and tears are awful. When I remember that I wrote the last twenty-six pages of *Thank You, Jeeves* in a single day, I sigh for the past. Pretty darned good if I get three done nowadays.

24 September 1971

But last night I was re-reading *Ring for Jeeves*, the novel I wrote from your play and I was stunned by its (mostly your) brilliance. If you remember, there was no Pongo, and the idea of the hero being a bookie was Jeeves's. What was so good in it was Rory, and I don't think we ought to lose him. He's terrific. And you have a version in which the Grand National is cut and Rory plays a big part.

15 August 1973

I'm afraid the difficulty is that the boys[1] regard Jeeves as sacred writ and think that the more of the stuff in the stories they can cram in, the better. I'm sure that CLARITY is the essential thing. Get a clear script and never mind how much good material you have to leave out.

[1] Andrew Lloyd Webber and Alan Ayckbourn

What I would like them to do is jettison all they have done and start again with *Thank You, Jeeves*, which has everything needed for a musical – a clear straightforward story with several good block comedy scenes.[1]

[1] *Jeeves*, a musical by Lloyd Webber and Ayckbourn, opened in London on 22 April 1975.

7 CRITICS

To Denis Mackail   23 Gilbert Street
4 December 1924   Mayfair
                                          London W1

Your letter was like the well-known balm in Gilead. I was sitting in
a corner, muttering to myself and licking my wounds, when it
arrived, and it cheered me up.

The bitter part of the whole affair is that, while I usually read
the *Times Lit Sup* at the club, this time I went out and bought a
copy, so that in addition to having my finest feelings gashed I am
threepence out of pocket, with no hope in sight of getting back at
them.

I have been analysing my feelings towards reviews, and my
position is this. I don't mind the review which says 'Why the devil
this ass sells a single copy, we cannot understand, but there is no
getting away from the fact that he sells thousands' but a notice like
this, which might have been that of the first book of an amateur,
cuts deep. It is particularly maddening because in a sense it is all
perfectly true. She – I agree with you that it was written by a
governess – simply omits to mention that I have gone to great pains
to cover each of the points she raises, so that in the book they are
quite plausible. But what's the use? I feel as if someone had flung an
egg at me from a bomb-proof shelter. But your letter has made me
feel ever so much better, and I am holding my head up again.

☆

At that time reviews in *The Times Literary Supplement* were
anonymous. In a short review of *Bill the Conqueror* on 14
November 1924, the writer describes how Bill is sent to London
by his uncle, an American millionaire, to investigate a falling off
of profits in the London office. Here he meets Flick and she
discovers the crook. The writer then continued: 'After a great

many more equally improbable episodes, Bill and Flick are at last married and when Mr Paradine appears on the scene, Bill is able to inform him that he has succeeded in his mission and is thereupon made manager himself, though he still knows nothing whatever about the business, at any salary he cares to name.'

☆

26 July 1929   Hunstanton Hall
                                                    Norfolk

In re what you say about the critics. I think I prefer 'hammocks' to 'this cheerful nonsense'. But what I want to ask you particularly is, what are we doing about this bird Priestley (J. B.)? I don't know if you read the thing he did about *Mr Mulliner* some time back. He said my ideas about love were those of a 'fifth form boy'. He now, though paying tribute to the 'Flower Show' (which may just save him from the vengeance) waggles his fat head at you and says 'But come, come, my boy, all this sort of stuff, I mean, what?', referring, blast him, to a book like *Another Part of the Wood*, which he ought to thank heaven for getting in the flood of bilge that usually comes his way.

What is it about light comedy that these fellows object to? Well, anyway, thank goodness the g.h. of the public is sound.

☆

Plum seems to have been unduly touchy about Priestley. Reviewing *Mr Mulliner Speaking* in the *Evening News* of 31 May 1929, Priestley said:

The Wodehouse characters, with their monocles and ability to imitate a hen laying an egg . . . are funny enough but they are nearly always the same in every story. Where Mr Wodehouse scores, where he is, in point of fact inimitable, is in his masterfully idiotic phrase-making. The talk of the thoughtless, the inarticulate, becomes in his hands an instrument of power. He has raised speech into a kind of wild poetry of the absurd. Any competent hack-writer can put a snake in a bedroom or a young man into a suit of armour, but only Mr Wodehouse can keep going such young men as Mr Finch, who greet the girls of their choice by crying 'Yo-ho! Yo frightfully ho!' This is where Mr Wodehouse enters literature.[1] And in the matter of wildly metaphorical slang he has beaten the Americans at their own game. Meet a New York crook of Mr

[1] Dudley Finch in 'Awful Gladness of the Mater' in *Mr Mulliner Speaking*.

166

Wodehouse's invention, and you find that he talks not as such crooks actually do talk, but as they would like to talk.

And in the *Evening Standard* of 18 August 1932, he wrote:

There are only about twenty people in this Wodehouse world and we all know them well. The henpecked little man, the masterful woman, the rough American crook, the smooth American crook, the female American crook disguised as an authoress or a maid, the absent-minded Duke, the monocled members of the Drones Club, the great Jeeves, there they are. In nearly every story these go through the same comic evolutions, usually round a diamond necklace, but we do not grumble at Mr Wodehouse's almost impudent lack of inventive power. We are fascinated, as ever, by the sublime idiocy of his comments on these puppets. . . . For a warm August afternoon this is the perfect literature. Hazlitt himself would have been content to pass such an afternoon with Mr Wodehouse's 'Soup' Slattery, the best safe-blower in Chicago.

☆

10 September 1933

I'm awfully glad you liked *Heavy Weather*. Reviews excellent, except for *Spectator* and *Week-End Review*, both inclined to sniff a bit and devote most of their space to an analysis of my defects. The *Week-End Review* one was by Gerald Bullett, co-author with Priestley of 'A Frolic' entitled *I'll Tell You Everything*, possibly the world's worst humorous novel – always excepting anything by our motoring pal, Raleigh, of course.

Don't you find yourself stunned by the nerve of critics. If I had written anything like *I'll Tell etc*, I wouldn't have the crust to criticize other people's efforts. The same applies to Ralph Strauss, of *Sunday Times*, who until presumably there were complaints, used to turn out a comic novel every year.

15 October 1934   Low Wood
                                   Le Touquet
I have at last come to a momentous decision. I am going to give up my press-clipping agency. I find that even a favourable notice makes me feel sick nowadays, while an unfavourable one, even from a small provincial paper, puts me off my work for days. I stopped reading American reviews of my books years ago, and now I'm going to stop reading the English ones.

11 December 1945

Looking back over the file of your letters (which are my constant reading) I find you have said bitter things about your present publishers, but it seems to me that there must be a lot of good in a firm that almost casually tells you it has printed 'another 10,000'. Congratulations! But isn't it extraordinary – and very pleasant as showing that the critics don't mean a thing – that you have not come across any reviews. In my latest novel – to be published in 1950 – I am amazingly funny about publishers who tell authors that it's no use advertising their books, as what counts is word-of-mouth advertising, but really it looks as if they were right.[1] I don't believe newspaper advertising or criticism affects an author at all.

28 March 1946

Who is this man Peter Quennell in the *Daily Mail*? Doesn't he ever read a book that is even faintly interesting to the general public?

20 April 1946

I resume this after tea, having walked down to the American Library to get books to see us through *les vacances*. One I got was *The Witch in the Wood* by T. H. White, author of *The Sword in the Stone*, which I picked up in the library the other day and took a chance on and simply loved. Now what all this is leading up to is this. When *The Sword in the Stone* first appeared, in 1937, it had a big critics' success, columns being written about it and in praise of it. But, mark this, the way the critics told its story and their damned pomposity not only gave me no idea of the merits of the book but put me right off it. Actually it is a story of the boyhood of King Arthur told in modern dialogue with lots of comic characters being really funny, but the impression I got from the reviews was entirely different, and what I want to know is, Is one missing lots of good books simply through the fatheadedness of reviewers? Can't these blighters even put over the books they like? Of course, the bright side is that more and more critics are becoming ignored and will shortly disappear altogether. Arising from this, don't you think

[1] *Uncle Dynamite*, p. 177.

film critics are the most futile people in the world? Do they really think that the public reads their criticisms and is influenced against a picture – because they always are against – by them? Faugh, if I may use the expression.

4 June 1946

I haven't seen any reviews yet, but imagine that if there are any they will be stinkers. But Watt tells me that Eagle of Jenkins told him that they had printed a first edition of 30,000 and expected to sell them quite soon, so to hell with the critics.[1] As a matter of fact, if this book gets over with the public, I am going to suggest to the Jenkinses that in future we deal direct with ye pub and ignore the critics. Marie Corelli did it, without, I believe, the slightest effect on her sales. Don't you loathe critics? I don't know if I hate them more when they praise me or when they roast me. Their appearing in the matter at all always seems to me an impertinence. Talking of critics, were you ever reviewed by (the late?) James Douglas? His method was to pinch all one's nifties from the book and use them as if they were his own.

4 July 1946

I saw that stinker in the *Observer* and for a couple of moments reeled beneath the coarse abuse, but it wasn't long before I was saying 'What the hell?' and realizing that the fact that a man who obviously hated my guts couldn't refrain from praising the book was all to the good. (In their advertisement ye Jenkinses have boiled the review down to the words 'Eminently readable', bless them!) Anyway, a few days later my spies inform me that the BBC of all people gave the book a terrific boost per V. S. Pritchett in his *Book Talk*, and the sales have been absolutely all right – 21,000 up to the morning of June 12 and who knows how many more as the result of Pritchett's praise. The *Times Lit Sup* also gave me quite a decent notice, and the heart of the *Yorkshire Post* and others seems to have been sound. So, as I say, what the hell!

[1] *Money in the Bank*, published by Herbert Jenkins, 1946.

To Denis Mackail   1000 Park Avenue
22 August 1950   New York

I say, the Jenkins people sent me the reviews of *Nothing Serious* and I note a distinct improvement in tone. I seem to be practically back to the 'dear old P. G. Wodehouse' days. My loathing for all critics, however, continues unabated. Damn their impertinence, praising my books. Don't they know that I just write them for you to read? What one strives for is some system whereby one can print a maximum of six copies and still be paid thousands a year.

27 November 1953

I find in this evening of my life that my principal pleasure is writing stinkers to people who attack me in the press. I sent Nancy Spain of the *Daily Express* a beauty. No answer, so I suppose it killed her. But what fun it is giving up trying to conciliate these lice. It suddenly struck me that they couldn't possible do me any harm, so now I am like a roaring lion. One yip out of any of the bastards and they get a beautifully phrased page of vitriol which will haunt them for the rest of their lives. . . .

Eileen tells me she is taking over a *Girls* for you to read. It doesn't come out in England till next spring. There is talk of the *Sunday Express* doing it as a serial, but I don't suppose it will come to anything. Apparently it is a riot out in California, where Groucho Marx is reported to be raving about it. Walter Winchell has promised to do a column review of it, provided he doesn't have to write it, so it is being done in the Simon and Schuster office and will, I imagine, be quite enthusiastic.

1 May 1954

A bastard named Alan Melville says in *Time and Tide* that I have been getting 'steadily unfunnier'. The trouble is I can't reply 'So are you', because he does write darned amusing stuff. I thought of writing him a stinker on general lines but abandoned the idea on picking up the life of Hugh Walpole and finding that he always wrote indignantly to unkind critics. I shall just have to put him on

---

¹ Printed as Appendix C.

the list as one of those marked for vengeance. But the funny thing is that his review came out in *Time and Tide*, who have just written me a grovelling letter begging me to contribute some articles. 'Not after what has occurred' is about my attitude.

8 DOGS

To William Townend
28 October 1930

Metro-Goldwyn-Mayer
Studios
Culver City
California

Listen, laddie, as life goes on, don't you find that all you need is about two real friends, a regular supply of books, and a Peke?

To Denis Mackail
28 December 1930

1005 Benedict Canyon
Drive
Beverly Hills
California

I wish I could see Victoria. Miss Winks is the light of the home. She seems to like it here. She has a nice garden to run about in and plenty of people to bark at. She is very fit.

To William Townend
19 May 1931

The Klaw Theatre
New York

Miss Winks is a weird dog. She lies absolutely torpid all the evening till we go to bed. Then she insists on sitting on my lap and licking my chin without stopping for a quarter of an hour.

To Denis Mackail
9 October 1932

Domaine de la Fréyère
Auribeau
Alpes-Maritimes

According to present plans, Ethel and I dash over to London at the end of the month for a week or two. This, of course, involves leaving Miss Winks here, and I doubt if, when the time comes, we shall be capable of it. What a curse that quarantine law is. It seems so

172

damned silly to extend it to Pekes, who couldn't possibly give rabies to anyone.

To William Townend
9 February 1933

I could go and stay at a hotel in Cannes, of course, but I have got a dislike of hotels after the Dorchester. Besides, Winky would be such a burden at a hotel. My God, she's bad enough here. She won't let me out of her sight. I feel rotten if I don't get an exercise walk in the afternoon, but every time I try to start on one Winky sits on the terrace and just looks at me. You can hear her saying 'Going to leave me, eh? Well, of all the dirty tricks!'. So I say 'Well, come along, too.' And she says 'No, I'm dashed if I do. What, sweat down that mountain and have to sweat up again? Not for me.' So it ends in my strolling about the garden.

2 August 1934   Low Wood
                                 Le Touquet
Ethel went over to England for a week the other day, and I was sitting in porch here waiting for her, and out of her cab wriggled a yellow object. Boo!! Snorky's Peke. It was a stroke of genius bringing her. She makes all the difference to Winky. They are the most tremendous friends. And here is a great fact of life which everybody should know – two Pekes are no more trouble than one. In fact, less, as you can leave two Pekes where it would break your heart to leave one alone.

15 October 1934

Boo is quite a different dog now. Her bad temper has quite gone, and she is all affection. I think the trouble at Snorky's place was that the other dogs were not Pekes. Pekes really are a different race and class. They may try to be democratic, but they don't really accept other dogs as their social equals.

10 December 1934   17 Norfolk Street
                                          Park Lane
                                          London W1

There's no getting away from it, female Pekes are human. You get to love them just as much as you would a child. I think it is partly because they are so absolutely dependent on you, and the way they combine bossiness with utter collapse when anything goes wrong. I shall never forget the time when I was going to air Boo and Winky at Norfolk Street and I started to pick Winky up and Boo flew at her, and I was so irritated that I gave a sideways kick and it caught Boo in the mouth. She dropped all her toughness in a second and lay down with her face between her paws and *screamed*. I've never felt such a hound and swine in my life. Of course, two seconds after I started petting her she was alright again and just as bossy as ever.

1 July 1935   Low Wood
                                          Le Touquet

That hound Boo as near as toucher got killed last night. We were walking on left side of road. Two girls on bikes came along on right side. Boo dashed across and gave chase, spilling one girl. I stopped to pick her up, and Boo legged it after the other one. I was twenty yards behind when I saw a car coming and at that moment Boo swerved to the left. I gave a yell and the car stopped with the wheel right over Boo. Another revolution would have killed her. She then trotted back to Ethel and lay on her back, which is her idea of passing off the most delicate situation.

20 January 1936

Winks and Boo do nothing nowadays but fight. I think it is because they aren't getting enough exercise. Have you ever studied the psychology of the Dirty Look in Pekes. Winks and Boo will be sleeping quite happily at different ends of the room and then suddenly one of them will lift her head and stare. The other then stares. This goes on for about ten seconds, and then they rush at one another. My theory is that dogs say things which the human ear can't hear. By the way, we're taking both Pekes to St Moritz.

28 December 1936   1315 Angelo Drive
                                           Beverly Hills
                                           California

PS   The pup is simply marvellous. Winky loves her and they play
together all the time. It has made Winky quite a young dog again,
having the pup.[1]

28 January 1937

Winks is very well. Also the puppy, who now has two names –
Wonder and Sixpence. My day starts when I hear the puppy bark in
Ethel's room. I open the door, and she, the puppy, comes leaping
out. Winky then pokes her head out of my bed, in which she has
been sleeping, and I take them downstairs and let them out. I bring
them in when I come down to breakfast, and they then have to be let
out again in order to bark at the gardener, whose arrival is always a
terrific surprise and shock to them, though he has turned up at the
same time every morning for four months.

They stand with their feet up against the window.

Puppy: Do you see what I see? Is that a man in the garden?

Winks: Egad, it is, and a low sinister, Mexican-looking man.
Should we tear him to pieces?

Puppy: Undoubtedly. We must keep the home safe.

Winks (to me): Hey! Open this door and let's get at him.

I open the door, and they fly out, yelling, to subside instantly as
the gardener pets them. Next day, the same.

The puppy is now in an interesting condition. Imagine – at six
months old! Nature seems to me an absolute ass. It appears to want
dogs to start breeding before they are out of the cradle.

28 November 1938   Low Wood
                                           Le Touquet

Winkie is dead. I can hardly bear to write about it, but I had to let
you know. The usual thing – tick fever. Same as Boo.

☆

[1] This was the most famous peke of all, named Wonder. She travelled with the
Wodehouses through Germany and Paris during the war and died at Remsenburg, aged
fifteen.

When Plum was released from camp during the war and went to Berlin, Ethel joined him, bringing Wonder with her.

☆

To William Townend   Berlin
11 May 1942

Wonder (the Peke) is in terrific form. Ethel brought her from France and she has settled down splendidly. All the children in the Tiergarten admire her enormously and follow her about shouting *'Kleine hunde!'*

8 November 1945   36 Boulevard Suchet
                                            Paris

I had to break off at this point to take Wonder for her walk. I find it almost impossible to get anything done in the mornings, as I have to suit my time to hers. What I would like would be to hoik her out of bed at 9.30, exercise her and be able to settle down to work at ten. But if I try to do this she curses so much that I desist. It is generally about eleven-fifteen, when I am just getting going, that there is a thud on my door and in she bounds. I wish you could come with me on one of my Wonder promenades. There is a spaniel who lives at No 72 and sits inside the front door, which is of thick glass, and every day Wonder toddles up to this door and she and the spaniel start a terrific fight through the glass, which lasts till I haul her away. The other day the spaniel nipped away and suddenly appeared at the open ground floor window, whereupon a scene of perfect camaraderie ensued, both dogs immediately becoming bosom friends. But the next day the fight started again.

27 November 1945

You know, I can hardly blame anyone in America for being hostile to me after the weird things that have been printed there about me. Yesterday Ethel got a letter from an old friend of hers in Boston, in which the latter mentioned an article which said that we used to lie in bed in Berlin feeding our dog with pork chops!! How on earth the writer was supposed to have got his facts, I don't know. Actually we used to victual Wonder just as you in similar circumstances would have victualled Tan – we had an ounce of meat each daily and we gave this to Wonder and ate vegetables ourselves. I don't think I ever saw a pork chop when I was in Germany. . . .

Rather a serious domestic problem has arisen owing to Wonder having decided that she objects to wood fires. We have to have one in the study, as otherwise we should freeze, and the moment it starts crackling Wonder rises in a marked manner and stalks out and goes into the passage, where she stands barking. We try to explain to her that it is impossible to get coal and that we are darned lucky to have wood, but she won't see it.

23 December 1945

By the way, a dishevelled Arab has just called at the back door with an illegal turkey, which Ethel promptly bought for two *mille*. And we already have a chci – chicken and a bit of beef, so Wonder's dinners are all set for some time to come, and she is the only one that matters. I remember you saying to me once that the only thing that kept Pekes from being perfect was that they were not vegetarians. Every day Ethel carefully mashes up vegetables with W's meat, and Wonder licks all round them without touching them, and then comes and barks for her lump of sugar.

To Denis Mackail
26 January 1946

The dog situation has become very complicated. I am now pledged to take the *concierge*'s terrier out with Wonder in the morning, and unfortunately there is a female hound down in the direction of Porte St Cloud and the terrier legs it off to her and comes back with the milk. So I ought to be following his every movement. But when I try to keep an eye on him Wonder goes off in the opposite direction. The thing always ends in my coming home without the terrier and saying to the *concierge* that Teddy has been '*pas sage*' and leaving it up to him to do something about it.

I passed on your story about the Peke and the rubber mat to Wonder, who seemed properly impressed. Wonder's latest performance has been to wolf a lot of powdered milk which Ethel had dropped on the kitchen floor and get herself white from head to foot. It got a big laugh out of our new cook (aged fourteen).

177

1 March 1946

The snow (*neige* we call it over here) began to fall in a mild, rather pleasant way yesterday afternoon but must have gone to town during the night, for today we are practically *neiged*-up. I have just taken Wonder for her walk, and we had to go up and down a tiny strip of pavement which had been cleared. Outside that it came over her back and she was buried. Yet would you believe it, that superb dog did her duty just the same as always, so now, thank goodness, that major worry is off my mind. I never hoped that she would be able to perform under existing conditions, and now she is all right for the day and needs only a couple more short terms. I still stick to it that three per day is enough – one in the morning, one at tea time, one at night. But they are real outings in the course of which she is expected to get into double figures.

To Sheran Hornby
13 January 1949

2 East Eighty Sixth Street
New York

Bunny[1] sails back on the Queen Mary on the 19th. She will have been away exactly five months. It will be a great day when we have her back. I don't believe Wonder has missed her at all. I don't think dogs can count, and so long as one of us is with her, it is the same as if we both were. But she will go mad when she does see her mother. She and I have been inseparable all these months. I have never left her alone for a minute. It has meant that I have never been able to go out at night, but it has been worth it to keep her happy.

To Denis Mackail
22 August 1950

1000 Park Avenue
New York

The first night I was back, Squeaky, the white Peke, slept on my bed and seemed to love it. But last night, just as I was dropping off to sleep, I heard her whimpering at the door. She wanted to go to Ethel. The solution seems to be that Ethel sits up all night reading and has developed a habit of setting up chocolate suppers at 4 a.m., and Squeaky suddenly realised that she might be missing something good. Gosh, what an angel that dog is. Wonder, rounding off her fourteenth year, still seems quite fit.

[1] Ethel

25 December 1950

Pekes. How understanding they are. When Squeaky is on my lap and sees that Wonder wants to get on, she instantly jumps off, as she knows that W. is the senior dog and nearly fifteen and must be put first. But then Squeaky is an angel from heaven. Sam, our coloured cook-butler-chauffeur adores her. Yesterday he turned up – an hour late as usual – and instantly disappeared. He was away for half an hour, with Ethel foaming at the mouth. When he came back, he said that he had had to take Squeaky down to the men in the basement to say Merry Christmas.

11 August 1951

Sad news to start my letter. Poor little Wonder had to be put to sleep. . . . So now Squeaky is our only dog. She gets more loveable every day.

To Guy Bolton
11 October 1951

Apropos of your taking Vicky out on the lawn, Ethel tells me Squeaky put up a regular circus last night. I started to go to bed at half-past one, having waited up to see a rotten picture on the television, and Ethel asked me to get her some chocolate from my room. I came back with a new Hershey slab, unopened. How Squeaky recognised it as chocolate I don't know, but the moment she saw it, she went crazy. Well, I went to bed, leaving Ethel and Squeaky to their party. Squeaky wolfed a lot of chocolate, then had a drink and wanted to go out on the roof. Ethel let her out and went back to bed. The next thing that happened was loud barking at the back door. The windows leading into the apartment in front were wide open, but though she has been out that way a hundred times, you can't drive it into S's head that there's any way of getting into the place except through the back door.

Well, Ethel let her in and she raced round and round the living-room and then began sniffing under the desk. She wanted her ball. Ethel finally found it wedged under the leg of the desk and gave it to her, and she settled down to make a night of it, chasing the ball all over the place. (This was about three in the morning.) Finally Ethel got her to bed and she seemed to settle down, and suddenly Ethel found that she had chewed a large hole in her best blanket. She gave her a good smacking, and Squeaky then called it a day.

She is terrifically fit now, though scratching a bit, and thank goodness is eating ever so much better. She still prefers a dinner of sugar, chocolate and broccoli, but will now eat other things.

To Denis Mackail   Remsenburg
7 June 1952   Long Island
                                                    New York

I am staying at the moment with Guy Bolton, and the houses are two miles apart. So every day when I go over to see Ethel, it means a four-mile walk. Oh, added to credit side: Squeaky, the Peke, loves the place. It's such a comfort not having to take her about on a leash. The day Ethel arrived a stray dog turned up – foxhound type – and firmly added himself to the strength. Nice dog and very respectful to Squeaky.

8 July 1952

The other night we went to one of those ghastly birthday parties where people bring cute presents, and one of the guests had brought host a couple of guinea hens. Ethels's horror on being told that they were going to be killed and eaten was terrific, and she at once offered to give them a home. So now the gardener and carpenter are putting up yards of wire at the end of the lawn, and we are saddled with two more protégés – possibly a protégé and a protégée, I don't know. The whole point of our buying this house was that we would have a place where we could turn the key and go away whenever we wanted to, and now I don't see how we are ever going to move even for a day.

15 July 1952

The other night Peggy, our maid, came in and said there was a wild animal in the garden making horrible noises. Ethel took the flashlight and went out, and there was a tiny kitten. Starving, of course, and so has had to be added to the strength.

Our great fear was that Squeaky and Bill would attack it, but they both took it to their bosoms at once. They really are angelic dogs. You ought to see the kitten lying on a cushion absolutely unmoved while Squeaky sniffs at its head and Bill at his backside. They both love it, and the kitten has settled down perfectly and is now the life of the party.

15 February 1953   1000 Park Avenue
                                                    New York

Do you want a foxhound? Our Bill is the most amiable and attractive dog in the world, but it's certainly a business having him in New York. I have to take him for a long walk before breakfast, a longer one in the afternoon and a final one after dinner, and even then, though his bowels have moved freely in the afternoon, he always does another one on the roof after bedtime, which I have to clear up or face the wrath of the superintendent. Still, we love him. The only trouble is, I don't see how we can ever travel anywhere unless we can find someone to take care of him. Squeaky continues more angelic than ever.

4 May 1953

You ask about the foxhound and the flat. The solution is that we have not only our terrace but the public roof – with its notice in large letters NO DOGS ALLOWED. We leave the french window on the terrace open at night, and some time during the small hours Bill trots out, does his business on the No-dogs-allowed roof and comes in again. Next morning I have to go and clean it up. He is scrupulous in never performing on the terrace.

18 May 1955   Remsenburg
                                                    Long Island
                                                    New York

A kitten turned up the other day and had to be added to the strength. It immediately started an affair with an orange cat from across the way and has been shipped off to the vet to be fixed. We Wodehouses are hospitality itself if you treat us right, but we simply can't put up three dogs and a family of kittens. (Three dogs because for the next six weeks we are housing Guy's Vicki. A superb dog, one of those active Pekes – in contrast to Squeaky, who nowadays seldom moves.)

181

17 December 1955

A crisis has arisen in the home and we shall need all our generalship to cope with it. Every morning I strew bread and fat for the birds, and then Bill the foxhound wants to go out, and once out he eats the damn lot. He was seen the other day leaping at a tree where we had hung a great chunk of fat for the birds and pulling it down and wolfing it. I think I may have outsmarted him by putting the stuff on top of the hedge.

18 April 1956

I have now completed a full year at Remsenburg, having arrived here on April 12, 1955. I have only spent one night away, and have loved the life. Not a bit dull. Always something to do – e.g. letting Bill the foxhound out and letting him in again, ditto with Poona the cat. Both are now out, and in a minute or two I shall hear a moaning at the side door like a foghorn, which will be Bill wanting to come in, and soon after that Poona will appear at the window. It all helps to pass the tikm – aha! – the time.

2 July 1956

I'm in a sort of dull stupor this morning owing to eccentricities of Bill the foxhound and Poona the cat. Bill, though aired at 12.30, woke me up at 3 a.m. clamouring to be let out, and I had just got to sleep again when Poona, whom we hadn't been able to bring in at bedtime, came mewing outside my window and when I let her in and put her on my bed insisted on biting my feet for half an hour, so that I got almost no sleep. How different from Vicki, Guy Bolton's Peke, now staying with us, who goes to bed at the normal time and stays there without moving till late in the morning.

16 December 1957

The Boltons had to go to New York on Christmas Day, so we have – until tomorrow, I suppose – in the home a hound, another hound, a dachshund, two Pekes and a cat. The second hound is one we have adopted. It belonged to some people who migrated to Florida and

'The Play's the Thing', Molnar's comedy, was adapted by P G Wodehouse and later revived. *Left to Right:* Edmond Breon, Henry Forbes–Robertson, Ursula Jeans, Gerald du Maurier, Henry Daniell.

Ivor Novello.

Lorenz Hart.

Jerome Kern, third in the great
triumvirate, 'Bolton and Wodehouse
and Kern'.

Top Cole Porter.
Above Florenz Ziegfeld.
Left George and Ira Gershwin.

FACING PAGE:

Left Plum with Ian Hay.

Right E. Phillips Oppenheim.

Below 'Anything Goes', the comedy by Plum and Guy Bolton with lyrics and music by Cole Porter. This shows Charles B. Cochran's production at the Palace Theatre in 1935.

THIS PAGE:

Right Plum with his foxhound, Bill.

Below Plum and Ethel relaxing in their drawing-room at Remsenburg.

Plum's step-grandson, Edward Cazalet, riding in the colours of Her Majesty Queen Elizabeth The Queen Mother, one of Plum's most ardent fans.

Sheran Hornby, née Cazalet, Plum's step-granddaughter, unveils a plaque over the house in Guildford where he was born.

Left Plum at Remsenburg.

Below Plum and Ethel at home. 'What is supposed to happen is that the County saunter in for a drink, and we mix it at the bar.'

Foot Plum at home, with Jed the Dachshund.

A big stretch!

Plum at work to the end. His famous old typewriter is now in the Wodehouse Library at Dulwich College.

wanted a home for it. A most charming – and very boisterous –
animal, who can't get it into his head that he is not a lap dog. The
moment I sit down, he is up on my lap, weighing a ton, and in the
mornings, after I have let him out, he makes a beeline for Ethel's
room and curls up on her bed. I used not to like the dachshund, but
he has won me over. But of course other dogs are not Pekes.

25 July 1958

We have spent a fortune rebuilding the house, the alterations
including a beautiful new carpet. End of Act One. Act Two – We
got a dachshund puppy over from England and it was completely
un-housebroken. Its mentality was rather like that of your famous
Pug – what was its name? We would keep Jed, the dachs, out in the
garden for three hours or so with no result, and the moment he was
in the house floods on the new carpet. It was not so much that he
was not housebroken as that he had apparently been carefully
trained to do it only on carpets. Fortunately he is practically all right
now, though we still hold our breaths and keep our fingers crossed.
    I now sleep with Poona the cat on my bed, Blackie the other cat
on a chair and Bill on the floor. The other morning I was aroused at
four-twenty by a terrific cat fight on my chest, Blackie having
apparently climbed on to the bed which of course belongs
exclusively to Poona.

To Guy Bolton
1 August 1961

Ethel and your Nora couldn't see eye to eye and N. has left. We
have now got a fat Irish cook from New York who so far seems
fine. But you never know. She is about fifty and says she likes the
peace of the country, so all may be well. But she stoutly refuses to
have Debbie, the boxer, sleeping on her bed, which is unfortunate.

9 BOOKS AND POETRY

To Denis Mackail
12 April 1921

1005 Benedict Canyon
Drive
Beverly Hills
California

I suppose you have been working as hard as ever. Don't you feel that what you need is some really definite break between jobs of work? I do. I find there is nothing in this world I really want to do except read. From here it would be easy to go to Japan, for instance. But what would one do in Japan? Thank heaven, I have three circulating libraries within easy walk. My only trouble is that so few writers ever do more than one decent book. Did you read *The Fool of the Family* and *A Note in Music* – the second innings of the authors of *The Constant Nymph* and *Dusty Answer*?[1] Frightfully disappointing. The fact is, practically every author is a damned amateur. They have one good book in them and can't repeat.

To William Townend
10 March 1928

17 Norfolk Street
Park Lane
London W1

I met John Buchan the other day. Nice chap, but I can't read his stuff, can you?

28 September 1928

Rogate Lodge
Rogate
Petersfield

I say, laddie, something really must be done about Kip's 'Mrs Bathurst'. I read it years ago and didn't understand a word of it. I

[1] Margaret Kennedy and Rosamund Lehmann.

184

thought to myself 'Ah, youthful ignorance.' A week ago I bought some old Windsors and re-read it. Result precisely the same. What did the villain do to Mrs B? What did he tell the captain in his cabin that made the captain look very grave and send him up country where he was struck by lightning? Why was the other chap who was struck by lightning introduced? And, above all, how was Kip allowed to get away with six solid pages of padding at the start of the story?[1]

12 May 1929   Hunstanton Hall
                                               Norfolk

What bloodstained books you seem to read. I haven't seen any of them. I spend all my time here re-reading old stuff from the seaside library in the town. e.g. Lucas and Maxwell.[2] Do you ever read Lucas's novels – *London Lavender* etc? They aren't really novels. He takes a character and sends him wandering about so that he meets all sorts of odd people. It's amazing how often one can read them. I should think I must have read each of them a dozen times.

I don't think any of those books you mention really amount to much. It seems to me that at least two-thirds of the stuff published nowadays are by one-book people. You know – a stirring revelation of a young girl, a soul by Emmeline Banks – who never writes another damn book in her life. The test is, can you write three?

I did read *Dodsworth*, and thought it fine. But, dash it, it's simply a vehicle for Lewis' travel notes.[3] He goes to Berlin with a notebook and then sets a couple of characters to cover the ground. I don't call it a story. Now, *Babbitt* was.

28 October 1930   Metro-Goldwyn-Mayer
                                               Studios
                                               Culver City
                                               California

What did Sheila Kaye Smith object to in *Angel Pavement*? I thought it was a corking book. Curious method of writing Priestley has, though. Have you noticed it? A lot of characters with practically no connection with one another, attended to, in turn. E.G. Smeeth and

[1] Kip was Rudyard Kipling. 'Mrs Bathhurst' is in a volume called *Traffics and Discoveries* and seems incomprehensible.
[2] E. V. Lucas and W. B. Maxwell.
[3] Sinclair Lewis. *Dodsworth* described the marital relations of a middle-aged American industrialist and his adventures in Europe.

Dersingham. You get fifty pages of Smeeth at home, then fifty pages of Dersingham at home. Then a chunk about some other character. I always feel that I have got to link up, and that I couldn't show Dersingham at home without having Smeeth pop through the window and play a scene with him. It makes it much easier to write solid novels if this sort of construction is all right. Why don't you do it? Start with a group of characters on a wharf, a ship coming in – crew scatter to their various homes, and you describe their life. Then you give the boss of the shipping firm a turn. You only need the slightest link between the characters.

16 January 1931

I am at last reading *The Good Companions* after two false starts. I love it. That's the sort of book I would like to write. I couldn't wade through *The Water Gypsies*.[1] After chapter one, the thing fell from my hand like lead.

PS I read some of those Dorothy Parker stories. She is a big noise over here among the intelligentsia. They sit round and roar at her wise cracks. I don't like her stuff much.

29 June 1931

I can't remember if you said you liked or disliked Dorothy Parker's *Laments for the Living*. I have just got it out of the library, and I must say I think it pretty good.

6 March 1932

Domaine de la Fréyère
Auribeau
Alpes-Maritimes

You're absolutely right about Kip. Gosh, what a rotten story that pig story was.[2] As a matter of fact, Kip was the outstanding case of the Infant prodigy. His stuff done in the early twenties was great, but he lost that terrific zest and got married and settled down and made his stuff too long and it's only the remnants of the old fire that make his later work readable.

I bought Aldous Huxley's book, but simply can't read it.[3]

---

[1] *The Water Gypsies*, a novel by A. P. Herbert, came out in 1930.
[2] 'Pig' is a tale of revenge in the Indian Civil Service.
[3] *Brave New World.*

Aren't these stories of the future a bore. The whole point of Huxley is that he can write better about modern life than anybody else, so of course he goes and writes about the future. Michael Arlen is down here, writing a novel, the scene of which is laid in 1980 or thereabouts!

I have had rotten luck with books lately. All my favourite authors have let me down. On the other hand, I have started learning French and find French books and weeklies like *La Vie Parisienne* fine.

10 October 1932

When we meet, I want to discuss Sapper with you.[1] His success just shows that what is needed is an absolute lack of all shame and self-criticism. His work is the pure magazine story.

To Denis Mackail   Hunstanton Hall
10 September 1933   Norfolk

Listen. This business of Compton Mackenzie and Margery Sharp. I usually follow your opinions like a Hollywood yes-man, but I thought both books fine. I admit *Water on the Brain* went on a bit too long and ended more or less nowhere, but surely funny? And I liked *Flowering Thorn* so much that I wrote to the female and got back rather a high brow response. You must have had a bad day among the oats or had some of your ricks burned down or something when you read them.

To William Townend   1315 Angelo Drive
24 March 1937   Beverly Hills
                               California

I agree with you about Kip's book and Noel Coward's. What is it that's wrong with Coward's? I admire his courage in facing those audiences when he had those two flops, but somehow I don't find myself liking him.[2]

[1] Author of *Bulldog Drummond*. His real name was H. C. McNeile.
[2] Noël Coward's book was *Present Indicative*.

24 February 1945   No address given

I have become very interested in Shakespeare and am reading books
about him, having joined the American Library here. A thing I can
never understand is why all the critics seem to assume that his plays
are a reflection of his personal moods and dictated by the
circumstances of his private life. You know the sort of thing I mean.
They say '*Timon of Athens* is a gloomy bit of work. That means that
Shakespeare was having a lousy time when he wrote it.' I can't see
it. Do you find that your private life affects your work? I don't. I
have never written funnier stuff than during these last years, when I
certainly wasn't feeling exhilarated.

22 April 1945   78 Avenue Paul Doumer
                                                 Paris

I have been reading Mark Twain's letters. Very interesting. He
thought an enormous lot of W. D. Howells' books.[1] Have you ever
read any of them? I have taken *The Rise of Silas Lapham* out of the
American Library here, and it certainly is good. It was written in
1884, but reads like a modern book.

To Denis Mackail
22 May 1945

Your story about Darlington and Topsy shocked me, though it is
only what might have been expected of a man who stole Anstey's
Brass Bottle plot and served it up as his own and made a packet out
of it. I have often wondered how you felt about Milne. I have never
really liked him myself, though I suppose we were friends of a sort
for a great number of years. I've always liked his books, though.
But don't these writers like Milne astonish what I might call a
'practising author' like you? I mean, they never seem to do any
work. You suddenly find they have produced nothing since the
autumn of 1929 or whenever it was. It must be at least ten years
since M's last novel and I suppose about the same since his last play.
I can't think how they fill in their time.

[1] W. D. Howells (1837–1920), novelist and magazine editor who gave much encourage-
ment to Henry James and other authors.

To William Townend
30 June 1945

Before I forget. In one of your letters you asked me if I had ever read anything by Trollope. At that time I hadn't, but the other day, reading in Edward Marsh's *A Number of People* that Barrie had been fascinated by a book of his called *Is He Popenjoy* I took it out of the American Library. I found it almost intolerably slow at first, and then suddenly it gripped me, and now I am devouring it. It is rather like listening to somebody who is a little long-winded telling you a story about real people. The characters live in the most extraordinary way and you feel that the whole thing is true. Of course I read Trollope's *Autobiography* and found it very interesting. But I still don't understand his methods of work. Did he sit down each morning and write exactly fifteen hundred words without knowing when he sat down and how the story was going to develop, or had he a careful scenario on paper? I can't believe that an intricate story like *Popenjoy* could have been written without very minute planning. Of course, if he did plan the whole thing out first, there is nothing so very bizarre in the idea of writing so many hundreds words of it each day. After all, it is more or less what one does oneself. One sits down to work each morning irrespective of whether one feels bright or lethargic and before one gets up a certain amount of stuff, generally about fifteen hundred words, has emerged. But to sit down before a blank sheet of paper without an idea of how the story is to proceed seems to me impossible. Anyway, I think Trollope is damned good and I mean to read as much of his as I can get hold of.

☆

Since Trollope's methods were in one way so different from Plum's, part of his description of them seems worth quoting. In this excerpt, he also answers Plum's questions about his methods of work. He writes:[1]

I have never troubled myself much about the construction of plots, and am not now insisting specially on a branch of work in which I myself have not been very thorough. But the novelist has other aims than the elucidation of his plot. He desires to make his readers so intimately acquainted with his characters that the creatures of his brain should be

[1] *An Autobiography*, Anthony Trollope, Oxford University Press, pp. 211–12.

to them speaking, moving, living human creatures. This he can never do unless he knows those fictitious personages himself, and he can never know them unless he can live with them in the full reality of established intimacy. They must be with him as he lies down to sleep and as he wakes from his dreams. . . . It is so that I have lived with my characters, and thence has come whatever success I have obtained.

☆

1 August 1945

I withdraw what I said about Anthony Trollope! He is too slow. I liked the characters in *Popenjoy*, but oh my aunt the way they loitered along. I don't think I shall ever be able to read him until life gets calmer and more settled. I find now I can't read a book unless it has action.

I see in the *Express* that poor Damon Runyon has had an operation which has left him unable to speak. It sounds pretty serious. Do you like his stuff? I have just been reading a book of his stories and some of them were fine, but he never seems to wait till he gets a good plot but just goes ahead and bungs down anything.

To Denis Mackail   36 Boulevard Suchet
27 November 1945   Paris

I don't know if it is a proof of my saintlike nature, but I find that my personal animosity against a writer never affects my opinion of what he writes. Nobody could be more anxious than myself, for instance, that Alan Alexander Milne should trip over a loose boot lace and break his bloody neck, yet I re-read his early stuff at regular intervals with all the old enjoyment and still maintain that in *The Dover Road* he produced about the best comedy in English.[1]

---

[1] A. A. Milne had written a very unfriendly letter to the *Daily Telegraph* when it was reported that Plum had broadcast on German wavelength to America.

190

To William Townend
29 April 1945

I had never heard of James Hadley Chase and *No Orchids for Miss Blandish*, but there seems to be a craze in America for that sort of book.[1] Incidentally I've just read Raymond Chandler's *Farewell, My Lovely*. It's good, of course, but it's awfully like an awful lot of other books – e.g. Dashiell Hammett and Peter Cheyney. A thing I've never been able to understand is how these detectives drink like fishes all the time and yet remain in the hardest physical condition. And also how Peter Cheyney's detectives manage to get all that whisky in London in war time. They must be millionaires, as I believe the stuff is at about four quid a bottle. Do you ever read Rex Stout's Nero Wolfe stories? A good many of them came out in the SEP.[2] They're good. He has rather ingeniously made his tough detective drink milk.

George Orwell. I wish I could get hold of that book of his, as it's just the sort of thing I like reading nowadays. He is a friend of my friend Malcolm Muggeridge and about a year ago or more came over to Paris and gave us a very good lunch at a dingy place down by Les Halles (the markets to you). He then sent me that article about me, which appeared in *The Windmill* and later in his book. I liked him very much indeed. Odd him being an old Etonian. He wrote a book once called *Down and Out in Paris*[3] and gave me the impression of somebody out of your novels, a sort of gentleman beach-comber. I thought that criticism he did of my stuff was masterly. I was tremendously impressed by his fairmindedness in writing such an article at a time when it was taking a very unpopular view. He really is a good chap. I wonder, though, how many people read a book of essays. I should think that article ought to help me with writing people, but I'm afraid the general public will miss it.

☆

Plum is speaking of the essay 'In Defence of P. G. Wodehouse'. He seems later to have changed his mind. On 11 August 1951 he wrote to Denis Mackail:

Another book which I have re-read is George Orwell's *Dickens, Bali and Others*, in which he has a long article entitled 'In Defence of P. G.

---

[1] This novel, published in 1939, shocked critics by its violence.
[2] *Saturday Evening Post*, American weekly that published Plum's stories for fifty years.
[3] *Down and Out in Paris and London*.

Wodehouse' which is practically one long roast of your correspondent. Don't you hate the way these critics falsify the facts in order to make a point? It is perfectly all right for him – or any other critic – to say that my stuff is Edwardian and out of date. I know it is. But why try to drive it home by saying that my out-of-touchness with English life is due to the fact that I did not set foot in England for sixteen years before 1939.

If only these blighters would realize that I started writing about Bertie Wooster and comic Earls because I was in America and couldn't write American stories and the only English characters the American public would read about were exaggerated dudes. It's as simple as that.

☆

To William Townend
27 August 1946

Incidentally, why do all these critics – e.g. George Orwell – assume that *The Light That Failed* was a failure and is recognized as such by the reading world. It certainly didn't fail in the sense of not making money, having been serialized, successfully dramatized and probably sold several hundred thousand copies in the ordinary edition. And if they mean that it is a failure because it doesn't grip you, they are simply talking through their hats. It's odd, this hostility to Kipling. I believe you pointed out in one of your letters that it was a bit hard on the poor bloke to tick him off for not having spotted the Future of the India Movement and all that sort of thing, when he left the country for ever at the age of about twenty.

30 August 1946

When you say you liked Priestley's book, do you mean *Bright Day*? I read that and liked it, and I also liked *Daylight on Saturday*. I haven't seen any others by him. Yes, I think he's a bit pompous, but he writes very well and is always readable. I am now reading Evelyn Waugh's *Put Out More Flags*, and am absolutely stunned by his brilliance. I think you said you didn't like *Brideshead Revisited*, which I haven't read, and I imagine it's different from his usual work. But I do think that as a comic satiric writer he stands alone. That interview between Basil Seal and the Guards Colonel is simply marvellous.

1 November 1946   Pavillon Henri Quatre
                                            St Germain-en-Laye

Do you ever read John O'Hara? I have got his last thing, 'Pipe
Night'. What curious stuff the modern American short story is.
The reader has to do all the work. The writer just shoves down
something that seems to have no meaning whatever, and it is up to
you to puzzle out what is between the lines. This, of course, applies
only to the *New Yorker* type of short story. The ones in *Collier's,* of
which I have recently got a few numbers, are simply ghastly – just
like the worst sort of English magazine story. I haven't seen the
Saturday Evening Post for ages, and don't want to.

To Guy Bolton   36 Boulevard Suchet
13 February 1946   Paris
                                            France

I haven't read *Brideshead Revisited*, but I've heard it is very good. I
always like Evelyn Waugh's stuff.

11 November 1948

I've discovered another gem in Keats. As follows:-

> When wedding fiddles are a-playing
> Huzza for folly O!
> And when maidens go a-maying
> Huzza etc
> When Sir Snap is with his lawyer
> Huzza etc
> And Miss Chip has kissed the sawyer,
> Huzza etc.

Well, John, I'll tell you. It's got the mucus, but it needs a lot of
work.

To Sheran Hornby   2 East Eighty-Sixth
28 March 1948   Street
                                            New York

What do you find to read these days? I simply can't cope with the
American novel. The most ghastly things are published and sell a

million copies, but good old Wodehouse will have none of them and sticks to English mystery stories. It absolutely beats me how people can read the stuff that is published now. I can't read any of the magazines except the *New Yorker*, and that has suddenly got deadly dull. I am reduced to English mystery stories and my own stuff. I was reading *Blandings Castle* again yesterday and was lost in admiration for the brilliance of the author.

To Guy Bolton
24 November 1948

I take it you will come back with the company. I shall meet you at the pier and immediately start to discuss Bysshe Shelley. I went out and blew three dollars on a book containing all his poems and Keats's, and I want you to tip me off as to which are his winners. I have always liked 'Epipsychidion' and 'Ozymandias', but last night I tackled 'The Revolt of Islam' and it was like being beaten over the head with a sandbag. I'm afraid I've got one of those secondrate minds, because, while I realize that Shelley is in the Shakespeare and Milton class, I much prefer Tennyson, who isn't.

Incidentally, what lousy prose Shelley wrote. I do hate the way people wrote in those days. 'It is an experiment on the temper of the public mind, as to how far a thirst for a happier condition of moral and political society survives, among the enlightened and refined, the tempests which have shaken the age in which we live. I have sought to enlist the harmony of metrical language, the ethereal combinations of the fancy, the rapid and subtle transitions of human passion, all those elements which essentially compose a Poem, in the cause of a liberal and comprehensive morality.' Block those double adjectives, Perce!

Why will people collect ALL a poet's work into a volume instead of burying the bad stuff? It's a nasty jar, after reading 'The Nightingale', to come on the following little effort of Keats:

> There was a naughty boy,
> And a naughty boy was he,
> He kept little fishes
> In washing tubs three
> In spite
> Of the might
> Of the maid
> Nor afraid

Of his Granny-good –
He often would
Hurly burly
Get up early . . .

I can see Keats shoving that one away in a drawer and saying to himself 'Thank God no-one will ever see *that* baby!' And then along comes some damned fool and publishes it.

To Denis Mackail   1000 Park Avenue
15 April 1950   New York

Getting back to writing, my trouble – and it is probably yours – is a sort of scornful loathing for the reading public. One feels What's the use of strewing one's pearls before these swine? I mean, if they like the muck which they apparently do like, why bother? I don't think it's quite so bad in England, where somebody does occasionally produce a decent book, but over here it's incredible, the awfulness of the best sellers. I go for my books to a library round the corner, and every time I scan the shelves and go out without anything, feeling that I'd rather read nothing than American best sellers. I just go home and read the forty-year-old books in my shelves. . . .

By the way, talking of Ma Thirkell, I think she is losing her public over here. People seem at last to have got on to the fact that her stuff is deadly dull. I used to read everything she wrote, but now I can't even begin a book of hers. Why is this? She used to be quite good. I still think *Wild Strawberries* good. But these dreary chronicles of dull people with nothing happening are too much for me now.

☆

Angela Thirkell, a best-selling novelist, was the sister of Denis Mackail and mother of Colin MacInnes, both of whom disliked her very much. On 7 November 1945 Plum had written to Mackail:

Talking of books, as we so often do when we get together, ought I to be ashamed of confessing to you a furtive fondness for Angela Thirkell? You told me once that she bullied you when you were a child, and for years I refused austerely to read her. But recently *Wild Strawberries* and *Pomfret Towers* have weakened me. I do think she's good, though if we are roasting her I will add that *August Folly* was rotten and I couldn't get through it.

25 December 1950

Recent discovery. Any English mystery story, however bad, is better than any American mystery story, however good.

24 May 1951

I am still seething with fury because I spent fifteen cents taking that new book of Priestley's (*Festival*) out of the library. Of all the lousy efforts.[1] I couldn't get through it. I refuse to believe Heinemann's statement that it has sold eighty-nine thousand copies. I had a letter from Townend the other day. He said he had paid a visit to Tunbridge Wells and there hobnobbed with manager of the big book shop, Goulden and Curry. Quote. 'I asked if he had seen the ads of Priestley's new book, 87,000 sold before publication. He had, he told me, and he asked me how many copies I thought he had bought. Remembering that two years ago I had found him debating whether to buy 100 copies of George Blake's latest book or only to give a first order for 50, I said he had bought perhaps 100. He said 6.' Somebody is lying, I insist. Incidentally, the Goulden and Curry manager spoke very highly of your books, if that's any comfort. . . .

I have just been reading Hesketh Pearson's little book supplementary to his book on Bernard Shaw. What a repulsive man Shaw was. At least, that is how he comes through in print. I believe people who knew him say he was charming. But what a damned Smart Alec. Don't you hate the sort of man who can never give a straight answer to a question? If you had said 'Good morning' to Shaw, he would have said 'Who are you to say whether a morning is good?'. By the way, just for the record, he wanted to call one of his plays *Bee, Beezy Bee*.

---

[1] *Festival at Farbridge* (published as *Festival* in the USA).

24 May 1951

I have been puzzling myself crosseyed over your criticism about the Keats quotation. You say 'Where did you get that 'wretched wight' stuff?'[1] I got it out of the published works of the late J. Keats. See enclosed, which I have cut out of my volume as evidence. I don't see what you are driving at? Do you mean that it is out of character for a man like Joe to quote Keats correctly? Or did you think the actual lines were different? Till I looked it up, I thought it was 'Alas, what ails thee, knight at arms' and was glad I had gone to the fountain head, as otherwise I should have made a bloomer. Of course 'Alas, what ails thee, knight at arms' is a damn sight better.

18 June 1951

I call that a very pleasing conclusion to the great Wight–Knight controversy. Both right. You know, I was so sure it was 'knight at arms' that I nearly didn't look it up, and when I did look it up, it was in this weird American volume. But Keats must have been an ass if he thought the wretched wight line was as good as – I mean better than – the other. I think you are right in calling the poem Wardour-Street. I've never really liked it. By the way, do you ever find that you have spells of loathing all poetry and thinking all poets, including Shakespeare, affected fools? I am passing through one now. Prose is the stuff. . . .

☆

The correct quotations are 'O what can ail thee, knight at arms' and 'Ah what can ail thee, wretched wight.' The latter was written second, and most critics agree with Plum that the former is the better.

☆

15 October 1951

I have just been re-reading A. A. Milne's *Chloe Marr*. One or two very good characters in it – notably Percy Walsh – but I wish he

[1] See p. 31 of *The Old Reliable* (1931).

197

wouldn't make every single one of his characters so damned clever. Chloe herself, of course, is the world's premier mess. He does write well, though.

You will be glad to hear that America at last seems to be rising in revolt against Mrs Thirkell. At one time all the critics did nothing but rave about her, but now a better feeling seems to be abroad. I have seen several stinkers about *The Duke's Daughter*, her latest.

7 February 1952

Also on the subject of books, have you read Daphne du Maurier's *My Cousin Rachel*? Book of the Month, serialized by *Ladies Home Journal* at about $60,000, sold to the movies for a couple of hundred thousand, and it floored me on page 6. Ethel got through it and said the first part was fine but it went off at the end, so my prospects of getting through it are dim. I simply can't make out the tastes of the present day reading public. They seem to like being bored. Look at those frightful productions of A. Thirkell. . . .

Apropos of the Milne cocktail party, is A. A. M. turning out any stuff these days? I wish he would, as he is one of the very few readable writers. I can always re-read him indefinitely. He had a flurry of short stories in the American magazines not long ago which were very good.

8 June 1953

Am happy to announce that the last Angela Thirkell is now out of the house. To my horror, after getting rid of the others, I found *The Schoolmistress* nestling in a shelf. I shipped it off to the library pronto.

1 May 1954

Are you following the McCarthy business? If so, can you tell me what it's all about? 'You dined with Mr X on Friday the tenth?' 'Yes, sir.' (keenly) 'What did you eat?' 'A chocolate nut sundae, sir.' (Sensation). It's like Bardell vs Pickwick, which reminds me. Do you hate Dickens's stuff? I can't read it.

24 June 1954   Remsenburg
                                                Long Island
                                                New York

Well, sir, I am giving Dickens a last chance. I am reading *Bleak House* for the first time, and it isn't as lousy as I had expected. But, oh my God, why can't he ever draw a straight character. Do you know *Bleak House*. Most of it is told by Esther Summerson, and every single character she meets is a freak of some kind. There's a boy in it who decides to study to become a surgeon, so a big surgeon is introduced. There's no earthly reason why he shouldn't be a straight character, but Dickens – you can see the sweat starting out on his brow – feels he's got to have whimsical comedy, so he gives him a wife who is always talking about her two previous husbands, Captain Swozzer of the Navy and Professor Dingo.

> 'When I was with Professor Dingo –' said Mrs Badger. ('A man of European reputation,' murmured Mr Badger) '– we used to throw our house open to the students. Every Tuesday evening there was lemonade and a mixed biscuit.'
> ('Remarkable assemblies, those, Miss Summerson,' said Mr Badger reverentially.)

Fine if the Badgers were the only comedy characters, but there are at least a million others, even worse freaks.

And what a gloomy devil old Charles is at heart. How he loves fog and dirt and general misery. Still, I suppose I shall stagger through all right.

☆

Trollope has this to say: 'To my judgement they [Dickens's characters] are not human beings. . . . It has been the peculiarity and marvel of this man's power that he has invested his puppets with a charm that has enabled him to dispense with human nature.'

☆

22 August 1954

According to the Evidence, by Henry Cecil. Good stuff. What happens is that *Harpers* send me page proofs of his asking for my views.

Fortunately I genuinely liked this one and the *Judge* one, so was able to come through without blckening (blackening) my soul with a lie. But what does one do if the book is lousy? Can one say so, do you think? H. C.'s stuff is *very* funny and a great relief from the usual mystery. . . .

Have you ever heard of an English reviewer and critic called Daniel George? I bought his last one because there was something about me in it. The 'something' turned out to be a nasty supercilious slam, but I liked the book and am getting his others. He seems to have read every ruddy book that was ever published. You know the sort of thing – '*The Road to Xanadu* is, for me, a treasure house as rich as, say, Trevisa's translation of *De Proprietatibus Rerum*, Bayle's *Dictionary* or Disraeli's *Curiosities.*' I think it must be that I am getting senile, but I enjoy that sort of book more than almost anything nowadays. As I often say, I am never happier than curled up with Trevisa's translation of *De Proprietatibus Rerum*.

21 December 1954   1000 Park Avenue
                                                New York

How I agree with you about the BBC. A loathsome institution. And one only gets about thirty quid for their starriest productions. Yes, I too have had my fill of Maugham. There is a book just published here called *Mr Maugham Himself*, and it consists of all his old stuff dished up again. A deliberate swindle, I consider, because it suggests some sort of autobiography, and I must say I do like M's autobiographical stuff. But Max.[1] What a louse. Simon and Schuster gave me his fat volume of dramatic criticisms, and that supercilious attitude of his made me sick. And do you realise that but for Max there would have been none of this *New Yorker* superciliousness. They all copy him.

6 March 1955

I'm seething with fury. Sir Allen Lane of Penguin was over here not long ago and told me that Agatha Christie simply *loved* my stuff and I must write to her and tell her how much I liked hers. So with infinite sweat I wrote her a long gushing letter, and what comes back? About three lines, the sort of thing you write to an unknown

[1] *The Incomparable.*

fan. 'So glad you have enjoyed my criminal adventures' – that sort of thing. The really bitter part was that she said the book of mine she liked best was *The Little Nugget* – a 1908 production. And the maddening thing is that one has got to go on reading her, because she is about the only writer today who is readable. . . .[1]

The only readable new book I have come across for months is Ben Hecht's autobiography. Published by Simon and Schuster, so I got a free copy. I don't suppose it will be published in England, Hecht being *persona non grata* there. Lots of it give you the shivers, but all of it readable.

17 December 1955   Remsenburg
                                          Long Island
                                          New York

I, too, have been reading *Life of Kipling*. I agree with you that it is a poor job. I wish these people wouldn't tell us that in some poem which we admire the author got stuck at the third line and had a hell of a job getting the thing finished. To me it takes all the charm out of it. What a depressing woman Mrs K must have been. K's whole work depended on messing around and talking to people, and she kept him rigidly excluded from the world.

2 July 1956

The catch about Max Beerbohm is that just as one is about to dismiss him as an overpraised fraud one remembers something really good that he wrote. Did you ever read *Seven Men*? It's excellent. But the man at Simon and Schuster's has given me the book of his collected dramatic criticisms, and they deserve everything derogatory that you have said about M. B. What a loathsome sub-species dramatic critics are.

10 September 1956

I'm still reading Max Beerbohm's dramatic criticism book, as it is in short spasms easy to read at breakfast before the papers arrive. I

---

[1] Things improved, and Plum kept up a friendly correspondence with Agatha Christie.

dislike it more every morning. What lice dramatic critics are, especially if they start off by being lice, like M. B.

16 September 1956

George Orwell. Why do the eggheads make such a fuss of him? He's quite good, of course, but surely not as good as all that. Weird fellow. I think he genuinely enjoyed being unhappy.

18 December 1956

I see by the papers that Peter de Vries's *Tunnel of Love* has been made into a play and is now in rehearsal. I can't imagine what sort of play they can have made of it. But never forget that I was the man who said that *Show Boat* and *On the Spot* couldn't possibly succeed and that no one could ever make *Pygmalion* into a musical. Incidentally, Lerner, who wrote the book and lyrics, has made a terrific job of it. He has even [made] Higgins an attractive character, which I would have said couldn't be done. . . .

I am now two books ahead and shall not have to publish anything else for about eighteen months, but I would like to get a plot of some kind going. So far not a gleam. I see, by the way, that Shaw's *Pygmalion* was lifted from Smollett. Did you know that? I suppose the thing to do is to read all those frightful old books. I inherited from the previous owners of this house a set of Fielding. Maybe I could rewrite *Tom Jones*.

17 August 1957

How are you on the classics? When we bought this house, a number of books came with it, including all Fielding's works. I have been trying to re-read *Tom Jones*, and my opinion is that it is lousy. Do people really think it's the greatest novel ever written? What I felt after reading a few pages was that if this son of a bishop goes on being arch like this, I'm through. And I was through. Can you stand him?

7 October 1957

A bit of a shock to hear that you didn't like Perelman's *The Road to Miltown*. (I'm not absolutely sure, but I think those American tranquillizing drugs are called Miltown.) He sent me a copy of the book with a most flattering inscription (which may have influenced me), and I thought it was pretty darned funny. Didn't even that thing about the Earl and his expense account make you laugh? You must be a man of iron.

Perelman, by the way, has a son who goes about sticking people with knives and getting put in the reformatory. Difficult to be funny in those circs. . . .

Dickens. A thing I've never understood about those Victorian birds is why the hell didn't they finish their novels before putting them out in serial form. Why wait till the June number was on the book stalls and then say 'By Jove, I must be thinking of something soon for the July instalment.' Dam fools.

To Guy Bolton   Remsenburg
3 August 1964   Long Island
                                        New York

How do you feel about literary classics? I have come to the conclusion that there must be something wrong with me, because I can't read them. I tried Jane Austen and was bored stiff, and last night I had a go at Balzac's *Père Goriot* and had to give it up. I couldn't take the least interest in the characters. Give me Patricia Wentworth.

18 February 1965

Love to Va. Tell her that against my better judgement I took *The Spy Who Came in From the Cold* out of the library and it was LOUSY. I couldn't get through it. And yet it's a best seller in both England and USA.

10 LYRICS

To Guy Bolton   78 Avenue Paul Doumer
3 September 1945   Paris

In the list of the songs for the Kern picture which Washburn sent to me was the item – No 10. 'Bill'. Isn't it Jerryesque to have given that impression! Of course, what actually happened was that Jerry called me up one day and asked in that bluff way of his if I would mind him using the lyric of 'Bill' to fill a spot in a show he was doing, and I said Go right ahead. I did the same thing with two lyrics for *Sally*, if you remember. We were always doing that sort of thing in those days. But to suggest that there was a definite sale is a bit thick. And naturally, as always, there was the understanding that the publishing rights of the lyric were retained by the author of the lyric. And, my God, if there is one thing that makes me froth, it is these fellows changing a couple of lines in a lyric and then calling themselves part-authors. Clifford Grey used to do it incessantly. If any changes had to be made in 'Bill', Jerry should have asked me to make them, and only if I had been too busy to do it would Oscar have had any right to touch the lyric.

It is so maddening, that tinkering with lyrics. Any ass can do it, once he has got the lyric in front of him. I'll do one now. The lyric:-

> Daisy, Daisy,
> Give me your answer, do.
> I'm half crazy
> All for the love of you.
> My version (entitling me to half the publishing rights)
> Maizie, maizie,
> Can't one and one make two?
> I'll go crazy
> If I don't marry you.

(I'm not sure that that brilliant idea of changing 'Daisy' to 'Maizie' doesn't rate a bit more than half the publishing rights.)

☆

In a letter to Denis Mackail dated 14 January 1946 Plum wrote:

That 'Bill' thing is quite a drama. As you say, I wrote it in 1917 for *Oh, Lady*. Right. But, as always happens when you get a real winner, it was cut out. I think it was considered too slow or something and I wrote a lousy waltz thing instead. All straight so far. Well, when *Show Boat* was in preparation Jerry asked me if he could use 'Bill', and I said yes, and he did. But Oscar Hammerstein went and changed about three words in it and for twenty years has been getting half the publishing royalties. I didn't pay any attention to this, not being particularly interested in lyrics during those years, but Guy Bolton, to whom – in exchange for a share of the book rights – I had given half my publishing royalties, started kicking and kept at it so assiduously that a few days ago I heard from America that Oscar has now relinquished all rights in the thing and in addition has coughed up $5000 for back payments.

☆

In 1989 in a production of *Show Boat* by the Royal Shakespeare Company and English Opera North, 'Bill' was sung superbly by Sally Burgess.

☆

25 December 1945   36 Boulevard Suchet
                                           Paris

I am concentrating now on writing lyrics, of the type that will fit in anywhere, but I find it awfully hard to get anything done without a book and a composer to inspire me. Somehow when you have the scene in front of you that has to be topped off with a duet, there is always something in the characters that gives you an idea, whereas doing a He and She duet cold is tough. Still, I'm at least getting what Friml[1] used to call sketches. I used to go and see him, yearning for a completed tune so that I could make a dummy, and he would play a couple of bars and then wander off into a lot of vague notes. 'Just a sketch,' he used to say, blast him! By the way, do you think the modern lyric has to be very different from the old ones? I mean, are there any new tricks one has to learn? It seems to me, listening to the radio, that verses seem to have disappeared. At least, on the radio the singer simply charges straight into the refrain. But in a show, I imagine, you still need a verse, though probably a short one. Do you realise that I haven't seen a musical show since 1937! What do you think are the prospects of your being able to get a commission for a B and W show? I am longing to get going on one.

[1] Rudolf Friml, the impresario.

9 January 1946

And now how are chances for a musical by us? I have abandoned all other forms of work and am spending my whole time working on lyrics and am pleased to report that the old Muse is in the real 1916–1918 form. So far I have completed three really good ones, a couple of light comedy duets and one of those trios for three men which used to go so well. I am hoping before long to have a large reserve into which we can dip when the moment arrives. Of course, the difficulty is that one is so handicapped, working this way without having a story and characters, and I have to stick to stuff that can be fitted in anywhere.

A fear that haunts me, of course, is that I may be thirty years behind the times and be turning out stuff that would have been fine for 1917 but no good for 1946. But I don't believe there is any reason to feel like this. The numbers I hear on the radio sound exactly like those of twenty and thirty years ago. My theory is that the business of keeping up to date is entirely the headache of the composer. If he is modern and the lyricist does his lyric to the music the lyricist can't go wrong. Where I may be out of date is in writing a thing like that trio for three men, for it is quite possible nowadays they are as much a back number as the old story song like 'Yip-i-addy'. What do you think? Can you get away today with trios like 'Sir Galahad' and 'It's a Hard World for a Man'? As regards the duets I feel happier. The only change there has ever been in the light comedy love duet is in the rhythm of the music. Anyway, I'm working away like the dickens.

To Ira Gershwin   36 Boulevard Suchet
31 May 1946   Paris

The other day I was asked to do book and lyrics for a show from Vienna in which Grace Moore is to star, Hassard Short directing – about Madame Pompadour, and I was torn between the desire to get in on what will presumably be a big production and a hit, especially as I was an old beachcomber trying to make a come back after thirty years, and the desire to put on a false beard and hide somewhere till the thing had blown over. I imagine you probably feel the same as I do when asked to work on a 'period' musical show – a sort of deadly feeling that you are going into a fight with one arm strapped to your side and hobbles around your ankles, because you won't be able to use anything in the nature of modern comedy lines or ideas and so are robbed of your best stuff. When I write a lyric I want to be able to work in Clark Gable and Grover Whalen's moustache and corned beef hash, and you can't when you are dealing with La Pompadour.

To Guy Bolton
4 April 1953

I have just read the published books of *Dial M for Murder* and *Pal Joey*. I was very disappointed in *Dial M* and *Pal Joey* made me absolutely sick. What a loathsome production! If that's the sort of thing the American public of today want, what's one to do? I felt particularly bitter about Hart's lyrics. I can't see him as a lyricist at all. He has no charm whatsoever, and all those trick rhymes of his which the intelligentsia rave about –

> 'Take your pa and ma: go
> To Chicago',

as an instance – are the easiest things to do in the world. Ira is worth ten of him.

Well, to hell with all editors and all musicals like *Pal Joey*. . . .

28 October 1961   Remsenburg
                                         Long Island
                                         New York

Here is the revised 'You're the Top' lyric. It was a pretty difficult job, as the lines were so short and one was confined to nouns and no chance of using adjectives, plus all those double rhymes. I think it has come out all right, but of course with a lyric like this one will probably get some much better ideas in the course of time. I'm not satisfied with some of the couplets like Cole's 'arrow collar' and 'dollar', which seem flat to me, and the poor devil got very exhausted after doing five refrains. Fancy letting a line like 'You're the baby grand of a lady and gent' get by. Not to mention 'Inferno's Dante'. What the hell does *that* mean? . . .

Secondly, I have always disliked *Anything Goes* heartily because the wrongness of the balance offends my artistic soul. Naturally, if you've got Ethel Merman starring, you have to give her something to do, but when the thing becomes non-Ethel-Merman, it's all wrong having Reno do all the three good numbers.

It throws everything out of kilter. You feel Why the hell doesn't Billy marry Reno if he thinks so highly of her? Is there no way we can give 'You're the Top' to Hope and Billy? (On second thoughts, no we can't. There's no way of making flip stuff like this suitable for the heroine.)

Thirdly, the score is so thin. Apart from the three song hits we have almost nothing. Even after twenty-seven years I can remember how lousy that 'Gipsy in Me' number was. All we have except for the three big ones are 'All Through the Night' (which is lyrically all wrong for the spot it's in, the love story not having advanced so far) and the comic song by Moon. Apart from those we have four sorts of opening choruses, a reprise and a finale. What we want are two good duets for Hope and Billy.

Surely 'Begin the Beguine' wouldn't fit into a show like this? In your letter you ask me to send you a 'list' of Cole Porter songs. But I don't know any except the well known ones. I think what we ought to do is go entirely for the melody. If you find one with a good tune, I can write an entirely different lyric and one that will fit the situation.

28 October 1961

I'm working on the 'A. Goes' lyric and have got a masterly couplet, as follows:

> 'When the courts decide, as they did latterly,
> We could read Lady Chatterley
> If we chose,
> Anything goes.'

(Darned sight better than anything old King Cole ever wrote.)

2 November 1961

The trouble with Cole is that he has no power of self-criticism. He just bungs down anything whether it makes sense or not just because he has thought of what he feels is a good rhyme. . . .

I have rewritten the verse, because Cole's verse seemed to me absolute drivel. What on earth does a line like 'Any shock they should try to stem' mean? And in the first refrain he has 'bare limbs', 'me undressed' and 'nudist parties' one after the other. It shows what a powerful personality Ethel Merman must have, to be able to put that sort of stuff over.

I always feel about Cole's lyrics that he sang them to Elsa Maxwell and Noel Coward in a studio stinking of gin and they said 'Oh Cole, *darling*, it's just too marvellous.' Why can't he see that you must have a transition of thought in a lyric just as in dialogue?

Do you remember a lyric of his with a line about 'a burning inside of me', followed by something about something being 'under the hide of me'? No taste!!

What do I do next? I feel I would like to rewrite every lyric in the show – at any rate to cut out some of the lines and substitute others.

To Ira Gershwin
10 November 1961

Thanks for the clipping. What a compliment! Everything these days is giving me swelled head. The *NY Times* and *Herald-Tribune* celebrated my eightieth birthday with long interviews, and there were reams of stuff in the London papers. But what gave me the biggest kick was the following telegram:

> 'On this happy day I wish to thank you on behalf of Larry Hart, Oscar Hammerstein and myself for all you taught us through the years. Please stay well and happy.
> Affectionately.
> RICHARD ROGERS

I nearly cried when I read it. I had only met him once and for a minute when he and Oscar passed the table where I was lunching with Max Dreyfus, and it never occurred to me that he would remember my existence. He must be an awfully nice chap. . . .

Talking of lyrics, they are going to review *Anything Goes* off B'way and I have been revising 'You're the Top' and other Cole Porter lyrics. Don't you think he's terribly uneven? He gets wonderful ideas, but he will strain for rhymes regardless of the sense. As for instance

> 'When Mrs Roosevelt with all her trimmins
> Can broadcast a bed by Simmons,
> Then Franklin knows
> Anything goes.'

What the hell does 'trimmins' mean? I always think, as you do, that the first thing a lyric has to do is make sense. As for instance

> 'Sober or blotto,
> This is the motto,
> Keep muddling through.'

11 PLAYS AND FILMS

To Denis Mackail   1000 Park Avenue
6 May 1952   New York

Well, well, so you have moved and are back in London. I hardly
know what to say about it. On the whole I should think it was a
good thing. Hove was never worthy of you, and there are things
about London which you will probably like. Of course, if you hate
going to the theatre, as I do, it cuts you off a good deal of the
London whirl. What you say about preferring a Punch and Judy
show is exactly how I feel. The other day a kind friend – equivalent
to your Yawx – dragged me off, kicking and screaming, to see Rex
Harrison and wife in a bloody thing (by an obviously bloody
author, Christopher Fry) called *Venus Observed*, and I never
suffered so much in my life. To start with, I dislike Rex Harrison on
the stage more than any other actor – I except actresses, as that
would include Beatrice Lillie, to avoid seeing whom I would run
several miles – and I can't stand Lilli Palmer (Mrs R.H.) and I think
Christopher Fry ought to be shot. I tried to go to sleep, but the
noise from the stage was too much. Incidentally, don't you hate
most of all created things actors and their wives who announce, as
the Harrisons did, that they cannot play this play for more than
sixteen weeks. They are sorry, they know this will be a disappoint-
ment to their public, but they really must take the thing off at the
end of the sixteenth week. I was delighted when *Venus Observed*
came off at the end of the eighth week for lack of popular
support. . . .
    But talking of television, do you see any future for it? We have
a set and I enjoy the fights, but everything else on it is too awful for
words. One odd thing about television is the way it shows people
up.

24 June 1954   Remsenburg
                                                Lond Island
                                                New York

Interesting, your reactions to the Morley play. I find I can't stand plays nowadays. I occasionally go to one and always when strolling outside after act one, I find myself saying 'If I leg it now, I can get home and read a book,' and I leg it. I left after the first act of *Guys and Dolls*, *Harvey*, *Brigadoon*, *The Solid Gold Cadillac* and half a dozen more.

22 August 1954

Were you ever misguided enough to go to the movie of *Gone With the Wind*? Edward lugged me there on Sunday. I left after three and a half hours of it and there was another half hour after that. Isn't it amazing that these movie people have no idea of construction and selection! Anybody could have seen, you would have thought, that there was an hour in the middle of the thing that could have come right out without hurting the story. After an eternity of it Clark Gable and Vivien Leigh fell into the embrace and I was just reaching for my hat, when blowed if they didn't start an entirely new story. I don't believe it was in the book at all. Brooding on this, I have come to the conclusion that Gable saw the rushes of what was supposed to be the complete picture and raised hell because he hardly appeared in it, so they wrote in a lot of new stuff. Significant that Gable refused to come to the original opening and again refused when it was revised.

8 November 1956

It's odd about TV. One starts, like you, by loathing and despising it and gradually becomes tolerant. Our set is up in Ethel's bedroom and I generally view for an hour or so while she is slowly getting ready for bed. The main thing that strikes me is that the 1930 movies were a damned sight better than those of today.

8 June 1957

Nice to hear from you again, but sorry you've been having this gouty-arthritic condition. I always have a feeling that almost anything foul can happen if you live in London. Guy Bolton, who is there now, writes to say it's wonderful, but I don't believe him. For about two years everyone has been telling me that *My Fair Lady* is wonderful, and I had to go to it last Wednesday, a prominent manager having got me house tickets, and I thought it was the dullest lousiest show I had ever seen. Even as *Pygmalion* without Rex Harrison it was pretty bad, but with Rex Harrison it's awful. Who ever started the idea that he has charm? I had always considered Professor Higgins the most loathsome of all stage characters, but I never realised how loathsome he could be till I saw Sexy Rexy playing him. Why everyone raves about the thing I can't imagine. I met a sweet clear-thinking woman the other day who told me she had walked out after the first act, which I would have done if I hadn't had Sheran with me, all dewy-eyed and saying 'Isn't this *magical*!'.

To Guy Bolton
7 June 1964

It is now three minutes to twelve, so I must go and watch *Love of Life*.

21 June 1964

Well *Love of Life* will be starting in a few minutes, so I'll close.

12 PERFORMING FLEA

To William Townend   Golf Hotel
4 August 1936   Le Touquet

Sorry I haven't written before. I was trying to get chapter one of my novel set.

I'll tell you what I feel about the letters book. I think it has all the makings, but the stuff as it stands is too private and intimate. I don't believe it would interest the general reader.

There is too much about Pekes and Dulwich footer. In short, the letters are what they were intended to be – of interest to you personally. What I feel is that we must fake them a lot. They must be anecdotes of celebrities and stuff about people the public will want to read about. Then I think the actual stuff about your stories should be fixed. This part will be up to you. What I suggest is that when I write about one of your stories, you in your comment should say 'This was the story suggested to me by old Joe Spelvin, the boatswain of the *Carioca*. Dear old Joe, I remember one evening in Santa Cruz. . . .'

You see what I mean. The whole book has got to be made more *generally* interesting. At present, it's like a private joke and would irritate the outsider. Critics would call it small beer, as they did that book of A. S. M. Hutchinson's *A Year that the Locust* –

The thing to do is to postpone publication and work on it. There are all the makings of a fine book, if we go for the idea of two parallel lives – mine among the wasters at Cannes etc and yours among the sailors. It ought to be terrific if we can get that idea into it.

See what I mean? We must chuck away the original scheme of preserving my letters intact and tune them up. I can shove in all sorts of stuff about people like Ziegfeld etc.

Do you approve?

It was ripping seeing both of you on Wednesday. It was a

master idea your coming over. I couldn't imagine how you were ever to see the dogs.

24 March 1937   1315 Angelo Drive
               Beverly Hills
               California

Bill, I've been brooding over those letters again. I must say they are absorbing – to me – but they're so infernally intimate. I pour out my heart to you, without stopping to weigh what I am writing, and the letters are full of stuff that I wouldn't want anyone but you to see. Still, I believe something could be done with them. But I have that feeling of not wanting to give myself away. All the best stuff would have to be cut, don't you think? And the point is – could one substitute anything for it.

☆

Plum changed his mind after the war.

☆

16 October 1951   1000 Park Avenue
               New York

I think the letters scheme is terrific. Even Ethel, who is usually so critical, approved of it wholeheartedly. I immediately sent your first letter to Ken McCormick, who is the boss of Doubledays now that Nelson Doubleday is dead, and you will see from the enclosed that he is very interested. I am lunching with him tomorrow.

The great thing, as I see it, is not to feel ourselves confined to the actual letters. I mean, nobody knows what was actually in the letters, so we can fake as much as we like. That is to say, if in a quickly written letter from – say – Hollywood, I just mention that Winston Churchill is there and I have met him, in the book I can think up some amusing anecdote, describing how his trousers split up the back at the big party or something. See what I'm driving at?

You see, all the letters I have written to you were written very quickly. I just poured out the stuff as if we were talking to each other. But for the book we need more carefully written stuff. (There's an example for you in that paragraph. I used 'written' three times and 'stuff' twice. The letters, as they appear in the book, must be much more polished. Naturally not artificial, but avoiding the same verb twice in a sentence.)

Also, these letters give me a wonderful opportunity of shoving thoughts on life to a much greater extent than I do in my actual letters.

The way to work this thing, as I see it, is for you to complete the book and then hand it over to me, and I will go through it and add stuff and make it all more vivid. I have always wanted to write my autobiography but felt too self-conscious. This will be a way of doing the thing obliquely. . . .

Well, laddie, I was seventy yesterday. I tried my hardest to think solemn thoughts like Somerset Maugham in *A Writer's Notebook*, but couldn't dig up any. I felt just the same as usual. (Now there's a case of what I mean when I say that we must fake a bit in the book. It ought to be possible, with thought, to turn out a complete letter dated Oct 15, 1951 which will be an amusing essay on How It Feels To Be Seventy. In fact, that is how the book ought to end. That should be the last letter in it. But an essay like that takes careful thinking out, and I can't possibly compose it in a letter which I want to get off to you this afternoon! See what I mean?)

13 BRING ON THE GIRLS

To Guy Bolton   36 Boulevard Suchet
21 January 1946   Paris

Listen. I've suddenly got the most terrific idea – a book of theatrical
reminiscences by you and me to be called
    BOOKS AND LYRICS
    by
    GUY BOLTON and P. G. WODEHOUSE
    BRING ON THE GIRLS[1]
I only got the idea an hour ago, so haven't thought out anything
about the shape of the thing, but I believe we could make a big thing
out of it. You have an enormous stock of theatrical stories and I
have a few myself. My idea would be to make it a sort of loose saga
of our adventures in the theatre from 1915 onwards, studded with
anecdotes. Think of all the stuff we could put into it! I remember
you telling me a priceless story about Bill McGuire, but I've
forgotten the details, and between us we must have a hundred
unpublished yarns about Erlanger, Savage etc. Do you think in
your spare time you could dictate a few to a stenographer – quite in
the rough, just the main points for me to work up? Meanwhile, I'll
be trying to shape the vehicle. I see something on the lines of
Woolcott's *When Rome Burns* – I mean *While Rome Burns*. Don't
give away the title to a soul, as it seems to me a winner and
somebody might pinch it. A book like this would be a cinch for
serial publication – always provided I am not barred by the
magazines! And I don't think I shall be long. Doubleday Doran are
bringing out my Jeeves novel soon, and if that sells well it ought to
establish me once more with the magazines.

31 October 1952   1000 Park Avenue
                                       New York
Brooding over the book, I believe we ought to carry on aziz to end
of *Oh, Boy* tour and then transpose *Oh, My Dear* and *Oh, Lady* so as

---

[1] In the original, this line was typed down the left-hand margin.

216

to make *Oh, Lady* come after *Oh, My Dear*. I want to get *Oh, My Dear*, *Kitty Darlin'*, *Miss 1917* (which we will retitle *The Second Century Show*) and *Riviera Girl* into one year. We shall thus get a funny 'failure' chapter, which will take the curse off the monotonous run of successes. Then we can get the happy ending by having *Oh, Lady* and *Leave It to Jane* come after this bunch of flops. And after *Oh, Lady* we go to London.

Do you like this? I think it will be an excellent thing to kid ourselves about failures. That plot of *Riviera Girl* will fit in fine.

4 November 1952

Here's an idea I've just had. Why not end the book with the crash of 1929 and show us both cleaned out. We discuss the situation and feel that we must face it bravely. You tell me the *Going Greek* plot. I like it, and we end the book with you writing on a blank sheet of paper:
GOING GREEK
Book by Guy Bolton, Lyrics by P. G. W.
This would make a neat finish, holding out promise of a sequel.

But the thing that is worrying me is this. Everything up to the end of the 'flop' chapter is so darned good and quick and funny that I don't see at present how we are to equal it with the rest of the stuff, much less top it. What have we that's as good as the Erlanger, Savage, Comstock, *Oh, Boy* tour stuff?

I think we shall have to let truth go to the wall if it interferes with entertainment. And we must sternly suppress any story that hasn't a snapper at the finish. I've been rereading Johnny Golden's book, and what's wrong with it – and almost all other theatrical reminiscence books – is that so many of the stories in it just aren't funny enough. He tells a long story, for instance, about how he went to a rehearsal of *Three Wise Fools*, saw an actor playing the part of the butler rather badly, had a chance of selling the show to London if Charlot liked it, took Charlot to it and found that the butler man was playing Claude Gillingwater's part as understudy, was greatly relieved to find that he played it well, and sold the show to Charlot. Now, of what possible interest is that to the reader or to anyone but Johnny? That is what I want to avoid in this book – shoving in stuff just because it happened. Even if we have to invent every line of the thing, we must have entertainment.

Thus, I don't think the rat and crazy maids story is strong

enough as it stands. (I got the last chunk of material all right.) I suggest that we are invited to Savage's house on Long Island for a couple of nights before the yacht tour. Crazy maids, Savage says they are tea drunkards and he got them cheap because they had no references. Then the rat. Then the yacht tour. Ties the whole thing in.

I'm awfully leary of playing any scene in which only you and I figure, as it seems to me to be making the mistake of the Johnny Golden book. You and I ought to be as much as possible *Alice in Wonderland*, appearing in the story only when we are up against some amusing and eccentric character (except for bits of dialogue between us from time to time). I may be wrong, but I don't think your jumping off the train story is strong enough as it stands. It's a good story, but it ought to be tied in with some other character – i.e. it should be a story Jerry tells us of somebody. (Jerry is going to be very useful all through as a teller of stories.)

As I say, I may be wrong about this, but that's how I feel.

Up to the end of the 'flop' chapter, everything is fine. We are two eager beavers engaged in making good and having a lot of amusing adventures on the way. But once we are solidly established as successful authors, we simply must have something more than 'Then we wrote *Hamlet*. It was a big hit. After that we wrote *Othello*. It ran for years on the road.' See what I mean? After *Oh, Boy* the Horatio-Alger-making-good interest does not exist, and we have got to have some very funny stuff to make up for it. Thus, there is nothing to say about *Oh, Kay*, for instance, if one sticks to the facts, except that it was a terrific success. What we want is to invent some amusing things that made it look as if it were bound to flop. In other words, we must handle this book just as we did the Ballymore stuff in *Derby Day*. We must manufacture suspense. Otherwise, we become like Johnny Golden with his stream of dull stories designed to show how good he is.

WE MUST BE FUNNY!!!!!!

What we want is a couple of days together, plotting the thing out as if it were a play or a novel. I'll come down as soon as I can.

I've unearthed your original notes for the book. You have probably forgotten half the stories you jotted down in it. The problem is, How to work those stories in without making the thing just a stream of anecdotes. I have got it just right in Chapter Three, where we are talking about managers. You tell a story to show how tough managers are, I tell another. (We could add others, if you have them.) Then I say 'Ah, but there is ONE manager, Henry W.

Savage, who etc.' Thus, the stories are not just dragged in but arise from what we were talking about.

We ought to be able to do this all through. We need a conference.

7 December 1952

The also enclosed you may have seen in today's *Herald-Tribune*. Rather encouraging as seeming to show that we are on the right lines. It also makes one feel that we must shove in every possible 'of those times' description that we can think of. This will be up to you, as I am so constituted that I never notice what is going on around me and if asked would say that there had been no changes in New York since 1916. The Palm Beach chapter is perfect, but what else can we put in?

Your letter about the diaries okay. Not easy to spot just where to put in the diary stuff, but we'll do it.

I wrote to Lee Shubert asking for figures about the *Oh, Boy* production, but so far a proud silence on his part.

The flop chapter has come out awfully well. I looked up my article on the *Century* Show in *Vanity Fair* and came on some other stuff which fits in. I am going to go through all those *Vanity Fair* volumes, the only catch being that I am not allowed to take them home with me, so have to copy the stuff out while there, which is a ghastly chore.

I think I shall have to go a buster and have the stuff – as far as we've got – typed again, blowing the expense. We simply must have a clean copy we can brood over. Nobody could read the script I now have, with all its interlinings and corrections. Maybe the thing is in such good shape that we shall have to make only small changes and additions for the final script which we send out, so that we needn't have the whole thing retyped but can insert pages.

I wish to heaven I could make up my mind about this book. To me, as I read it, it seems the most marvellous thing ever written, every line of it absorbing. Then comes the gloomy mood, when I tell myself that the public today knows nothing of the people we are writing about and doesn't care a damn. Then again I say If Morehouse can get away with it, why not us? I think some figures will help a lot – e.g. costs of production in those days, number of theatres etc.

6 February 1953

BUT I fear very much that he is going to jib at the Marion–Justine stuff.[1] We don't want any risk of having to suspend publication while the thing is argued out by lawyers, so we must either get Marion's approval or cut the stuff out. Of course, there is a lot of good material in the chapter without Justine and Marion. Anyway, we won't worry about it till we have to. The book is long enough for us to cut ten thousand words, if necessary, so it might be a good plan to skip straight from the end of the chapter where Ray gives us the *Oh, Boy* contract to the start of the flop chapter. We lose some great stuff, but we certainly speed the thing up. But don't worry. I suppose it wouldn't be possible to tell the J–M party story without giving names or by inventing other names? On the lines of your 'Baa'. They might have nicknames like Pat and Mike or something, and we could explain this and label them thus throughout.

16 March 1953

I finished the script yesterday and am taking it to be typed tomorrow, as I want to go over it again today. We have added fifty-three pages – i.e. about 16,000 words, so the thing is now about as long as the Bible. The last chapter came out superbly. I wrote it at such a pace that I wondered if it would be all right, and I was stunned when I read it just now and found how good it was. It ends the book with a real snap. It involved changing the last three pages of our old last chapter, and I think it's a great improvement.

In a previous letter Grimsdick made several suggestions for cuts, which I will attend to. He has sent me the script by air mail and doesn't want it back before September, so there is lots of time for concentrating on it. He says he would like some more English stuff if possible and picks out as the gem of the book the chapter where I throw the letters out of window. Odd. It's good, I know, but I should have thought we had half a dozen funnier scenes. It just shows you can't ever tell what will slay people.

10 April 1953

I lunched with Scwed – sorry, Schwed – yesterday. He was very

---

[1] Marion Davies and Justine Johnstone.

pleasant and enthusiastic about the book. He said that they first decided to publish the Jeeves novel, and then Scott sent in the *Girls* script, and Jack Goodman asked Schwed what it was. Schwed said 'Well, I haven't read it yet, but it seems to be a sort of joint autobiography of Guy Bolton and P.G. Wodehouse.' And Jack Goodman said 'I can't imagine anything more lousy. You damn well read it. I'm not going to.' And next day Schwed arrived at the office trembling with excitement. 'This is the book,' he said. 'This is the one we must start with. The novel can come later.' Then Goodman read it and was just as enthusiastic as Schwed. And that was before we put in the yachting trip and the final chapter (which really is a pippin. It gives the book just the lift it needed at the end).

27 April 1953

You will see from enclosed that Grimsdick is much more critical than Schwed – who seems to be worried principally by 'Who is Bob Barbour?'! I have made the cuts he suggests, as I always think one is wise to defer to a publisher, but if you feel they should stay in, you can go and argue with him. (Of course I haven't cut the story of Armand's musical education. Why cut one of the best things in the book?)

To Denis Mackail   Remsenburg
24 June 1954   Long Island
                                   New York

I agree with everything you say about the *Girls* book. I must say I'm surprised at the enthusiastic tone of the reviews. I was expecting to get slated on all sides, but I've had about twenty so far and all good.

It's an odd book. Of course, the things we say happened to us didn't really, but they did happen to somebody and are all quite true. Thus, it was Fred Thompson who used to throw his letters out of window, Arthur Hopkins who played golf with Ziegfeld in the dark and so on. Legitimate, I think. Anyway, we have avoided that awful 'We opened in Philadelphia with the following cast – that sterling actor George Banks as the Prince . . .' which make theatrical reminiscences so boring.

To Ira Gershwin   1000 Park Avenue
14 January 1953   New York

The thing I found hardest was getting used to calling ourselves Guy and Plum. I wanted to say 'Bolton' and 'Wodehouse' throughout, but Guy overruled me. It came quite natural, of course, to write of 'Flo' and 'Ira' and so on, but I found myself jibbing at 'said Plum with a quiet smile'. Maybe it'll read okay, though. By the way, if you want to get into the act and have any good George stories, send them along.

14 MISCELLANEOUS

To William Townend
26 June 1926

Hunstanton Hall
Norfolk

I have been spending two weeks at Bexhill, the spot which God forgot, but am now in my beloved Hunstanton and am writing this sitting in a punt on the moat with my typewriter on a bed-table balanced on one of the seats. There is a duck close by which makes occasional quacks that sound just like a man with an unpleasant voice saying nasty things in an undertone.

17 May 1927

'She spoke as though drowning *were* the most etc', but I am still wondering what the rule is after 'as though'. Michael Arlen in his last book (God! What muck! Have you read it?) uses 'as though' every second paragraph and always puts 'was' after it. I'm nearly sure 'were' is right.[1]

27 March 1928

Edgar Wallace, I hear, now has a Rolls Royce and also a separate car for each of the five members of his family. Also a day butler and a night butler, so that there is never a time when you can go into his house and not find a butler. That's the way they live. But why not two day butlers and two night butlers, so that they could do cross-talk and perhaps a song?[2]

---

[1] Fowler has this to say on the subject: *As if, as though*. These should invariably be followed by past conditional, and not by a present form (*would* not *will*; *could*, not *can*; *did*, not *does*; *was* or *were*, not *is* . . .).

[2] Edgar Wallace had two butlers because he wrote at night.

8 January 1930   17 Norfolk Street
                                                 Park Lane
                                                 London W1
Isn't it great to think that Christmas is over! I am resolved to spend
next Christmas on a liner. I came in for the New Year festivities at
Hunstanton and had to wear a white waistcoat every night.

29 June 1931

We are toying with a scheme for going round the world in
December on the *Empress of Britain*. Sometimes we feel we should
like it, and then we ask ourselves if we really want to see the world.
I'm darned if I know. I have never seen any spectacular spot yet that
didn't disappoint me. Notably the Grand Canyon. Personally, I've
always liked wandering around in the background. I mean, I get
much more kick out of a place like Droitwich, which has no real
merits, than out of something like the Taj Mahal. I suppose what it is
really is that one only likes the places which appeal to one as having
possibilities in the way of locations for stories.

6 March 1932   Domaine de la Fréyère
                                                 Auribeau
                                                 Alpes–Maritimes
The above is our new address. We moved in on Thursday. We have
taken it for a year. It is a sort of Provençal country-house, with a
hundred acres of hillside and large grounds and a huge swimming-
pool. It ought to be lovely in summer. Just at the moment it is a bit
bleak.
    Gosh, what a sweat it is learning French! A woman comes to
me for two hours a day and we talk French to each other. I am really
getting darned good, but the strain is awful and lays me out for the
rest of the day.

1 April 1932

We have a German butler, an Alsatian footman, a Serbian cook, a
French chauffeur, an Italian maid, and an English odd-job man.
Good material for the next war. But they all seem to get on well
together.

13 August 1932

We have been seeing a lot of Maurice Chevalier. Not a bad chap, but rather a ham. I can't ever really like actors, can you?

10 October 1932

Plans at present: – A visit to London in early November. Then probably a dash to America. Ethel is very keen on living at Norfolk Street again, which I am all for. Our only trouble is Winks. Isn't that quarantine law a nuisance. I think they ought to make an exception in favour of Pekes, who couldn't possibly give anyone rabies. Meanwhile, they give driving licences to anybody who can prove that he is deaf and very short-sighted, so that the death-roll can be kept up.

1 December 1932   Dorchester Hotel
                                               London
Don't you find, as you get on in life, that the actual things you really want cost about two hundred a year? I have examined my soul, and I find that my needs are a *Times* Library subscription and tobacco money, plus an extra bit for holidays. If only you were making a couple of thousand a year steady, I shouldn't have a worry in the world.

Talking of the world, what a place! What one really wants is some method by which America could be reduced to ruin without it affecting the ability of American magazines to pay big prices. Isn't it amazing that the mugs can't see that their high tariffs and insistence on these debts are what is making everything the way it is.

16 August 1934

Have you ever considered how difficult it is to select a pseudonym? Now that I may have to, I can think of no name that sounds like anything. My mind dwells on things like Eustace Trevelyan. (Old Brook has just written a story under the name of Batt Rimes!) I think the thing is to combine two actual names – such as Reeves Grimsdick.

28 December 1936   1315 Angelo Drive
                                                    Beverly Hills
                                                    California

What about old Pop Windsor? A dashed good riddance, I think.
George will make a much better king. Good gags about it over
here, which may not have penetrated to England, are 'Gone with
the Windsor' and 'You can't abdicate and eat it'.

4 January 1938   Low Wood
                                                    Le Touquet

I say, rather funny. When I left for Hollywood in 1936, I left a
hundred quid with Peter to be doled out in bets on the horses in his
stable, when he thought he had a winner. When I got there for
Christmas, he showed me the figures and I was down to ten
pounds. All the rest had gone. Well, Anthony Mildmay was riding
a horse at Kempton next day which he thought might finish in the
first three, so I told Peter to put my tenner on it, five to win and five
for a place. It won at 100 to 7, being the complete outsider of the
race, and I scooped in ninety quid and so am exactly as I was at the
start. Bit of luck, what?

To Guy Bolton   78 Avenue Paul Doumer
30 May 1945   Paris

Are you beginning to feel at all old nowadays? I am now on the
verge of sixty-four and for the first time am starting to abandon the
illusion that I am really a sprightly young fellow in the early forties.
The way it affects me as regards my work is to make it increasingly
difficult to write quickly. I used to rattle off the stuff on my
machine, but now I have to do each paragraph in pencil first and it is
only after about half a dozen shots that I get the thing right.

To William Townend
30 June 1945

By the same post as yours I had a letter from Watt – my Watt –
saying that he is now all right again, his cataract cured. He says that
the idea of having Collins publish my books is off, as the Jenkins
people refuse to consider giving me up and want to publish *Money
in the Bank* as soon as possible. I am sorry in a way, but it is nice to

feel that the Jenkins people want me, and after all they have done extraordinarily well with my stuff. It is only their jackets that jar one, and I suppose you are apt to get a pretty foul jacket from any popular publisher. I sometimes wish I were one of those dignified birds whose books come out in grey wrappers with the title and author's name on them and nothing else. God may have forgiven Herbert Jenkins Ltd for the jacket of *Meet Mr Mulliner*, but I never shall.

7 March 1946

I often wonder if you and I were exceptionally fortunate in our school days. To me the years between 1896 and 1900 seem so like heaven that I feel that everything since has been an anti-climax. Was the average man really unhappy at school? Or was Dulwich in our time an exceptionally good school? . . .

What always amazes me about Denis is why he lives in London.

He doesn't like the place and doesn't do any of the things that people live in London for. Personally I feel that I would rather be back in camp than live in London again. The atmosphere of Paris, even nowadays, is entirely different. Even now there is a sort of gaiety in the air. But London seems to me so heavy and dismal. You have been wise always to stick to the country. I think London does something bad to the soul.

Do you ever feel bored? I was thinking it over the other day and I was surprised to find that I couldn't recall a single day in the last twenty years when I have been bored. I find that I get into a routine of work and walks and reading which makes the time fly. I never want to see anyone – except you, of course – and I never want to go anywhere or do anything.

To Guy Bolton   36 Boulevard Suchet
17 June 1946   Paris

Good news from the London front. *Money in the Bank* has sold 21,000 copies in two weeks and my publishers are confident that the whole first edition of 30,000 will go off before long. And a leading critic, giving a *Book Talk* on the BBC on June 12, delivered a perfect eulogy of the book.[1] This is particularly good, because the BBC is a

[1] V. S. Pritchett.

Government show and this looks as though the Govt were offering an olive branch. Until now they have been very hostile. They refused to allow my lyrics to be sung on their programmes and then went and featured 'Bill', ascribing it to Oscar! I got my agent to write them a stinker, asking them either to refrain from using my lyrics or else not to credit them to somebody else. So I presumed that brass rags had been definitely parted. And now comes this stupendous boost of my book, which I should think would do wonders for the sales.

2 October 1946

I'm so glad you liked *Joy in the Morning*. Its reception in the USA has been a great relief. Except for a very mild stinker in *Time*, I hear the reviews have been excellent. I have only seen the *NY Times* one (very good) and a marvellous one in rhyme that Ogden Nash did for the *Herald-Tribune*.[1] The sales have been fine, several thousand more already than the total sales of anything I have had published in America in the last ten years. I am hoping that this will encourage the magazines to buy my stuff again.

24 January 1947   Pavillon Henri Quatre
                                       St Germain-en-Laye

In case I don't get to NY before you sail, let me impress it upon you with all the emphasis at my disposal that England is no place to be in at the moment and you will be far better off in France. (I can help out as regards francs, as I am now allowed to get my English income over here.) The only person I know who says a good word for life in England at present date is an American girl who went over there some time ago. She says she is having a swell time, but the fact remains that you simply can't buy a thing in the shops and the food situation is bad. Here, if you have the money, you can live almost a pre-war life. Now that the brutal and licentious military have buzzed off, all the restaurants are running again and you can get anything you want. The prices are big, though not, I suppose, particularly so by American standards.

[1] Given as Appendix C.

25 May 1947   53 East 66th Street
                                                New York
Everything has gone absolutely marvellously for me since I arrived.
I was swamped by reporters on the boat at Quarantine, but
fortunately I struck up a bosom friendship with the P.M. representative, who gave me a wonderful notice. I believe the leftist press
takes its tone from P.M., so that must have helped a lot. Anyway, I
don't think there have been any unpleasant cracks in any of the
papers.

　　A couple of days after I landed I held a sort of reception from
the literary columnists, and they printed nothing but stuff about my
work. I then did a radio talk to about three hundred stations which I
believe was a success. I did another yesterday on that *Lunchtime at
Sardi's* set-up. Finally, my new novel, *Full Moon*, which came out
last Thursday, got splendid notices on day of publication in *NY
Times* and *NY Sun*, and there is another terrific boost in today's
Herald-Tribune, and my agent has just sold a short story to
Cosmopolitan for only a little under my pre-war price and tells me
that at least six of the leading magazines are anxious to have my
stuff, so I am hoping that I shall shortly be all right with the
magazines.

7 August 1949   1000 Park Avenue
                                                New York
Do come back soon. New York is a desert without you.

29 January 1950

Harry Tierney wants me to make a musical with him of Barrie's
Admirable Crichton, which sounds a great proposition till you read
the play again, as I have just done. I remember being entranced with
it in 1904 or whenever it was, but now it seems like a turkey of the
first water. I believe the best bet for a musical would be *The Cave
Girl*.

To Denis Mackail
25 December 1950

Oh, glory, glory! I feel like a Salvation Army Colonel seeing a sinner come into the fold. Yours of Dec 1 announcing that at last you have seen the light and resigned from the Pest Hole. Golly, what a club!, as R. L. Stevenson said of your other haunt, the Athenaeum. . . .

Christmas. Gosh, what a season! Thank goodness it will be over after today. I wish the radio wouldn't be so damned hearty about Christmas. Ethel insists on having it on, and yesterday it was too awful for words. . . .

Ethel has been given an electric blanket for Christmas. You can imagine how Squeaky and Wonder love it. . . .

I am feeling a little sobered by the reflection that I have only got another four months to go before becoming seventy. Then I look at Pétain and feel more encouraged. But how on earth does a man who has lived a life like Pétain's – Verdun, sentenced to death (quite a nerve strain, that) and prison – live to 95?

I had forgotten that you knew Shaw. Everyone says he was charming in private life. But he is the most maddening public character I know. I met him twice, once at lunch at Lady Astor's (another maddening louse) and again on the platform at the Gare whatever that station is – ah yes, du Lyon, when I was off to Cannes and he was starting on his world tour. Ethel, silly ass, gave him an opening by saying 'My daughter is so excited about your world tour,' and he said 'The whole world is excited about my world tour.' I nearly said '*I'm* not, blast you.'

9 February 1951

How difficult it is to nurse a grievance. For the last few years, as the result of my being in the doghouse, the BBC coldly refused to consider doing anything by me, and I said to myself 'One of these days they'll want something of mine, and then I'll draw myself up to my full height and write them a stinker.' I had even drafted out a few specimen lines for the stinker. I have now had a letter from my agent saying the BBC want to do my *Damsel in Distress* as a bedtime story or something, and I simply can't bring myself to take the trouble to be haughty about it. It's a pity, because the stinker would have been terrific.

25 March 1951

I came out of hospital yesterday, my six doctors having decided that I had not, as they thought at first, got a tumor on the brain or, as they thought later, a ditto on the spine. They still don't seem to know what has caused these giddy attacks I have been having, but it is either a noram hardening of the arteries or something to do with my eyes. (That word 'noram' is supposed to be 'normal'.) At intervals of about a year or more I suddenly find I can't control my legs, just as if I were drunk, but recover directly I am sick. At first it was supposed that the trouble was in my middle ear, but I don't think it is. Anyway, I have had every possible test and they can't find anything wrong, so I suppose I now carry on just as usual. I feel quite all right, but very weak, which is not surprising after all they did to me, including twice taking fluid out of my spine, a loathsome operation which involves lying flat on one's back for twenty-four hours! Have you ever tried to drink tea lying on your back?

15 October 1951

Well, laddie, I'm 70 today. Silver threads among the gold, what? The odd thing is that I don't feel a bit different. Somerset Maugham, if one can believe *A Writer's Notebook*, felt all sorts of solemn thoughts on his seventieth birthday, but I can't seem to pump up any. It's just another day to me.

7 February 1952

I wonder how you are going to like having to read the *New Yorker* every week. As it only costs fifteen cents, I buy it weekly, but it's a long time since I found anything in it worth reading. I think what I hate most are the stories. Why do they all begin 'When my father and I were living in Singapore, my aunt Georgina used to stay with us. She had grey ringlets and a pug dog'? I thought that sort of thing went out in the eighties. And what price those Letters from Czechoslovakia and other places? And those yards of stuff about shops? And the Profiles of dull people you've never heard of? I think you're darned lucky if only the wrapper arrives.

231

27 November 1953

You are quite right about Malcolm.[1] He is everywhere these days. I think *Punch* must be beginning to catch on in America, for you see page advertisements of it all over the place. But don't break my heart by saying you really *enjoy* that deadly production, The *New Yorker*, with its Letters From Malaya and Our Far Flung Correspondents? Except for Wolcott Gibbs – or is it Wolcot? – it is the dullest bloody thing ever published. I buy it each week, skim through it in five minutes, skipping the twenty pages of unreadable stuff which they always have in the middle and chuck it away. Do you mean to say you have found something amusing in it? . . .

To Guy Bolton
26 January 1953

I've had a great triumph with *Pigs Have Wings*. A trade paper asked twenty booksellers throughout England to name the ten books they thought would sell best at Christmas, and not one in twenty named *Pigs*. The results are in, and *Pigs* was the biggest seller in five districts, coming third on the list after *The Cruel Sea* and another book and miles ahead of *Giant* and John Steinbeck's new book and also Agatha Christie's new book. This ought to pave the way nicely for *Ring for Jeeves*, which will be out in the spring, and if that gets a good sale *Bring on the Girls* will be in a great spot.

4 June 1953

Brilliant parody of Jeeves in *Punch* May 20. It ought to help the sale of the book.[2]

To Denis Mackail   Remsenburg
15 October 1954   Long Island
                                   New York
I am 73 today. Oddly enough I feel younger than I did yesterday. Relief from the suspense of waiting to be 73, I suppose. I once read a book by Hugh Walpole where an author aged 70 sits down to write

[1] Malcolm Muggeridge was editor of *Punch* 1953–7. See p. 92.
[2] Given as Appendix D.

a story, and I remember thinking H. W. was crazy. How could a man write a story at that age? He would be doing well if he could walk across the room, but now I look on men of seventy as kids and am a bit annoyed by their juvenile exuberance.

17 December 1955

Only another nine days and it will be over. But of course there will be another one next year, so how can you beat the game? I don't know if it is a sign of old age, but I find I hate Christmas more every year.

To Guy Bolton   1000 Park Avenue
1 May 1958   New York

Ethel suddenly decided to have the alterations for which she has always yearned done on the living room, and of course this had led to a complete rewrite of the whole house! My bathroom is being modernised, the door from my bedroom to the living-room has been done away with and I now have a big cupboard with sliding doors, and the kitchen is now twice the size with a new door leading into the garden! It's hell, of course, at the moment, with five workmen in the place, but the results are going to be terrific. Those pillars in the living room which we always hated have disappeared, and the fireplace has been done over. The two cats nearly went cuckoo for the first week or so, but seem to have settled down now.

We miss you both very much. Remsenburg seems lost without you. Apart from tripping over workmen, our main interest these days is watching the pheasant which comes into the garden and eats the bread we put out. It is a very stately bird, and the first few times it brought its wife with it. Now it seems to feel that the bread is too good to be shared with the little woman, so she stays at home, thus avoiding being chased by Bozo and Blackie the cat.

To Denis Mackail
22 April 1959

I find myself shaking my head a bit over the England of today, if the populace can read the national newspapers. A man I was in camp with sends me great bundles of *Mirrors*, *Expresses*, *Sketches* etc every week, and they really are abysmal. I think I dislike the *Express* most, it apparently being written entirely by bounders. Don't you hate that modern newspaper habit (a) of always giving a woman's age – '59-year-old Lady whoever-it-is' (b) using Christian names, especially in reporting cricket and football. Why the hell have they always got to say 'Reggie Smith' and 'Phil Brown' played well (or badly) in the scrum? And those big headlines to a story of some shop girl in Wigan or somewhere having sprained an ankle or fallen off her bicycle. There'll always be an England, but who wants an England full of morons reading the *Express*?

To Guy Bolton
7 July 1959

Damn and blast the English working classes! I see in the *Herald-Trib* this morning that the printers' strike is going to close down every form of publishing in Great Britain from national newspapers to bottle tops and bank notes, which means that the day I live for – Saturday, when the *Observer*, *Sunday Times*, *Punch* etc arrive – will be a blank. What a curse these strikes are. My latest opus was scheduled to start as a serial in *John Bull* on July 12, and there won't be any *John Bull* apparently. Still, I've got the money for it, which is the main thing.

8 August 1959

We have got Edward with us for a few days, but unfortunately he has to go and settle down in NY as he is joining some legal firm till October. But we shall have him for week ends. He's wonderful to have staying with us, and we both love him.

17 September 1959

I'm frothing with fury because this blasted Khrushchev keeps interrupting my *Love of Life* programme. It happened yesterday and again today just at the most exciting part of the story. I can't see why the TV people think there is entertainment value in watching a chap who looks like a blend of Rudolf Friml and Bobby Denby

234

arrive at Pennsylvania station. I wish to heaven he wouldn't time his appearances for 12 to 12.30.

16 October 1959

We all miss you both sadly. Edward Cazalet is now with us till early November and is a tremendous success.

To Denis Mackail
7 January 1960

The editor of *Punch* was over here the other day, and I gave him lunch and he told me he was putting me on the *Punch* table, which of course is an honour, though I should have appreciated it more fifty years ago.

Ethel and I have become very keen on bridge, a game from which I have always hitherto held off. We play double dummy every night and during the day I study Goren's bridge books. Does this mean that I have become senile?

6 June 1960

How I agree with you about going to parties. Ethel and I never see a soul these days and thank goodness the neighbours have stopped inviting us to their binges. About three times a year I motor up to New York, lunch, buy books and return the same day. It's odd about living in the country, there always seems such a lot to do. Work in the morning, at twelve watch a television serial in which I am absorbed, lunch, take the dog to the post office which covers two till three, brood on work till five, bath, cocktails, dinner, read and play two-handed bridge, and the day is over. The same routine day after day, and somehow it never gets monotonous.

To Guy Bolton
4 June 1971

I typed these yesterday, but didn't send them off as I wanted to write you a letter and was too exhausted to do it. Some TV people came down and I had to read an article I had written, to be done in Channel 4 at six p.m. It was supposed to be an impromptu, but I couldn't read that gadget they use with my distance glasses, and they said 'Then read it, but keep the paper well down' and I found I couldn't read with my reading glasses unless the paper was well up. I started and got halfway, when Ethel coughed and I had to start again. I did, and some workmen next door began hammering, so I started again. In all I read the damned thing seven times, by which time it seemed to me about as funny as an obituary notice. However, they said it would be all right. Blast them. They had told me the thing would take half an hour. It took two hours and three quarters and left me as limp as a rag.

2 August 1973

I'm glad about Ira. I thought he must have had a stroke. What I meant about his lyrics being pedestrian was that when *Oh, Kay* was done he wasn't really a lyricist but a Tin Pan Alley song writer. He had no notion of getting a situation and fitting a lyric to it; he just turned up with a bundle of lyrics like 'Do Do Do' and 'Clap Your Hands' and expected you to fit the book to them, which you did miraculously. He improved a lot later on.

9 August 1973

I can't make myself out. I have never felt fitter in my life, and my brain is super, but I can only hobble about with a stick. It's not that my legs are weak, it's a matter of balance. Take the stick away from me and I'm liable to topple over sideways. But to hell with the legs, it's the brain that counts.

18 September 1974

My walking has become awful. I daren't move without my stick, and I never know when I am going to get the staggers. I suppose some sort of falling apart is inevitable at 93, but I don't like it. (My back seems more or less all right. Sorry you have been having trouble with yours.)

15 CASSANDRA

As Cassandra, William Connor had been responsible for the vicious and scurrilous broadcast on the BBC after Plum's wartime broadcasts to America on German wavelengths. This gave a completely false picture of what had happened, and because of it there are people even today who believe that Plum broadcast propaganda for the Germans. In 1961, to commemorate Plum's eightieth birthday, Evelyn Waugh broadcast a 'national salute' to him in which he rebutted the charges made by Cassandra and revealed for the first time that the BBC had broadcast his talk only because the Minister of Information used wartime powers to enforce it. Evelyn Waugh said: 'It is therefore with great pleasure that I take this opportunity to express the disgust the BBC has always felt for the injustice for which they were guiltless and their complete repudiation of the charges so ignobly made through their medium.'

The following letters reveal that, to many people incomprehensibly, Plum had later made a friend of William Connor.

☆

To William Connor   Remsenburg
10 May 1961   Long Island
                                     New York

Dear Walp[1]

A rather embarrassing situation has arisen. (For me, I mean. I don't suppose you will turn a hair over it.)

Some time ago I had a letter from Evelyn Waugh, saying (quote) 'I have arranged for the BBC to make an act of homage to you on July 15th, the twentieth anniversary of their attack on you.'

I thought that was fine, but I have just had a letter from Guy

[1] In his broadcast Connor spoke with derision of the names Pelham Grenville. In return Plum expressed the hope that Connor's initials stood for 'Walpurgis Diarmid or something of that sort', and afterwards addressed him as Walp.

237

Bolton, recently arrived in London, and he says that somebody told him 'that Evelyn Waugh is making a TV appearance which will be an attack on Cassandra in answer to what he wrote of you.'

Well, dash it, you and I are buddies, and if the above is correct, I don't want you thinking I had anything to do with this. I value our friendship too much. I'll do what I can to halt the proceedings, though, as I say, you probably won't give a damn.

Even before I met you, I had never had any ill-feeling about that BBC talk of yours. All you had to go on was that I had spoken on the German radio, so naturally you let yourself go. And what the hell! It's twenty years ago.

I hope the cats are flourishing. We have just had to add a stray boxer to the establishment. So now we have two cats (both strays), a dachshund and this boxer. Fortunately they all get on together like old college chums.

When are you going to make another of your trips to this side.

Yours ever

To Evelyn Waugh
10 May 1961

I'm a bit concerned about this TV appearance of yours on July 15. I've just had a letter from Guy Bolton, who said that somebody had told him that you were going to make an attack on Cassandra of the *Mirror*. And the embarrassing thing (to me) is that for several years past he and I have been great friends. I had a very amiable letter from him one day when he was over here and we lunched together and got on fine. He sent me that *Mirror* book with a charming inscription, and since then we have been on first name and Christmas card terms. So I am hoping you will see your way to make your talk not so personal as you had planned. Is this possible? If not, okay. But I thought I would mention it. . . .

To Guy Bolton
14 May 1961

That was rather disquieting what you said in your letter about Evelyn Waugh going to make an attack on Cassandra of the *Mirror*, because for some years Cassandra and I have become quite buddies, lunching together when he visits NY and swopping Christmas cards. I wrote to him explaining that I had nothing to do with the attack and also to E. Waugh asking him to make his speech less personal. That's all I could do, and if Waugh goes ahead as planned, I can't help it. What a blessing it is to come to an age where nothing matters much except one's work!

24 July 1961

Evelyn Waugh certainly started something! Fancy posters all over London. The papers here were on to it, of course, and the telephone never stopped ringing. The *NY Herald-Trib* had a front page thing on it, headed by your photo of me in the chair with Squeaky on my lap. I wish in some ways that E. Waugh hadn't disinterred the thing, but I imagine it's good on the whole.

13 August 1961

About the Evelyn Waugh broadcast my feelings are a bit mixed. I think he did a wonderful job, but it's a bit like the soup in that show of yours. . . . I'm sorry he stirred it. Still, what the hell.

16 RICHARD USBORNE

When Richard Usborne was preparing *Wodehouse at Work*, he wrote some questions for Plum. These are the answers.

☆

To Richard Usborne   1000 Park Avenue
14 January 1955   New York

Heavens! You can't expect me to remember the set books at school after fifty-five years!! We did the usual ones, I suppose, certainly including Homer, and I sweated at Homer then, but I have never read him since. BUT interesting news item. . . . When I was six years old, I read the whole of Pope's *Iliad*. I can't have been more than six, because I read it at my grandmother's in Worcestershire, and she died when I was eight and the house was sold. So it must have been when I was either six or seven, and I remember loving it.

I did reams of Greek and Latin verse, and enjoyed it more than any other work. I was two years in the Sixth – or top – form, never rising to any great eminence – I was about fifteenth of a form of thirty – but I should probably have got a scholarship at Oxford or Cambridge, as several of my inferiors got them. But there was not enough money to send me to the University even with a scholarship. I don't remember much about the English books we read. And I can't remember any examination on English books. I suppose one read a good bit of Shakespeare, and I seem to remember Carlyle ('I, mine Werther, am above it all'). Where I got *Rem acu tetigisti*, I can't say. It just stuck in my mind.

Blandings is purely imaginary, but a composite, I suppose, of a number of country houses I visited as a child. My parents were in Hong Kong most of the time, and I was left in charge of various aunts, many of them vicars' wives who paid occasional calls on the local Great House, taking me with them. Why, I can't imagine, as I

240

had no social gifts. But those visits made me familiar with life in the Servants' Hall, as I was usually sent off there in the custody of the butler, to be called for later. So I got a useful insight into the ways of Beach etc. The lake and the bushes and all that I put in as I needed them. Probably my subconscious supplied the lake from Lord Methuen's house at Corsham, Wilts, where I used to go and skate as a child.

30 December 1955   Remsenburg
                                    Long Island
                                    New York

No, I don't keep a notebook about those factual things, but I am always re-reading my books and keep them well in mind. I am writing a novel now in which Lord Uffenham from *Money in the Bank* is one of the principal characters, and it is quite a job keeping the same as he was in the first book. . . .[1]

That thing about me and the typewriter paper was in *Bring on the Girls* and was fathered on me by Guy Bolton. It was somebody else actually who did it, I forget who. Still, I don't see any reason why you should not use it. It has been attributed to me in print and makes a good story.

Guy did that sort of thing all through *Bring on the Girls* – I mean, making him or me the hero of some story which had really happened to someone else. I approved, as it knitted the book together so well. But I don't see any reason why you shouldn't use those stories as having happened to me.

1 September 1956

(e) 'Smiling, the boy fell dead'. Mr Usborne, *really*! I thought everybody knew Robert Browning's poem 'An Incident in the French Camp'. Young lieutenant comes to Napoleon with the news that they have taken Ratisbon. Napoleon quite pleased. He notices that the young man isn't looking quite himself.

> 'You're wounded!'. 'Nay,' the soldier's pride
> Touched to the quick, he said:
> 'I'm killed, Sire!' and his chief beside
> Smiling the boy fell dead. . . .

[1] *Something Fishy* (1957), published in the USA as *The Butler Did It*.

241

(g) I was at one time a member of Garrick, Beefsteak, Constitutional, and over here Coffee House. I now belong only to Coffee House and the Lotos of New York. At a very early stage I was a member of a ghastly little bohemian club called the Yorick, and later, of course, the Dramatists' Club. But I hated them all and almost never went into them. I have not been inside the Coffee House for three years, though I sometimes lunch at the Lotos when in New York. I think I hated the Garrick more than any of them. All those hearty barristers! I did resign from the Garrick.

17 SPIRITUALISM

To William Townend   Granville Hotel
17 December 1925   Bexhill
                                Sussex

I've got the Bradley book. I want to talk to you about Spiritualism.
I think it's the goods.

15 March 1927   Hotel Impney
                                Droitwich
                                Worcestershire

That was rather queer about the planchette and Kate Overy. Do
you remember she and her brother both committed suicide. I knew
her fairly well. Have you had any more results?

☆

The Bradley book was *The Wisdom of the Gods* by H. Dennis
Bradley. When Wodehouse died, an additional list of sixty-one
other books on spiritualism or mysticism were found on his
shelves. He also received several letters 'dictated' by Townend
to a medium after his death. These letters run from 17 October
1967 to 13 January 1970 and they are full of statements like the
following:

Life continues here in the most delightful way with interests of all
kinds, everything one wants. You have to understand that mind plays a
very large part in this. People formulate their desires according to their
enlightenment and ability to do this, so have they little or much.
    It has nothing to do with cleverness as we know it on earth. It is sort
of soul awareness which comes about in the first instance from having
been able to help others – to have compassion or love and unselfishness.

There is also the surprising statement that 'There is

243

swimming and diving – if that is what one likes to do – in water which is superlatively blue, but, unlike the Mediterranean, not static but full of change.'

To what extent Plum believed all these things is not known to anyone, but the papers concerning them were found after his death.

18 THE END

To Denis Mackail   Remsenburg
7 January 1960   Long Island
                             New York

I got quite a shock the other day when my New York publisher told me he was going to do a huge anthology of my stuff next September, to be called *Eighty Years of Wodehouse*. I suppose, being a mathematician, I had known that anyone born in 1881 has to be eighty in 1961, but having my octogenarianism hurled at me like that shook me a bit. I consoled myself with the thought that I can still touch my toes fifty times every morning without a suspicion of bending knees, which I'll bet not many octogenerians can.

To Edward Cazalet
1 November 1970

I had a quiet birthday as usual, working all the morning, going for a walk with Guy in the afternoon, watching *Edge of Night*, which was rotten for a time but has now bucked up, a girl having been found in the doctor's bed stabbed with a carving knife (doc not yet arrested but going through a bad spell).

To Thelma Cazalet-Keir
25 May 1973

What a wonderful surprise!!! I feel deeply grateful to all the contributors and even more so to you for all the trouble you must have taken assembling them. And how sweet of Sheran coming all the way over here to bring it to me. It was a joy to see her again, and looking so well and pretty, too. . . .

    Who is Richard Ingrams? I think I liked his contribution best of all of them. BUT THEY WERE ALL TERRIFIC.

☆

Thelma Cazalet-Keir had made a collection of essays on Wodehouse by various people which was published as *Homage to Wodehouse*. Richard Ingrams was at that time best known as editor of *Private Eye*.

☆

To Ira Gershwin
19 December 1973

I would have written sooner to thank you for that magnificent book about George, but I have had to have a tooth out and it robbed me of all my vim. What a nuisance it is being 92 and gradually decaying.

This book I am sending you with my love is my latest, but not yet published over here. I hope you and Lee will like it.

☆

Plum died in 1975, at the age of ninety-four. Four new books were published between his ninetieth birthday and his death – *Much Obliged Jeeves; Pearls, Girls and Monty Bodkin; Bachelors Anonymous* and *Aunts Aren't Gentlemen*. He continued to work until the end, taking the manuscript of what was later given the title *Sunset at Blandings* with him to the hospital in which he died.

Fifteen years later his novels are kept regularly in print, his place in the history of literature is assured, and his characters are household words. Few people are privileged to give as much pleasure to others as he did, and his death was mourned all over the world.

APPENDIX A
'Engaged? Consult Me First'
Daily Mail, 5 September 1935, by P. G. Wodehouse

Whenever a question of nation-wide interest comes up vitally affecting the welfare of the community, the first thing people want to know is, What Does Wodehouse Think About It? I was not surprised, therefore, to find beside my breakfast kipper a communication from the Editor of *The Daily Mail* asking me to put the public straight on the Killick Millard business.

Fair Exchange
Dr Killick Millard – try saying that ten times quickly – is the medical officer for health in Leicester – and a jolly good one, too, I believe – and it is his opinion that there should be a form of Health Certificate to be exchanged by engaged couples before marriage – a questionnaire, if you know what I mean, which each would fill up and hand to the other, telling each other the worst.

There is a good deal in this, of course. My only complaint is that it does not go far enough. Let us go deeper into the thing is my advice.

If I were a young man starting life and contemplating matrimony, there are certain points on which I would require definite assurance before I put up so much as a single bann.

I would be reasonable. I would not ask too much. Robert Louis Stevenson advised young men not to marry a woman who wrote. It would be enough, in my opinion, to refuse to marry a woman who wrote bad imitations of Evelyn Waugh.

The Shifters
But there is one thing that would keep me from the altar even if matters were so advanced that I had bought presents for the bridesmaids and selected the actual carnation to be worn in the buttonhole, and that is the discovery that my bride-to-be, whether from some inherited family taint or otherwise, was a Shifter – or to use the Harley-street term, a victim of Furor Interio-Decoratus – that is to say, one who moves furniture.

247

The primary symptoms are an abstracted restlessness and a sort of rummy look in the eye. The sufferer wanders about the drawing-room chewing the under lip. She then takes a picture from over the mantelpiece and shifts it to the opposite wall, almost immediately afterwards saying, 'No, I don't like that so well,' and shifting it back.

At this point, prompt treatment may effect a cure. But let the thing get a grip and before long she will be shifting tables, foot-stools, what-nots, and even arm chairs from under her unfortunate partner's very trousers-seat.

Professor Nunally Johnson, the American specialist, tells of a case where a husband, returning home late and not wishing to disturb his wife, undressed in the dark and flung himself backwards on to the bed, only to discover that during the day she had shifted it to where the chest of drawers used to be and shifted the chest of drawers to the other end of the room – with the result that he hit the floor, bounced twice, and was never the same man again.

Beware of Didusis

Furor Interio-Decoratus is perhaps the worst scourge that can devastate a home, but there are not many happy days in store for a husband whose wife is a victim of Didusis.

This generally breaks out during the summer vacation, when the husband, who has always considered his mate normal, is shocked to hear her pour forth a stream of questions of which 'Did you lock up everything?' 'Did you turn off all the taps?' 'Did you tell the milkman to stop delivering?' and 'Did you leave the cat with the people at The Acacias?' are fair samples. I knew of one case where the husband of a Didusis victim was so nervously affected that he would shy like a startled horse every time he saw her lips begin to part.

That particular story, however, has a happy sequel. One day when they were driving in their two-seater she suddenly turned to him and said, 'Did you remember to post that letter?' As a matter of fact he had, but the shock was so severe that he gave the steering wheel a sharp twist and the car went straight up the side of the house, falling back as it reached the second storey window. Since that day she has never again used the words 'Did you.'

Pfaff's Disease

Space is too short for me to dwell on such common maladies of women as Breakfast Brightness, Whatulism (where the sufferer, when addressed, puts her head on one side like a canary and says 'What?'), Spectaculosis (the losing of spectacles), Pfaff's Disease (the tidying of desks), Pocketisis (asking husband to put things in his pocket, such as the subject's vanity case, cigarette case, purse, and, in some instances, brown paper parcels containing dress materials), and Mikophobia (the inability to listen to husband when he starts telling stories about two Irishmen named Pat and Mike).

It may seem in the above that I have devoted myself too closely to the female side of the questionnaire, but a moment's thought will show that that is the only side that matters. All husbands are practically perfect. The only thing you ever find wrong with a husband is Ashma (the scattering of tobacco ash on carpets), and in these days of feminine smoking most wives have been down with Ashma themselves for years.

APPENDIX B

Introduction by P. G. Wodehouse to *'The Ship in the Swamp' and Other Stories* by W. Townend

It is with some diffidence that I take typewriter in hand to inscribe these few words. The position of an author – call him Author A. – who writes an introduction to a book by another author – call him Author B. – must alway be a little embarrassing. He inevitably runs the risk of seeming to claim for himself an importance and a right to speak which may be resented by a public consisting largely of cold-eyed men with tight lips and sneering eyebrows. In one way, however, he is unquestionably on velvet. He cannot be interrupted or heckled.

If I were to try to introduce these short stories of W. Townend verbally, the scene would run more or less as follows:-

MYSELF (starting well): It has been frequently said, gentleman, that there is no public for a volume of short stories. I venture to think, however, that an exception will be made in favour of the book which I am presenting to your notice. The sea, gentlemen, is our heritage, and a writer who, like Mr Townend, can bring home to us the glamour of the sea, can fill our nostrils with the salt breath of the sea, can put on paper the splendour, the mystery, the tragedy of the sea. . . .

A VOICE: One moment. Just one moment.

MYSELF: Sir?

A VOICE: Did you say the splendour, the mystery, the tragedy of the sea?

MYSELF: I did.

A VOICE: What do you know about the splendour, the mystery, the tragedy of the sea?

MYSELF (weakly): That's all I know about the splendour, the mystery, the tragedy of the sea. Gentlemen, I venture to say. . . .

A VOICE: Is it not a fact that, when you go to America, you travel first-class on the *Majestic*?

MYSELF: . . . venture to say, gentlemen. . . .

A VOICE: And have breakfast in bed?

MYSELF: . . . to say, gentlemen. . . .

A VOICE: And the only time anything tragic ever happened to you at sea was when the boat was so full you couldn't get a table at the Ritz Café?

MYSELF (wisely changing the subject): But not all the stories in this volume are set among the leaping billows and the flying scud of perilous seas. What, in my opinion, is the gem of the collection – I allude to the story entitled 'Bolshevik' – is a tale of London's submerged – a gripping, biting tale that reveals in a few short pages the Soul of England. . . .

A VOICE: Just one moment.

MYSELF: That England, gentlemen, which never did nor never shall lie at the proud foot. . . .

A VOICE: What do you know about London's submerged?

MYSELF: I. . . .

A VOICE: Is it not a fact that for years you have made your living writing about younger sons of dukes tripping over door-mats? I appeal to this audience to tear up the benches and throw them at the speaker.

[The crowd rush the platform, and I am roughly handled before being rescued by the police.]

In print, of course, one is safe from this sort of thing. Nevertheless, it is difficult not to be conscious of that voice floating somewhere in the background and, realising my inadequacy as an introducer of a book like Townend's, I think it best to scamp the task and hurry on. I could say – but will not – that I think 'Bolshevik' one of the greatest short stories written in the last few years. I will refrain from giving my opinion of 'Overseas for Flanders' and 'In the Stokehold'. I will go on at once to the part of this introduction where I am on safe ground, the personal details about the author.

Bill Townend shared a study with me at school. We brewed tea together, shoved in the same scrum, and on one occasion put on eighty-seven together for the fourth wicket in a final house match. (I must tell you about that innings of mine one of these days when I have more time.) Shortly after this feat, our school career ended, and Townend started out in life as a black-and-white artist, in which capacity he contributed to *Punch* and other papers, and illustrated one of my books.

But all this while the writer in him was popping its head out at intervals. I was doing the 'By-the-Way' column on the old *Globe* in those days, and could always rely on him to pitch in for a day or two when a holiday seemed imperative. For several weeks, till a directors' meeting was called and we were thrown out simultaneously, we wrote the 'Answers to Correspondents' in *Tit-Bits* together. Everything that is any good in a novel entitled *Love Among the Chickens* was supplied by Townend. And we also collaborated – under a pseudonym – in a lurid serial in *Chums*. It was obviously only a question of time before a man capable of helping English Literature along to that extent would feel the urge to get going on his own account. And this happened just after Townend went to sea.

He had been to sea before, he had been taken about the world quite a good deal: but this time he went in a tramp steamer, was nearly wrecked off the coast of Wales, messed about in the engine-room, and came back, looking perfectly foul in a stained tweed suit and a celluloid collar, resolved to write stories about men of the deep waters. His first long sea-story was 'A Light For His Pipe', and his best, 'The Tramp', published by Messrs Jenkins last year. He also contributed largely to American magazines.

His connection with America came about through his being offered a job out there. Some years ago, after a long separation, I met him in the Strand and immediately noticed something peculiar in his appearance and bearing. 'That man,' I said to myself, 'has been sorting lemons.' And so it proved. He had just returned from a long stay on a ranch in Chula Vista, California, and the only thing you do on a California ranch is sort lemons. You get up at about five, breakfast, and go out and sort lemons. Lunch at twelve-thirty, followed by a long afternoon of lemon-sorting. Then dinner, and perhaps sort a few small ones before bed-time and the restful sleep. Next morning you get up at five, breakfast, and go out to sort lemons. Lunch at. . . . But you have gathered the idea and will understand why in some of the stories written by him at that time there is a strong lemon-motive. His heroes were usually young lemon-sorters who fell in love with the daughters of their employers, and the big scene was where the villain rang in a bad lemon on them and got them sacked.

This phase lasted only a brief time, and he was soon back again in his proper element, the sea. I have hinted above that I am not the best man to come to for authoritative pronouncements on the sea, but I take it a fellow, however scanty his knowledge, can make a remark if he wants to, and I maintain that nobody today writes better sea-stories than Old Bill Townend. Read 'The Tramp'. And read the sea-stories in this book.

And, whether he is writing of sea or land, he writes as man whose artist schooling has trained his eye to observe details. He can make you visualise a background.

Gentlemen, I trust I have not detained you over-long. We old buffers are a bit inclined to drool on when we get on a subject that interests us. What I have been trying to convey is that W. Townend, when he writes, writes with knowledge. If he lays the scene of a story in a stokehold he writes personally, no doubt encouraging the stokers with word and gesture. When he writes of soldiers, remember that soldiers flocked about his cradle. And if lemons creep in, bear in mind that here speaks a man who was known all through California, from distant wherever-it-is far-off I-forget-the-name-of-the-place, as 'The Prince of Sorters'.

Gentlemen, I have finished. Mr Townend will now rise to reply.

APPENDIX C

'P. G. Wooster Just as He Useter'
New York Herald-Tribune, 22 May 1946, p. 2, weekly book review:
Joy in the Morning, by P. G. Wodehouse, 281 pp., New York,
Doubleday and Company, $2; reviewed by Ogden Nash

Bound to your bookseller, leap to your library
Deluge your dealer with bakshish and bribary,
Lean on the counter and never say when,
Wodehouse and Wooster are with us again.
Flourish the fish-slice, your buttons unloosing,
Prepare for the fabulous browsing and sluicing,
And quote, till you're known as the neighbourhood nuisance,
The gems that illumine the browsance and sluicance.
Oh, fondle each gem, and after you quote it,
Kindly inform me just who wrote it.
Which came first, the egg or the rooster,
P. G. Wodehouse or Bertram Wooster?
I know hawk from handsaw, and Finn from Fiji,
But I can't disentangle Bertram from P. G.
I inquire in the school room, I ask in the road house,
Did Wodehouse write Wooster, or Wooster write Wodehouse?
Bertram Wodehouse and P. G. Wooster.
They are linked in my mind like Simon and Schuster.
No matter which fumbled in ' 41,
Or which the woebegone figure of fun.
I deduce how the *faux pas* came about;
It was clearly Jeeves's afternoon out.
Now Jeeves is back, and my cheeks are crumply
From watching him glide through Steeple Bumpleigh.

APPENDIX D

'Good Lord, Jeeves'
Punch, 20 May 1953, by J. Maclaren-Ross

All unconscious of impending doom I was gnawing a solitary bone at the Drones Club and wistfully recalling that golden age when coves like Catsmeat Potter-Pirbright and Barmy Fotheringay-Phipps had reigned supreme, filling the air around with snappy dialogue and bread rolls bandied to-and-fro. I'd reached the point, after a few shots of cognac imbibed to assist the gastric juices, when a less reserved chappie would have burst into the chorus of 'Auld Lang Syne' or wondered, with the poet, where the jolly old *neiges* of *a.* had got to nowadays, and it was in this mellow mood that I became suddenly aware of two birds in formal attire bearing down on me from across the banqueting hall – now, alas, empty save for the last of the Woosters.

Though the advancing figures were clearly recognizable as Sir Roderick Glossop and Sir Watkyn Bassett CBE, JP, respectively, it took me some moments to realize that these knights were actually present in the flesh, and by the time it'd sunk in that they weren't mere shades conjured up from the mists of m. or the pages of a cheap edition chronicling some past kick of the heels, they were already standing over my table with expressions that betokened business.

Sir Watkyn was the first to give tongue, and at his tone of voice even my iron nerve began to describe a graceful arc. I felt a kinship with those private eyes of American lit., who glance up from a newly-discovered stiff to find the boys from the Homicide Squad standing around, idly swinging their black-jacks in preparation for a cosy chat about the case.

'Mr Wooster,' said the former bane of Bosher Street, 'we are from the Ministry of Rehabilitation. We were informed that the club secretary was to be found lunching in this room.'

'I'm the Hon. Sec., Sir Watkyn,' I said: an honest admission received by Sir Roderick with what brothers of the PEN qualify as a mirthless chuckle.

255

'A suitable nominee for an institution so named, do you not concur, Bassett?' he said.

'Especially apt in view of the establishment's future function,' Sir W. agreed. 'You are, of course, aware, Mr Wooster, that these premises have been requisitioned w.e.f. today's date as a State Home for the Mentally Deficient . . .'

'. . . and that I, as Governmental Psychiatrist,' said Sir Roderick, coming in pat on his cue, 'will be in charge of the scheme, which is to be implemented forthwith.'

'Here, I say,' I protested, rallying from the ropes, as one who recovers from a right cross, 'you can't do that, you know! The members won't stand for it!'

'There are no members, Mr Wooster,' Sir Watkyn said, planting another banderilo in the quivering hide. 'We've already ascertained that. And if it is the free board and lodging which as club secretary you receive here that causes your patent anxiety, why, you are in no danger of losing it. Sir Roderick, I am sure, will gladly sign the certificate insuring your future as an inmate of the Home – eh, Glossop?'

It was the KO delivered with full force to the softer parts of the anat. I had crumpled over the table, gasping for breath, when through the loud singing in my ears a familiar and well-loved voice spoke sharply, scattering the opponents to right and left.

'Gentlemen,' it said, 'I wish to have a word in private with Mr Wooster, if you please.'

The big fight was over. Before you could say Sugar Ray Robinson, Sir Roderick and W. Bassett had beaten it, murmuring 'Yes, Minister,' and 'Certainly, Lord Jeeves,' in the most obsequious of accents, and the hand, it seemed, of a ministering angel was holding a beaker of brandy to my lips.

'Jeeves,' I said fervently, 'lives there a man with soul so dead as to resist the incomparable Jeeves?'

'Thank you, sir. The tribute is much appreciated.'

'I merely quote from The *Daily Herald*. But wait a sec.,' I said, as full consciousness flooded back to the brain, 'didn't I hear those two blighters address you as Minister? And Lord Jeeves? Or was it a dream?'

'The Government has been kind enough to reward my trifling services with a peerage, and also by inclusion in the Cabinet, sir.'

'As Minister of Re-Thing?'

'Habilitation, sir. A little more brandy, if I might so suggest? I feel this news has come as a grave shock to you, sir.'

'Worse than that, Jeeves. The loss of this job would be the last straw.' I raised my measure on high. 'To your success, Jeeves, which you dashed well deserve.'

'Thank you, sir. But you were saying about your position as secretary here, and its importance to you . . .'

'Supreme importance, Jeeves, financially speaking. Nationalization and surtax have taken their toll. The Wooster millions are, in fact, down the drain. Need I say more?'

'It is a plight shared by many in these times, sir. Your friends are unable to assist?'

'Friends,' I echoed bitterly. 'Shall I show you the typed note I had from Mrs Bingo Little's secretary? Or the stern refusal received from Stiffy Byng's spouse, the Bishop of Blandings, formerly the Rev. Stinker Pinker? The receipt of such missives is souring to one's sunny nature, Jeeves.'

'Man is an ungrateful animal, sir. But perhaps I might be of some little help, if you'd allow me . . .'

'How?'

'The offer of employment, sir?'

'What kind of employment?'

'I hesitate to say, sir.'

'Don't hesitate. Out with it. Beggars can't be c., Jeeves.'

'Well, sir, the post of secretary to the Junior Ganymede Club has fallen vacant in the past week. I could confidently promise you the appointment if you so desire.'

'But the Junior Ganymede's a club for gentlemen's personal gentlemen. How could I get in?'

'By accepting a temporary position as my personal attendant, sir. . . . If I may say so, you would not find me too exacting an employer.'

We Woosters are nothing if not adaptable. My hesitation was of the briefest. 'Jeeves,' I said, 'you're on! Let's drink to that!'

'Thank you,' said Jeeves, as I ladled out liberal portions. 'Er – . . . not all the soda, Wooster.'

'No, sir,' I said, falling without effort into the new role. 'I will endeavour to give you satisfaction, sir . . . I mean, m'lord.'

ACKNOWLEDGEMENTS

For help in compiling and editing this volume of letters I wish to thank the following: Sir Edward Cazalet; Lady Hornby; Margaret Slythe, Head of the Wodehouse Library and Archive at Dulwich College, and The Master and Governors of Dulwich College for access to the original correspondence between P.G. Wodehouse and Bill Townend; James Heineman; Richard Usborne; Lieutenant-Colonel N.T.P. Murphy, whose knowledge of the Wodehouse oeuvre was of great assistance in identifying characters in the letters; and Douglas Matthews, Librarian of the London Library, who also compiled the Index.

Any mistakes remaining are my own.

Frances Donaldson
June 1990

INDEX